If You're Trying to
Get Better Grades
&
Higher Test Scores
in Social Studies,
You've Gotta Have This Book !

Grades 6 & Up

by Imogene Forte
& Marjorie Frank

Incentive Publications, Inc.
Nashville, Tennessee

Illustrated by Kathleen Bullock
Cover by Geoffrey Brittingham
Edited by Charlotte Bosarge

ISBN 0-86530-590-0

3   4   5   6   7   8   9   10   06   05

PRINTED IN THE UNITED STATES OF AMERICA
www.incentivepublications.com

Contents

GET SHARP . . . ON CULTURE & SOCIETY   59

GET SHARP . . . ON GLOBES & MAPS   77

GET SHARP . . . ON WORLD GEOGRAPHY 93

GET SHARP . . . ON U.S. GEOGRAPHY 129

GET SHARP . . . ON WORLD HISTORY 151

GET SHARP . . . ON U.S. HISTORY, GOVERNMENT, & CITIZENSHIP 183

GET SHARP . . . ON ECONOMICS 219

INDEX 233

✔ Get Ready ———————————————➤

Get ready to get sharper in social studies. Get ready to be a better student and get the grades you are capable of getting. Get ready to feel better about yourself as a student. Lots of students would like to do better in school. (Lots of their parents and teachers would like them to, also!) Lots of students CAN do better. But it doesn't happen overnight. And it doesn't happen without some thinking and trying. So, are you ready to put some energy into getting more out of your learning efforts? Good! The first part of getting ready is wanting to do better–motivating yourself to get moving on this project of showing how smart you really are. The **Get Ready** part of this book can help you do just that: get inspired and motivated. It also gives you some wonderful and downright practical ways to organize yourself, your space, your time, and your social studies homework. Even more than that, it gives tips you can use right away to make big improvements in your study habits.

✔ Get Set———————————————➤

Once you've taken a good, hard look at your goals, organization, and study habits, you can move on to other skills and habits that will get you set up for more successful learning. The **Get Set** part of this book starts out with an overview of the themes of social studies. Then it gives a quick tune-up on the thinking skills that will help you get the most out of your brain, followed by a reminder about good places to find information for your social studies research. The section is topped off with a great review of skills you need for good studying. It's all right here at your fingertips–how to listen and read carefully, take clear notes, study for tests, and take tests. Take this section seriously, and you'll start making improvements immediately in your social studies performance.

✔ Get Sharp ————➤

Now you're ready to mix those good study habits and skills with the content that you need to learn. The **Get Sharp** sections of this book contain all kinds of facts, people, places, events, lists, and definitions, lists and how-to information. These sections cover the basic areas of social studies that you study–social and cultural concepts, map skills, world geography, U.S. geography, world history, U.S. history, U.S. government and citizenship, and economics. The **Get Sharp** sections are loaded with the information you need to understand social studies homework and get it done right. This part of the book is a handy reference tool PLUS a *how-to-manual* for many social studies topics and assignments. Keep it nearby whenever you do any social studies homework or project. It is sure to help you keep all those concepts, definitions, dates, places, persons, and events clear and distinguished from each other!

How to Use This Book

Students

This can be the ultimate homework helper for your social studies instruction and assignments. Use the *Get Ready* and the *Get Set* sections to improve your attitude and sharpen your organizational and study skills. Then, have the book nearby at all times when you have social studies work to do at home, and use the *Get Sharp* sections to . . .

. . . reinforce a topic you've already learned.

. . . get different and fresh examples of something you've studied.

. . . check up on a fact, definition, event, skill, process, or detail of social studies.

. . . get a quick answer to a social studies question.

. . . get clear on something you thought you knew but now aren't so sure about.

. . . guide you in social studies thinking, research, or projects.

. . . review a topic in preparation for a test.

Teachers

This book can serve multiple purposes in the classroom. Use it as . . .

. . . a reference manual for students to consult during learning activities or assignments.

. . . a reference manual for yourself to consult on particular events, facts, or concepts.

. . . an instructional handbook for a specific social studies topic.

. . . a remedial tool for anyone needing to sharpen a particular social studies concept.

. . . a source of advice for parents and students regarding homework habits.

. . . an assessment guide to help you gauge student mastery of social studies concepts.

. . . a source of good resources for making bridges between home and school.
   (Use the letter on page 17 and any other pages as take-home pieces for parents.)

Parents

The *Get Ready* and *Get Set* sections of this book will help you to help your child improve study habits and sharpen study skills. These can serve as positive motivators for the student while taking the burden off you. Then, you can use the *Get Sharp* sections as a source of knowledge and a guide for yourself. It's a handbook you can consult to. . .

. . . refresh your memory about a person, place, event, era, or idea in social studies.

. . . get a clear definition of a social studies term.

. . . end confusion about concepts, facts, dates, changes, processes, and many other
   social studies questions.

. . . provide useful homework help to your child.

. . . reinforce the good learning your child is doing in social studies class.

. . . gain confidence that your child is doing the homework right.

GET READY →

Get Motivated

Dear Student,

Nobody can make you a better student. Nobody can even make you WANT to be a better student. But you CAN be. It's a rare kid who doesn't have some ability to learn more, do better with assignments and tests, feel more confident as a student, or get better grades. You CAN DO THIS! You are the one (the only one) that can get yourself motivated.

Probably, the first question is this: "WHY would you want be a better student?" If you don't have an answer to this, your chances of improving are not so hot. If you do have answers, but they're like Joe's (page 15), your chances of improving still might be pretty slim. Joe figured this out, and decided that these are NOT the goals that really motivate him. Now, we don't mean to tell you that it's a bad idea to get a good report card, or get on the honor roll, or please your parents. We're not saying that getting into college is a poor goal or that there's anything wrong with preparing for high school either.

However, if you are trying to motivate yourself to be a better student, the reasons need to be about YOU. The goals need to be YOUR goals for your life right now. In fact, if you are having a hard time being motivated, maybe it is just BECAUSE you're used to hearing a lot of "shoulds" that seem to be about what other people want you to be. Or maybe it's because the goals are so far off in some hazy distant future that it's impossible to stay focused on them.

So it's back to the question, "Why try to be a better student?" Consider these as possible reasons why:

- to make use of your good mind (and NOT short-change yourself by cheating yourself out of something you could learn to do or understand)

- to get involved—to change learning into something YOU DO instead of something that someone else is trying to do TO you

- to take charge and get where YOU want to go (It's YOUR life, after all.)

- to learn all you can for YOURSELF–because the more you know, the more you think, and the more you understand–the more possibilities you have for what you can do or be in your life RIGHT NOW and in the future

Follow the "Get Motivated" tips on the next page as you think about this question. Then write down a few reasons of your own to inspire you toward putting your brain to work, showing how smart you are, and getting even smarter.

Sincerely,

Imogene and Marjorie

Get Motivated Tips

1. Think about why you'd want to do better as a student.

2. Think about what you'd gain right now from doing better.

3. Get clear enough on your motivations to write them down.

4. Set some short-term goals *(things you can improve in a few weeks).*

5. Think about what gets in the way of doing your best as a student.

6. Figure out a way to change or eliminate something that interferes with your efforts to reach your goals. *(Use the form on page 16 to record your thoughts and goals.)*

Why Should I be a better student?

To please my parents
To please my teachers
To impress other kids
To impress my parents' friends
So people will like me better
To keep from embarrassing my parents
To do as well as my older brother
To do better than my sister
So teachers will treat me better
To do as well as my parents did in school
To get the money my parents offer for good grades
To be well-prepared for high school
To make a lot of money when I finish school
To get a good report card
To get into college

None of these really motivate me much at all.

Get Ready Tip # 1
Set realistic goals. Choose something you actually believe you can do. And if you set a short time frame for your goal, you'll have a better chance of success.

15

I can do this!

Why do I want to be a better student? What difference would it make for me, now and in the future?
(Write a few reasons.)

1._____

_____

2._____

_____

3._____

_____

What changes could I make in the near future?
(Write two short-term goals—things that, realistically, you could improve in the next month.)

1._____

2._____

What gets in the way of good grades or good studying for me?
(Name the things, conditions, or distractions that **most often** keep you from doing your best as a student.)

1. _____

2._____

3._____

4._____

What distraction am I willing to eliminate ?
(Choose one of the interferences above that you'd be willing to try changing or getting rid of for the next month.)

1._____

16

Dear Parent,

What parent doesn't want a child to be a good student? Probably not many! But how can you help yours get motivated to do the work it takes? You can't do it for her /or him. But here are some ideas to help students as they find it within themselves to get set to be good students:

• Read the letter to students (page 14). Help your son or daughter think about where he/she wants to go, what reasons make sense to her or him for getting better grades, and what benefits he/she would gain from better performance as a student.

• Help your child make use of the advice on study habits. (See pages 18-28.) Reinforce the ideas, particularly those of keeping up with assignments, going to class, and turning in work on time.

• Provide your child with a quiet, comfortable, well-lighted place that is available consistently for study. Also post reminders, display schedules, and provide a place to keep materials.

• Set family routines and schedules that allow for good blocks of study time, adequate rest, relaxing breaks, and healthy eating. Include some time to get things ready for the next school day and some ways for students to be reminded about upcoming assignments or due-dates.

• Demonstrate that you value learning in your household. Read. Learn new things. Show excitement about learning something new yourself. Share this with your kids.

• Keep distractions to a minimum. You may not be able to control the motivations and goals of your child, but you can control the telephone, computer, Internet, electronic games, and TV. These things actually have on-off switches. Use them. Set rules and schedules.

• Help your child gather supplies for studying and resources for projects, papers, or reports. Be available to take her/him to the library, and offer help tracking down sources. Do your best to provide standard resources in the home (dictionary, thesaurus, computer, encyclopedias, maps, supervised Internet access to good educational sites, etc.).

• DO help your student with homework. This means helping straighten out confusion about a topic (when you can), getting an assignment clear, discussing a concept or skill, and perhaps working through a few examples along with the student to make sure he/she is doing it right. This kind of involvement gives a chance to extend or clarify the teaching done in the classroom. Remember that the end goal is for the student to learn. Don't be so insistent on the student "doing it himself" that you miss a good teaching or learning opportunity.

• Be alert for problems, and act early. Keep contact with teachers and don't be afraid to call on them if you see any signs of slipping, confusion, or disinterest on the part of your child. It is easier to reclaim lost ground if you catch it early.

• Try to keep the focus on the student's taking charge for meeting his/her own goals, rather than on making you happy. This can help get you out of a nagging role and get some of the power in the hands of the student. Both of these will make for a more trusting, less hostile relationship with your child on the subject of schoolwork. Such a relationship will go a long way toward supporting your child's self-motivation to be a better student.

Sincerely,

Imogene and *Marjorie*

Get Organized

9:00 p.m.

Joe has a geography project due tomorrow. He plans to make a papier-mache globe of the world. He spent a lot of time collecting information and making plans, but he hasn't put it together yet.

JOE! Stop the video games, and do your homework.

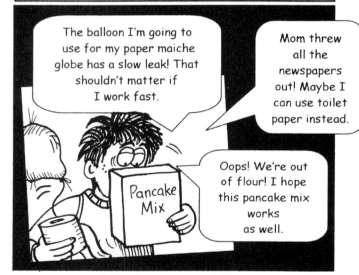

The balloon I'm going to use for my paper maiche globe has a slow leak! That shouldn't matter if I work fast.

Mom threw all the newspapers out! Maybe I can use toilet paper instead.

Pancake Mix

Oops! We're out of flour! I hope this pancake mix works as well.

11:00 p.m.

I should have started earlier! This will *never* dry by tomorrow!

Joe's project is far from finished! He'll have to start over another day. Now, the project will be late. What happened to his good intentions?

Joe has done plenty of research about the features of Earth's surface. However, since he is so disorganized, he is not able to show what he's learned. Don't repeat Joe's mistakes.

Get Your Space Organized

Find a good place to study. Choose a place that

. . . is always available to you.

. . . is comfortable.

. . . is quiet and as private as possible.

. . . has good lighting.

. . . is relatively uncluttered.

. . . is relatively free of distractions.

. . . has a flat surface large enough to spread out materials.

. . . has a place to keep supplies handy. *(See page 19 for suggested supplies.)*

. . . has some wall space or bulletin board space for posting schedules and reminders.

Get Ready Tip # 2

Set this up before school starts each year. Make it cozy and friendly—a safe refuge for getting work done. Put a little time into making it your own, so it's a place you like and not a place to avoid.

Get Your Stuff Organized

Gather things that you will need for studying or for projects, papers, and other assignments. Keep them organized in one place, so you won't have to waste time running around looking. Here are some suggestions:

Handy Supplies

- a good light
- a clock or timer
- bulletin board or wall
  (for schedule & reminders)
- pencils, pens, erasable pens
- erasers
- colored pencils or crayons
- markers, highlighters
- notebook paper, typing paper
- scratch paper
- drawing paper
- index cards, sticky notes
- poster board
- folders, report folders

- ruler, compass
- tape, scissors
- glue, glue sticks
- paper clips, push pins
- stapler, staples
- standard references:
  - globe
  - world atlas
  - history textbook
  - geography textbook
  - encyclopedia (books, CD, or online)
  - homework hotline numbers
  - homework help websites
  - good social studies websites

Get Ready Tip # 3

Have a place to put things you bring home from school. This might be a shelf, a box, or even a laundry basket. Put your school things in there every time you come in the door, so important stuff doesn't get lost in the house or moved (or used up) by other family members.

Get set with a place to keep supplies.
(a bookshelf, a file box, a paper tray, a drawer, a plastic dish pan, a plastic bucket, a carton, or plastic crate)

- Keep everything in this place at all times.
- Return things to it after use.

Also have:
- an assignment notebook (See page 22)
- a notebook for every subject
- a book bag or pack to carry things back and forth
- a schedule for your week (or longer)

Get Your Time Organized

It might be easy to organize your study and space and supplies, but it is probably not quite as easy to organize your time. This takes some work. Here's a plan you can follow right away to help you get your time organized.

Think about how you use your time now.

1. For one week, stop at the end of each day, think back over the day, and write down what you did in each hour-long period of time for the whole day.

2. Then look at the record you've kept to see how you used your time. Ask yourself these questions:

Did I have any clear schedule?

Did I have any goals for when I would get certain things done?

Did I even think ahead about how I would use my time?

How did I decide what to do first?

Did I have a plan or did I just get things done in haphazard order?

Did I get everything done or did I run out of time?

How much time did I waste?

3. Next, start fresh for the upcoming week. Make a plan. Include. . .

. . . time that will be spent at school.

. . . after-school activities.

. . . meals and family activities.

. . . study time.

. . . fun, sports, or recreational activities.

. . . social activities or special events.

. . . time for rest and sleep.

4. Make sure you have an assignment notebook. When you plan your weekly schedule, transfer assignments from that notebook into your study time. *(Did you leave enough time to do all these assignments?)*

5. Make a daily *To Do* List *(For each day, write the things that must be done by the end of that day.)*

Better Grades & Higher Test Scores / SOCIAL STUDIES
Copyright ©2003 by Incentive Publications, Inc., Nashville, TN.

Mon. TO DO List

Study for Math test.
Finish English short stories.
Review for Grammar quiz.
Finish History Ch 11.
Schedule weekend study time.
Wash tennis clothes.
Return library books.
Work on Spanish essay.
Check Internet for History
   info on Cold War.

Wed. TO DO List

Finish History timeline.
Read Health, Ch 8.
Math problems, pg 221.
Work on autobiography.
Get book of short stories.
Start English, Ch 8.

**Get Ready
Tip # 5**
At all times—keep
a copy of class
outlines,
schedules,
or long-range
class assignments
at home.

	M 5th	T 6th	W 7th	TH 8th	F 9th
8 am–3 pm School	Due: Science project Math: pg 215 Health: pg 78 *check History website*	Math test, Ch 7 Due: English: 3 short stories History: Read Ch 12	Grammar quiz Due: Spanish essay Math: pg 219	Due: History time-line Health: Ch 9 Math: pg 221 *Yes! Got an A— on Grammar Quiz!*	Due: English: autobiography English: Ch 8 myths
4-7 pm	tennis practice relax dinner	tennis match 4 pm relax dinner	tennis practice relax dinner *Heath test tomorrow*	tennis practice relax dinner	tennis match 4 pm dinner
7-10 pm Study Time	Math Test, Ch 7 English: Read short stories Grammar quiz Start Spanish essay History: finish Ch 11	**Study Time** Math: pg 219 Grammar quiz finish Spanish essay Health: Ch 8 9:00 TV show	**Study Time** Math: p 221 Health: Ch 8 review quest. finish History timeline English: work on autobiography *too bad my life is boring!*	7 pm Computer Club **Study Time** English: read Ch 8 English: finish autobiography	Football Game 7 pm *Sleep over at Carrie's house. Bring History Homework!*

Weekend: Tennis Match 10 am Sat., soccer game Sat. night, get supplies for Health project; 7 – 9 pm Sun. Study Time: finish English Ch 8, start Health project

Long-Range Assignments (due next week): Health project—immune system, finish biography, English report on short stories

Better Grades & Higher Test Scores / SOCIAL STUDIES
Copyright ©2003 by Incentive Publications, Inc., Nashville, TN.

Get Ready: Get Organized

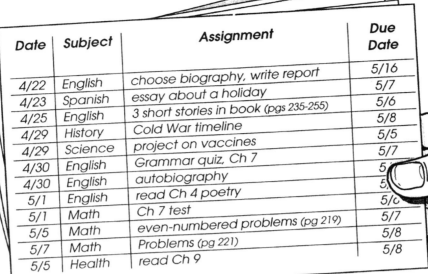

Date	Subject	Assignment	Due Date
4/22	English	choose biography, write report	5/16
4/23	Spanish	essay about a holiday	5/7
4/25	English	3 short stories in book (pgs 235-255)	5/6
4/29	History	Cold War timeline	5/8
4/29	Science	project on vaccines	5/5
4/30	English	Grammar quiz, Ch 7	5/
4/30	English	autobiography	5/
5/1	English	read Ch 4 poetry	5/c
5/1	Math	Ch 7 test	5/7
5/5	Math	even-numbered problems (pg 219)	5/8
5/7	Math	Problems (pg 221)	5/8
5/5	Health	read Ch 9	

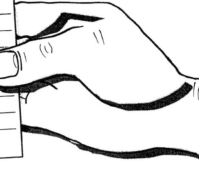

Get Your Assignments Organized

You can't do a very good job on an assignment if you don't have a clue about what it is. You can't possibly do the assignment well if you don't understand the things you're studying. So, if you want to get smarter, then get clear and organized about assignments. It takes 7 simple steps to do this:

1. Listen to the assignment.

2. Write it down in an assignment notebook. *(Make sure you write down the due date.)*

3. If you don't understand the assignment—ASK. *(Do not leave the classroom without knowing what it is you are supposed to do.)*

4. If you don't understand the material well enough to do the assignment—TALK to the teacher. *(Tell him or her that you need help getting it clear.)*

5. Take the assignment book home.

6. Transfer assignments to your weekly or monthly schedule at home.

7. Look at your assignment book every day.

Get Ready Tip # 6

Don't count on anyone else to listen to the assignment and get it down right. Get the assignment yourself. Find a reliable classmate to get assignments when you are absent, or contact the teacher directly.

Get Yourself Organized

Okay, so your schedule is on the wall—all neat and clear. Your study space is organized. Your study supplies are organized. You have written down all your assignments, and you've got all your lists made. Great! But do you feel rushed, frenzied, or hassled? Take some time to think about the behaviors that will help you feel as organized as your stuff and your schedule.

Before you leave school . . .

STOP, take a few calm, unrushed minutes to think about what books and supplies you will need at home for studying. ALWAYS take the assignment notebook home.

When you get home . . .

FIRST, put your school bag in the same spot every day, out of the way of the bustle of your family's activities.

STOP – After relaxing, or after dinner, take a few calm, unrushed minutes to look over your schedule and review what needs to be done. Review your list for the day. Plan your evening study time and set priorities. Don't wait until it is late or until you are very tired.

Before you go to bed . . .

STOP, take a few calm, unrushed minutes to look over the assignment notebook and the to-do list for tomorrow one more time. Make sure everything is done.

THEN, put everything you need for the next day IN the book bag. Don't wait until morning. Make sure you have all the right books and notebooks in the bag. Make sure your finished work is all in the bag. Also, pack other stuff (for gym, sports, etc.) at the same time. Put everything in one consistent place, so you don't have to rush around looking for it.

In the morning . . .

STOP, take a few calm, unrushed minutes to think and review the day one more time.

THEN, eat a good breakfast.

Get Ready Tip # 7

It doesn't do any good to get your homework done if you don't turn it in.

Maxine finally finished her report on the *Constitution*. It's due today. She worked on it for three weeks. She typed it perfectly and included great illustrations She added creative cartoons and a complete timeline. Her cover and title are smashing! She remembered to take her lunch and math homework along to school. She remembered the makeup she promised to loan her friend Anya. Guess what Maxine forgot to take to school today?

oh no!

I can't believe I forgot it! I remembered everything else!

Get Healthy

If you are sick, or tired, droopy, angry, nervous, weak, or miserable, it is very hard to be a good student. It is hard to even use or show what you already know. Your physical and and mental health is a basic MUST for doing as well as you would like to in school. So, don't ignore your health. Pay attention to how you feel. No one else can do that for you.

Get plenty of rest.

If you're tired, nothing else works very well in your life. You can't think, or concentrate, pay attention, learn, remember, or study. Try to get 7 or 8 hours of sleep every night. Get plenty of rest on weekends. If you have a long evening of study ahead, take a short nap after school.

Eat well.

You can't learn or function well on an empty stomach. And all that junk food (soda, sweets, chips, snacks) actually will make you more tired. Plus, it crowds the healthy foods out of your diet—the foods your brain needs to think well and your body needs to get through the day with energy. So eat a balanced diet, with lean meat, whole grains, vegetables, fruit, and dairy products. Oh, and drink a lot of water—8 glasses a day is good.

Exercise.

Everything in your body works better when your body gets a chance to move. Make sure your life does not get too sedentary. Do something every day to get exercise—walk, play a sport, play a game, or run. It's a good idea to get some exercise before you sit down to study, too. Exercise helps you relax, unwind, and de-stress. It's good for stimulating your brain.

Relax.

Your body and your mind need rest. Do something every day to relax. Take breaks during your study time and do anything that helps you unwind.

OHMM

Find relief for stress.

Pay attention to signs of anxiety and stress. Are you nervous, worried, angry, sad? Are your muscles tense, your stomach in a knot? Is your head aching? Are you over-eating or have you lost your appetite? All these are signs of stress that can lower your success in school and interfere with your life. If you notice these signs, find a way to de-stress. Exercise and adequate rest are good for stress relief. You also might try these: stretch, take a hot bath, take a nice long shower, laugh, listen to calming music, write in a journal. If you're burdened with worries, anger, or problems, talk to someone—a good friend, teacher, parent, or other trusted adult.

Get a Grip (on Study Habits)

Here's some good advice for getting set to improve your study habits. Check up on yourself to see how you do with each of these. Then, set goals where you need to improve.

. . . in school:

1. Go to class.
You can't learn anything in a class if you are not there. Go to all your classes. Show up on time. Take your book, your notebook, your pencil, and other supplies.

2. Choose your seat wisely.
Sit where you won't be distracted. Avoid people with whom you'll be tempted to chat. Stay away from the back row. Sit where you can see and hear.

3. Pay attention.
Get everything you can out of each class. Listen. Stay awake. Your assignments will be easier if you've really been present in the class.

4. Take notes.
Write down main points. Write down definitions or examples of events. If you hear it AND write it, you'll be likely to remember it.

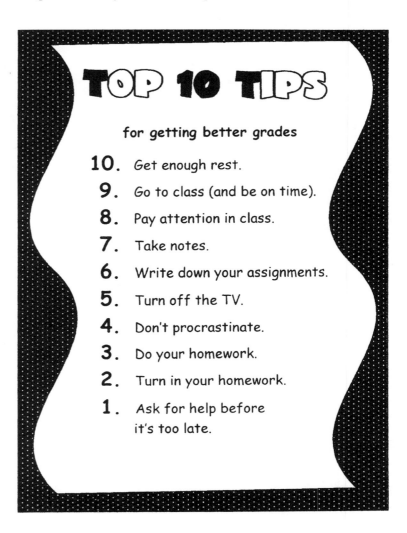

TOP 10 TIPS
for getting better grades

10. Get enough rest.
9. Go to class (and be on time).
8. Pay attention in class.
7. Take notes.
6. Write down your assignments.
5. Turn off the TV.
4. Don't procrastinate.
3. Do your homework.
2. Turn in your homework.
1. Ask for help before it's too late.

5. Ask questions.
It's the teacher's job to see that you understand the material; it's your job to ask if you don't understand.

6. Use your time in class.
Get as much as possible of the next day's assignment done before you leave the classroom.

7. Write down assignments.
Do not leave class until you understand the assignment and have it written down clearly.

8. Turn in your homework.
If you turn in every homework assignment, you are much closer to doing well in a class—even if you struggle with tests.

. . . at home:

9. Gather your supplies.

Before you sit down to study, get all the stuff you'll need: Assignment book, notebook, notes, textbook, study guides, paper, pencils, etc. Think ahead so that you have supplies for long-term projects. Bring those home from school or shop for those well in advance.

10. Avoid distractions.

Think of all the things that keep you from concentrating. Figure out ways to remove those from your life during study time. In other words: Make a commitment to keep your study time uninterrupted. If you listen to music while studying, choose music that can be in the background, not the foreground of your mind.

I'm doing my homework.

11. Turn off the TV.

No matter now much you insist otherwise, you cannot study well with the TV on. Plan to watch TV before or after study time, not during it.

12. Phone later.

Plan a time for phone calls. Like TV watching, phoning does not mix with serious studying. The best way to avoid this distraction is to study in a room with no phone. Call your friends when your work is done.

13. Hide the computer games.

Stay away from the electronic game playing stations, computer games, email, and Internet surfing. Plan time for these when studies are done, or before you settle into serious study time.

14. Know where you're going.

Review your weekly schedule and your assignment notebook. Be sure about what it is that needs to be done. Make a clear *To Do* list for each day, so you will know what to study. Post notes on your wall, your refrigerator, or anywhere that will remind you about what things you need to get done.

15. Plan your time.

Think about the time you have to work each night. Make a timeline for yourself. Estimate how much time a task will take, and set some deadlines. This will keep your attention from wandering and keep you focused on the task.

16. Start early.

Start early in the evening. Don't wait until 10 PM to get underway on any assignment. Whenever possible, start the day before or a few days before.

17. Do the hardest things first.

It's a good idea to do the hardest and most important tasks first. This keeps you from procrastinating on the tough assignments. Also, you'll be doing the harder stuff when your mind is the most fresh. Study for tests and do hard tasks early, when your brain is fresh. Do routine tasks later in the evening.

18. Break up long assignments.

Big projects or test preparations can be overwhelming. Break each long task down into small ones. Then take one small task at a time. This will make the long assignments far less intimidating, and you'll have more successes more often. Never try to do a long assignment all in one sitting.

19. Take breaks.

Plan a break for your body and mind every 30-45 minutes. Get up, walk around, stretch, do something active or relaxing. However, avoid getting caught up in any long phone conversations or TV shows. You'll never get back to the studying!

20. Cut out the excuses.

It's perfectly normal to want to avoid doing schoolwork. Just about everybody has a whole list of techniques for work avoidance. And the excuses people give for putting off or ignoring it are so numerous, they could fill a whole book. Excuses just take up your energy. In the time you waste convincing yourself or anyone else that you have a good reason for avoiding your studies, you could be getting some of the work done. If you want to be a better student, you'll need to dump your own list of excuses.

21. Plan ahead for long-range assignments.

Start early on long-range assignments, big projects, and test preparations. Don't wait until the night before anything is due. You never know what will happen that last day. You could be distracted, sick, or unexpectedly derailed. Get going on long tasks several days before the due date. Make a list of everything that needs to be done for a long-range assignment (including finding information and collecting supplies). Then, start from the due-date and work backwards. Make a timeline or schedule that sets a time to do each of the tasks on the list.

22. Don't get behind.

Keeping up is good. Many students slip into failure, stress, and hopelessness because they get behind. The best way to avoid all of these is simply not to get behind. This means do your assignments on time.

Getting behind is often caused by procrastination. Don't procrastinate. The more you do, the worse you feel, and the harder it is to catch up.

If you do get behind because of illness or something else unavoidable, do something about it. Don't get further and further into the pit! Talk to the teacher. Make a plan for catching up.

23. Get on top of problems.

Don't let small problems develop into big ones. If you are lost in a class, missed an assignment, don't understand something, or have done poorly on something—act quickly. Talk to the teacher, ask a parent to help, find another student who has the information. Do something to correct the problem before it becomes overwhelming.

24. Ask for help.

You don't have to solve every problem alone or learn everything by yourself. Don't count on someone noticing that you need help. Tell them. Use the adults and services around you to ask for help when you need it. Remember, it is the teacher's job to teach you. Most teachers are happy to help a student who shows interest in getting help.

25. Reward yourself for accomplishments.

If you break your assignments down into manageable tasks, you'll have more successes more often. Congratulate and reward yourself for each task accomplished, by taking a break, getting some popcorn, going for a walk, bragging to someone about what you've done, or any other way you discover. Every accomplishment is worth celebrating!

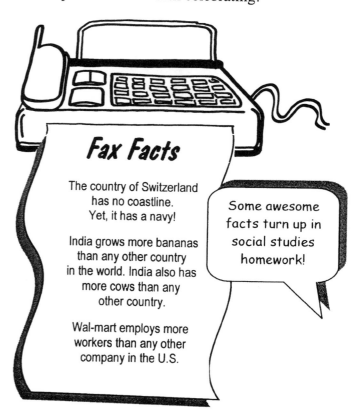

Fax Facts

The country of Switzerland has no coastline. Yet, it has a navy!

India grows more bananas than any other country in the world. India also has more cows than any other country.

Wal-mart employs more workers than any other company in the U.S.

Some awesome facts turn up in social studies homework!

GET SET →

Get Familiar with Social Studies Themes

Social studies includes many different sciences and areas of study–all of them related to people. Without people, there can be no study of anything *social*! The subject of social studies describes, examines, and explains how and where and when people live, their groups, relationships, and institutions. To get an overview of the social studies, you can divide the subject into these themes, or big ideas.

> Psychology and sociology are social sciences that study the growth, development, and behavior of people.

> Sociology and anthropology are social sciences that study culture.

Culture

. . . the features that contribute to culture traits
. . . how culture is learned
. . . relationships between values, behavior, and ideologies
. . . characteristics of specific cultures
. . . similarities in cultures and differences between cultures
. . . the multicultural nature of a country
. . . how cultures change
. . . how cultures affect other cultures

People in Societies

. . . how personal identity is shaped
. . . various forms of social interaction and groups
. . . how individuals function in groups
. . . roles of individuals in institutions
. . . the role of institutions in the lives of individuals
. . . the need for rules, laws, and authority in groups
. . . changes in institutions and how institutions change society

Places

. . . the different places and regions of the world
. . . physical and human characteristics of different regions
. . . why people live where they do
. . . interrelationships between people, cultures, and places
. . . reasons for movement of people and materials
. . . how technology affects places

> Geography and anthropology are social sciences that study the relationships between people and places.

Time and Change

. . . the location of people, cultures, and events in time
. . . chronological relationships between events
. . . significant contributions of individuals and groups to historical events
. . . causes and effects of historical events
. . . what has happened in the past and how it has affected people
. . . things that have changed over time; things that have stayed the same
. . . relationships between past and present conditions, events, or institutions
. . . differing interpretations of historical events and issues
. . . the role of science and technology in changes

> History is a social science that focuses on time and the changes that occur over time in human societies and institutions.

Power, Authority, and Government

. . . structures of power, authority, and government
. . . different forms of power
. . . the origins, purposes, functions, and formations of governments
. . . the function of power and authority in social groups
. . . different forms of government and political systems
. . . individual rights within political systems
. . . features of American democracy
. . . structures and functions of different governments

Citizenship

. . . individual participation in society
. . . rights and responsibilities of citizens
. . . the principles and origins of different governments
. . . the electoral process and importance of voting
. . . role of individuals as citizens of cities, states, nations, and the world

> Political science, sociology, and history are social sciences that study power, authority, and government.

> Political science and history are social sciences that study the roles of citizens in political systems.

> Economics, political science, and sociology are social sciences that study the role of economics in the lives of individuals and societies.

> History, economics, political science, anthropology, sociology, and geography are social sciences that study global connections.

Economics

. . . the dilemma of scarcity and why decisions must be made about use of resources
. . . benefits and consequences of choices about use of resources
. . . the wants and needs of individuals and societies
. . . what different individuals, groups, and societies consume
. . . the relationship between production and consumption
. . . how goods are produced and distributed
. . . how different economic systems make use of resources
. . . how different economic systems produce, distribute, and exchange goods and services
. . . the results of trade and economic interdependence
. . . the interrelationships between economic, political, and social systems or events

Global Connections

. . . how nations and cultures interact, cooperate, and clash
. . . issues that concern many or all nations; problems that affect the globe
. . . different kinds of connections–political, economic, cultural, environmental
. . . political and military divisions, clashes, and alliances
. . . roles of international institutions and agreements

Get Tuned-Up on Thinking Skills

Your brain is capable of an amazing variety of accomplishments! There are different levels and kinds of thinking that your brain can do—all of them necessary to get you set for good learning. To answer social studies questions, your brain must use many different processes. Here are some of the thinking skills that will freshen up your mental flexibility and keep your mind sharp as you learn concepts and investigate events in the many areas of social studies.

Recall – To **recall** is to know and remember specific facts, names, processes, categories, ideas, generalizations, theories, or information.

> **Examples:** *Recall helps you remember such things as the branches of the U.S. government, the location of Malaysia, the meanings of symbols for maps, who first landed on the Moon, the latitude of the North Pole, the length of a senator's term of office, or the difference between a stock and a bond.*

Classify – To **classify** is to put things into categories. When you classify ideas, events, topics, or things, you must choose categories that fit the purpose and clearly define each category.

> ### Example: *Russia, Vietnam, North Korea, Cambodia, Indonesia, China*
>
> *There are many different ways to classify these items. They are all countries. They are also countries in Asia, and countries that border the Pacific Ocean.*

Over 2000 jellyfish traveled into space in 1991 on space shuttle STS-40. I guess that means I could classify jellyfish as astronauts.

It would be faulty to generalize that all space shuttles have carried jellyfish.

Generalize – To **generalize** is to make a broad statement about a topic based on observations or facts. A generalization should be based on plenty of evidence (facts, observations, and examples). Just one exception can prove a generalization false.

> **Examples:**
>
> **Safe generalization:**
>
> *Climates at high latitudes are likely to be cooler than those at low latitudes.*
>
> **Invalid generalizations:**
>
> A **faulty generalization** is invalid because there are exceptions.
>
> *Average temperatures at latitudes of 45° are lower than temperatures at latitudes of 25°.*
>
> A **broad generalization** suggests something is *always* or *never* true about *all* or *none* of the members of a group. Most broad generalizations are untrue.
>
> *The climate is hot and dry at all locations between 0° and 10° latitude.*

Elaborate – To **elaborate** is to provide details about a situation (to explain, compare, or give examples). When you elaborate, you might use words or phrases such as these: *so, because, however, but, an example of this is, on the other hand, as a result, in addition, moreover, for instance, such as, if you recall, furthermore, another reason is.*

> **Example:** *Many thinkers, such as Galileo, Newton, and Copernicus, made contributions to scientific advances during the Renaissance.*

Predict – To **predict** is to make a statement about what will happen. Predictions are based on some previous knowledge, experience, or understanding.

> **Example:** *After September 11, 2001, many U.S. citizens were willing to have their rights to privacy reduced in efforts to increase security from terrorist attacks. Charlie predicts that if threats and acts of terrorism increase, citizens will continue to tolerate these kinds of restrictions on their freedoms.*

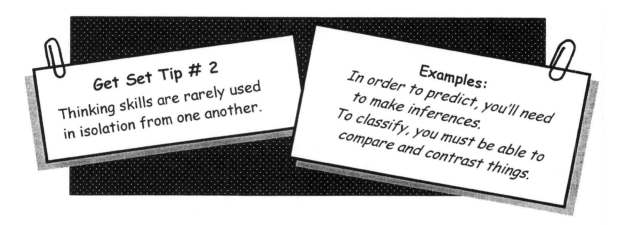

Get Set Tip # 2
Thinking skills are rarely used in isolation from one another.

Examples:
In order to predict, you'll need to make inferences.
To classify, you must be able to compare and contrast things.

Infer – To **infer** is to make a logical guess based on information.

> **Example:** *Alex has noticed that stock prices have fallen steadily for the last several months. He infers that buyers have lost confidence in the stock market.*

Recognize Cause and Effect – When one event occurs as the result of another event, there is a **cause-effect relationship** between the two. Recognizing causes and effects takes skill. When you read or hear about an event or group of events, pay careful attention to words or symbols that give clues to cause and effect (*the reason was, because, as a result, consequently, so*).

> **Example:** *Because of hurricane damage to the fields, this year's crop production was greatly reduced.*

Extend – To **extend** is to connect ideas or things together, or to relate one thing to something different, or to apply one idea or understanding to another situation.

> **Example:** *A group of students read the "U.S. Constitution," including all amendments. Afterwards, they wrote a "Student's Bill of Rights" for their school, modeled after the principles in the "U.S. Constitution's Bill of Rights."*

33

Distinguish Fact from Opinion - A **fact** is a statement that can be proven to be

true. An **opinion** expresses personal attitudes or beliefs. Many opinions tell what
a person believes or wishes should be so. It is not always easy to tell the difference
between fact and opinion. Good thinkers will analyze statements carefully in order
to keep from accepting opinions as fact.

Examples:

An investment in the stock market does not yield a guaranteed profit. (Fact)

It is not wise to invest in the stock market. (Opinion)

A savings account is a better investment than buying real estate. (Opinion)

Think Logically (or Reason) - When you think **logically**, you take a statement or

situation apart and examine the relationships of parts to one another. You reason **inductively**
(start from a general principle and make inferences about the details) or **deductively**
(start from a group of details and draw a broad conclusion or make a generalization).

> I served shredded pork, potato salad, pineapple slush, creamed cabbage, and baked beans to twenty-six guests at my luau. Everyone consumed some of the pork, the beans, and the pineapple slush. Half of the guest ate the potato salad, but only four ate the creamed cabbage. Thirteen got food poisoning. I wonder what caused it?

> Since half of the guests ate potato salad and half of them got sick, I **deduce** that the potato salad was the culprit.

Compare & Contrast - When you **compare** things, you describe similarities.

When you **contrast** things, you describe the differences.

Examples:

Compare: *Russia and China are huge countries with long coastlines. Both border the Pacific Ocean and have extensive fishing industries.*

Contrast: *Russia extends into the continent of Europe, while China does not. China's government is a Communist dictatorship. Russia's government moved away from communist control many years ago.*

Draw Conclusions - A **conclusion** is a general statement that someone makes after analyzing examples and details. A conclusion generally involves an explanation someone has developed through reasoning.

> **Example:** *Maxie reviews the maps of several countries, looking for the locations of large cities. She notices that most of the largest cities in these countries lie along coastlines or major rivers. She concludes that cities developed in areas where goods and people could be transported by water.*

Analyze - To **analyze,** you must break something down into parts and determine how the parts are related to each other and how they are related to the whole.

> **Examples:** *You must analyze to . . .*
> *. . . identify different institutions in a culture and describe their functions.*
> *. . . describe the ethnic groups within a society.*
> *. . . explain the difference between characteristics of a fjord and a lake.*
> *. . . discuss the role of each house of Congress in making a law.*

Synthesize - To **synthesize,** you must combine ideas or elements to create a whole.

> **Examples:** *You must synthesize to . . .*
> *. . . explain how the movement of political, economic, and religious conditions led to mass emigrations from Europe to America.*
> *. . . describe the process by which a president is elected in the United States.*
> *. . . understand how factors and events combined to start the World War I.*
> *. . . create a map to show the average monthly rainfall in various parts of Australia.*

You've said that the invention of the microchip had a more significant effect on modern society than any other event of the 20th century.
The reason you gave was that it turned the children of the world into video game players.
I think your conclusion may be right, but you only gave one example of the effects of the microchip. I need to hear more examples and more evidence.

Evaluate - To **evaluate** is to make a judgment about something. Evaluations should be based on evidence. Evaluations can include opinions, but these opinions should be supported or explained by examples, experiences, observations, and other forms of evidence.

> **Examples:** *When you evaluate an argument, an explanation, a decision, a prediction, an inference, a conclusion, or a generalization, ask questions like these:*
> • *Are the conclusions reached based on good facts?*
> • *Is there evidence for the generalization or inference?*
> • *Is the evidence substantial? (Is there enough?)*
> • *Does the explanation make sense?*
> • *Are the sources used to make the decisions reliable?*
> • *Did the writer or speaker give clear examples?*
> • *Is the argument effective?*
> • *Is it realistic?*

35

Identify Faulty Arguments – An **argument** is **faulty** when it is based on an error in logic. This means the information is misleading, or there are exceptions to the statement, or the statement is not supported by evidence.

Examples:

Once you visit Congress, you'll want to run for public office.

Any business that does not display a flag has owners that are unpatriotic.

People who invest in the stock market have a lot of money.

Identify Biases – A **bias** is a one-sided attitude toward something. Biased thinking does not result from facts, but from feelings or attitudes. Learn to recognize biases. Biased information may not be reliable, especially if it's presented as fact or nonfiction.

Example: *I just know that anyone who has a tattoo is a person of low moral standards.*

Identify Propaganda –

Propaganda is a form of communication intended to make listeners or readers agree with the ideas of a group. Unlike ordinary persuasive writing, propaganda often focuses on an appeal to emotions. Propaganda often uses faulty arguments, exaggeration, or information that distorts or confuses the truth. To identify propaganda, look for faulty arguments, exaggeration, manipulation of facts, manipulation of emotions, or unsupported claims.

Identify Stereotypes – A **stereotype** is an oversimplified opinion or belief about a group, person, or event. A stereotype makes a generalization (often faulty or broad, or both) about someone or something as a group, without paying attention to individual circumstances or characteristics. A stereotype is often negative or critical in nature.

Examples:

People of that religion are untrustworthy.

Teenagers don't care about important issues. They are all selfish.

Get Brushed-Up on Information Skills

If you're going to get set to be a good student, you need sharp skills for finding and using information. You're fortunate to live in a time and place of almost unlimited resources for finding information. You can only make use of those resources well if you know what they are and what's in them. Here's a quick review of some of the most common sources of information available for students. Get to know these references well.

Which Reference is Which?

Almanac: a yearly publication that gives information, basic facts, and statistics on many topics. Almanacs are organized with lists of information by topics. They have an alphabetical index. Much of the information is about current or recent years, but some of it is historical. Almanacs cover current events, famous people, sports, countries, geographic records, and many other categories. They usually have an index that lists information by categories.

Atlas: a book of maps. Atlases give geographical information in the forms of maps, tables, graphs, and lists. They include information about geography, including population, climate, weather, elevation, vegetation, regions, topics, topography, and much more. Some maps in atlases show political information such as countries and cities.

Bibliography: a list of books, articles, and/or other resources about a certain topic. Often a bibliography is found at the end of a book or article, giving a list of the sources used in the publication.

Biographical Dictionary or Biographical Reference: a book that gives a brief summary of the lives and accomplishments of famous persons. Entries are listed alphabetically. *Contemporary Authors, The Dictionary of American Biography*, and *Who's Who in America*, are examples of this kind of reference.

Dictionary: a book that lists the standard words of a particular language alphabetically, and gives their meanings and pronunciations. Many dictionaries also provide other information about the word, such as the part of speech, uses, antonyms, and etymologies.

Special Dictionaries: dictionaries of words related to one subject only. There are many special dictionaries, listing such things as slang, scientific terms, historical terms, geographical features, biographies, foreign words, or abbreviations.

Glossary: a listing of the important terms used in a specific book or article, accompanied by their definitions. A glossary is arranged alphabetically and generally located at the end of the book or article.

Encyclopedias: a set of books providing information on many branches of knowledge. Usually there are many volumes. Information is presented in the form of articles, and consists of a survey of the topic. The information is arranged alphabetically according to the topic or name of a person, place, or event. It is best to use key words to search for a topic in an encyclopedia.

Special Encyclopedias: There are many encyclopedias that contain information about one subject rather than about many subjects. Individual volume encyclopedias or whole sets cover such topics as science, art, music, history, and sports. Don't miss this one: *The Encyclopedia of American Facts and Dates.*

Get Set Tip # 2

Guide words are a great help in using dictionaries, glossaries, and encyclopedias. All the words on a page fall alphabetically between the two guide words.

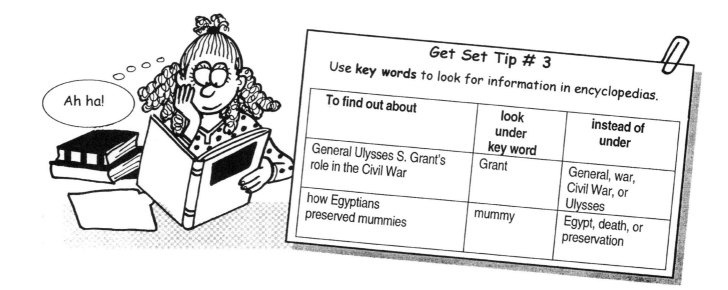

Ah ha!

Get Set Tip # 3

Use key words to look for information in encyclopedias.

To find out about	look under key word	instead of under
General Ulysses S. Grant's role in the Civil War	Grant	General, war, Civil War, or Ulysses
how Egyptians preserved mummies	mummy	Egypt, death, or preservation

Famous First Facts: a book that lists facts about firsts (first events, accomplishments, discoveries, and inventions) of many kinds in America, listed alphabetically. There is also an international version.

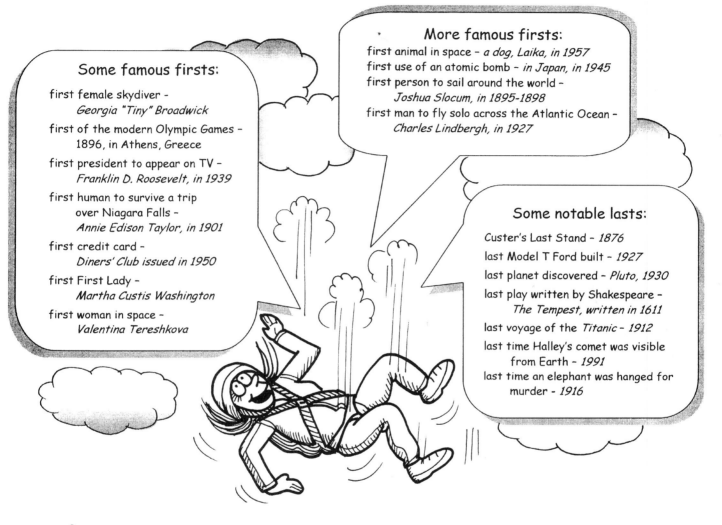

Some famous firsts:

first female skydiver - *Georgia "Tiny" Broadwick*

first of the modern Olympic Games – *1896, in Athens, Greece*

first president to appear on TV – *Franklin D. Roosevelt, in 1939*

first human to survive a trip over Niagara Falls – *Annie Edison Taylor, in 1901*

first credit card – *Diners' Club issued in 1950*

first First Lady – *Martha Custis Washington*

first woman in space – *Valentina Tereshkova*

More famous firsts:

first animal in space – *a dog, Laika, in 1957*

first use of an atomic bomb – *in Japan, in 1945*

first person to sail around the world – *Joshua Slocum, in 1895-1898*

first man to fly solo across the Atlantic Ocean – *Charles Lindbergh, in 1927*

Some notable lasts:

Custer's Last Stand - *1876*

last Model T Ford built – *1927*

last planet discovered – *Pluto, 1930*

last play written by Shakespeare – *The Tempest, written in 1611*

last voyage of the *Titanic* - *1912*

last time Halley's comet was visible from Earth - *1991*

last time an elephant was hanged for murder - *1916*

Gazetteer: a geographical dictionary, listing information about important places in the world. Subjects and places are listed alphabetically.

Guinness Book of Records: a collection of information about the best and worst, most and least, biggest and smallest, longest and shortest, and other facts and records.

Index: a list of information or items found in a book, magazine, set of books, set of magazines, or other publications. The index is generally located at the end of the resource. Information is listed alphabetically. Sometimes a resource has an index that is a separate book. A specific magazine or journal sometimes has its own index, as do most encyclopedia sets. To find the volume and page location of information in a set of encyclopedias, you would consult the encyclopedia index accompanying the encyclopedia set. When a reference is on CD or online, a CD or online index accompanies the reference.

Get Set
Tip # 4

When you find a site that gives good information, add it to your list of favorites (or bookmark it) so you can get there quickly next time.

Internet: an extensive computer network that holds a huge amount of information from organizations and groups around the world as well as government agencies, libraries, schools and universities, educational organizations, businesses. Information can be located by browsing through categories and sites assembled by your Internet service provider and by searching the Web with the help of a good search engine. The Internet can connect you to information on a vast number of topics related to all sorts of subject areas.

Library Card Catalog:

a file of cards that has three cards for every book in the library. These cards are filed separately in sets of drawers. For each book or item, there is an author card, which is filed alphabetically by the author's last name; a subject card, which is filed alphabetically according to the subject of the book, and a title card, which is filed alphabetically according to the title of the book. In many libraries, card catalogs have been put into computer databases.

Library Computer Catalog:

a computer file or database of author, title, and subject listings for all books (and other materials) in a library. The computer system usually allows you to search by title, author, subject, or key words. It shows a list of materials on your subject or by your author available in the library, and the current status of the item (whether it is checked out or available for you to check out). Often the computer system also connects to databases of articles or books online that you can read and/or print.

Periodicals: publications that are issued at regular intervals, such as daily, weekly, monthly, quarterly, or annually. Magazines, newspapers, and scholarly journals are types of periodicals. Periodicals are an excellent source of current news and information.

Periodical Index: a book or computer database that lists the subjects and titles of articles in a particular magazine or newspaper, or a particular group of magazines or newspapers.

Newspapers: periodicals published frequently, containing current information on national, international, and local news. Newspapers provide a wealth of information on sports, financial trends and figures, weather, book reviews, editorial comments, reviews of film, theater, and other entertainment events. Other features (such as classified ads, comics, puzzles, restaurant reviews, recipes, horoscopes, and listings for TV, radio, and movie programs) add to the list of information available in newspapers.

Quotation Index: listing of famous quotations and the persons who said them, listed alphabetically by the first word of the quotation and by the last name of the person. A popular quotation index is *Bartlett's Familiar Quotations*.

Table of Contents: an outline of the information contained in a book, listed in order that the information occurs in the book. The Table of Contents is found at the beginning of the book.

Thesaurus: a reference book that groups synonyms or words with similar meanings. A thesaurus is sometimes organized by idea or theme with an alphabetical index. Other versions organize the words like a dictionary. Some thesaurus editions contain antonyms as well as synonyms.

Yearbook: a book that gives up-to-date information about recent events or findings, or that reviews events of a particular year. One such yearbook is the *World Book Yearbook of Facts*. Many encyclopedia sets publish a yearbook to update the set each year. This reduces the need to update the entire set to keep information current.

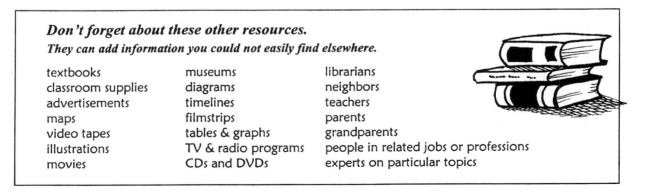

Don't forget about these other resources.
They can add information you could not easily find elsewhere.

textbooks	museums	librarians
classroom supplies	diagrams	neighbors
advertisements	timelines	teachers
maps	filmstrips	parents
video tapes	tables & graphs	grandparents
illustrations	TV & radio programs	people in related jobs or professions
movies	CDs and DVDs	experts on particular topics

Finding Information on the Internet

It's a skill to use the Internet well for finding reliable information. It takes practice. Here's some good advice for smart use of the Internet.

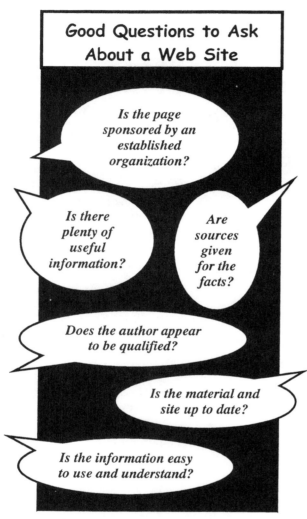

Good Questions to Ask About a Web Site

Is the page sponsored by an established organization?

Is there plenty of useful information?

Are sources given for the facts?

Does the author appear to be qualified?

Is the material and site up to date?

Is the information easy to use and understand?

That's a Good Question!

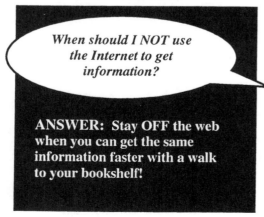

When should I NOT use the Internet to get information?

ANSWER: Stay OFF the web when you can get the same information faster with a walk to your bookshelf!

Browse – Your Internet provider gathers pages on general topics. These give you quick access to information on several of the most popular topics, such as news, weather, health travel, music, and sports. Most providers also offer links to kids' pages and reference materials.

Search – For a more advanced search, use a good search engine such as google.com or yahoo.com. Try different engines until you find your favorite. To use a search engine, type in a key word (such as **nuclear**). To make your search more specific, type in a phrase (such as **nuclear weapons**) or more than one word connected by AND (**nuclear** AND **weapons** AND **treaties**).

Be selective – Use your time wisely to get the best information by choosing reputable sites. Sites from the government, established companies or organizations, and universities are usually reliable *(Examples: National Hockey League www.nhl.com; Field Museum of Natural History www.fmnh.org; NASA www.nasa.gov; National Geographic for Kids www.nationalgeographic.com/kids)*.

Be smart – Learn to evaluate the websites you visit, and don't waste time on sites that won't yield information that is reliable or substantial.

Be cautious – If you download information, beware of viruses. Download information only from sites that seem reputable. If you are going to download software, it is safest to do it directly from the company that publishes the software. Be very careful what you download from individuals. Never open an email or download a file unless you know the source of the document. Keep a good anti-virus program on your computer, and keep it updated.

Be safe – NEVER give any personal information away on the Internet.

Better Grades & Higher Test Scores / SOCIAL STUDIES
Copyright ©2003 by Incentive Publications, Inc., Nashville, TN.

Good Stuff on the Web

The Internet has wonderful social studies facts, explanations, and discussions, if you know where to look. There are hundreds of good sites. Check out a few of these to find fascinating information related to culture, society, geography, economics, civics, or history.

American Memory, Library of Congress:
memory.loc.gov

American Museum of Natural History, Ology:
ology.amnh.org

Hands On History:
www.angelfire.com/ma4/handsonhistory

Atlapedia Online (World Maps Online):
www.atlapedia.com

BBC History for Kids:
www.bbc.co.uk/history/forkids

Ben's Guide to U.S. Government for Kids:
bensguide.gpo.gov

CIA Kids Page:
www.cia.gov/cia/ciakids

CIA Kids Page History:
www.cia.gov/cia/ciakids/history

CIA Kids Page Geography:
www.cia.gov/cia/ciakids/geography

FirstGov for Kids (with links to Geography, History, Government, Money & Finances):
www.kids.gov

Geography 4 Kids:
www.geography4kids.com

History Channel:
www.historychannel.com

H4K (History for Kids):
www.historyforkids.org

Infoplease.com:
www.infoplease.com

KidsClick:
sunsite.berkeley.edu/KidsClick!

The Internet Public Library: States Facts:
www.ipl.org/div/kidspace/stateknow

Library of Congress Geography & Maps:
lcweb.loc.gov/rr/geogmap

NASA's Visible Earth:
www.visibleearth.nasa.gov

National Geographic Kids:
www.nationalgeographic.com/kids

National Geographic for Kids GeoSpy:
www.nationalgeographic.com/geospy

National Geographic Maps & Geography:
www.nationalgeographic.com/maps

Netstate.com:
www.netstate.com/states

Smithsonian Institute:
www.si.edu

U.S. Geological Survey Education Site:
www.usgs.gov/education

U.S. Census Bureau Fact Finder Kids' Corner:
factfinder.census.gov/home/en/kids/kids.html

U.S. Mint Site for Kids:
www.usmint.gov/kids

U.S. Treasury for Kids:
www.ustreas.gov/kids

The United Nations:
www.un.org

Welcome to the White House:
www.whitehouse.gov

Get Serious about Study Skills

Let's face it–good learning and good grades don't happen without some sharp study skills. Take advantage of every opportunity you get to strengthen skills like the ones described on pages 44-58.

Better Listening

Keep your ears wide open! Here are some tips for smart listening. They can help you get involved with the information instead of letting it just buzz by your ears.

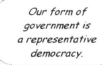

Our form of government is a representative democracy.

That's right! Where have I heard that before?

Get Set
Tip # 3
Stop talking!
(You can't listen while you talk!)

1. Realize that the information is important.

Here's what you can get when you listen to someone who giving you information:

. . . details about a social studies concept or event
. . . help answering social studies questions
. . . examples of projects done correctly
. . . hazards or difficulties you might face when doing a social studies project
. . . meanings of terms used in social studies questions or assignments
. . . directions for certain assignments

2. Be aware of the obstacles to good listening.

Know ahead of time that these will interfere with your ability to listen well. Try to avoid them, alter them, or manage them, so they don't get in the way.

. . . fatigue
. . . surrounding noise
. . . uncomfortable setting
. . . personal thoughts or worries

. . . wandering attention
. . . too many things to hear at once
. . . missing the beginning or ending
. . . talking

3. Make a commitment to improve.

You can't always control all obstacles (such as the comfort of the setting or the quality of the speaker's presentation), but there are things you can control. Put these to work to gain more from your listening.

. . . Get enough rest.
. . . Do your best to be comfortable while you listen.
. . . Cut out distractions. Keep your mind focused on what is being said.
. . . Look directly at the speaker.
. . . Take notes. Write down examples that the speaker gives.
. . . As the speaker talks, think of examples or relate the information to your life.
. . . Pay special attention to opening and closing remarks.
. . . Pay special attention to anything that is repeated.
. . . Soon after listening, summarize or review what you have heard.

Careful Reading

There is plenty of reading in social studies. Textbooks and other materials explain concepts and processes. Many social studies lessons include details from lists, maps, charts, graphs, or captions that you need to read closely and interpret. All social studies questions or assignments include some sort of instructions to follow.

Before you read a social studies article or assignment, have a clear idea of the purpose for reading. Are you reading to find directions for the assignment? Are you reading to gain general understanding of a concept? Are you reading to solve a problem or answer a question? Are you reading to find a particular fact? You can accomplish some purposes by skimming quickly. For other purposes, you need to read closely, paying attention to every detail. In some cases you may need to read the information more than once–possibly even several times.

Renaissance means "rebirth." This is the name given to a period of time in European history when there was a renewed interest in the art, architecture, and learning of classical Greece and Rome. This period of great interest in exploring new ideas marked the end of the Middle Ages and the beginning of the modern age. The Renaissance began in Italy in the 14th century and spread throughout all of Europe in the 15th and 16th centuries. During this time, there were many exciting accomplishments and advancements in science, medicine, art, literature, architecture, music, and theater. Wealthy patrons such as the Medicis, a family of Florentine bankers, gave money to support artists and scholars, luring artists to work in their cities. Michelangelo and Leonardo da Vinci were two of the artists who made Florence their home. Architect Filippo Brunelleschi and writer Dante Alighieri also benefited from the patronage of the Medici family. Perhaps mainly due to the support of the Medicis, Florence was a center of activity where many of the arts flourished during the Renaissance. Florence is also known as the birthplace of opera, which began there about 1600.

Skimming

By skimming the passage, a reader can quickly gain the main ideas:

. . . *The Renaissance was a period of renewed interest and accomplishments in art, science, and learning.*

. . . *Patrons gave financial support to enable artists and thinkers to do their work.*

. . . *The Renaissance ended the Middle Ages and began the modern age.*

Reading Closely

With a closer, slower reading, the reader will discover specific details, such as:

. . . *the time period over which the Renaissance spread*

. . . *where the Renaissance began*

. . . *what it was that was "reborn" during the Renaissance*

. . . *the city where the Medici family lived*

. . . *the profession of the Medici family*

. . . *some of the artists and scholars supported by the Medici family*

. . . *the function of patrons of the arts*

. . . *when and where opera was born*

Summarizing & Paraphrasing

What's the Difference?

Hey Joe! I have to summarize some stuff for economics class. Then, I'm supposed to write a paraphrase of the information, too. What's the difference between a summary and a paraphrase?

Well Gina, a **paraphrase** is a restatement of someone else's ideas in your own words. It covers ALL the ideas from the original statement.

A **summary** is a short statement of the MAIN IDEAS of a speech or piece of writing.

Can You Trade Your Dollars for Gold?

The U.S. dollar used to be backed by gold and the country's money system was called the gold standard. This is a system of currency in which paper money can be exchanged for a fixed amount of gold. The purpose for this system was to be sure that the money was worth something.

As the United States government and economy got stronger, the currency was strengthened also. The need for gold to back the money was not so strong. So, the United States gave up the gold standard in 1971. Without the gold standard, the amount of money in circulation does not have to depend on the amount of gold in storage.

However, the U.S. government still has plenty of gold; the amount is in the billions of dollars. The gold is stored at Fort Knox, Kentucky, in a bomb-proof building. Alarm systems and many armed guards keep the building and gold secure. No one has ever broken into Fort Knox.

Yes, there was a time when you could bring your paper money to a bank and exchange it for gold; but that time is gone!

Summary:

At one time, the U.S. dollar was backed by a gold standard, where each dollar was worth a fixed amount of gold. Though the government still holds billions of dollars worth of gold, the gold-backed system has been abandoned.

Paraphrase:

The United States used to have a money system that used gold to back each dollar. To assure that paper money had a stable value, the money could be exchanged at a bank for a fixed amount of gold. As the government and economy grew stronger, the need for a gold-backed system disappeared. The gold standard was abandoned in 1971, and the amount of money in circulation is not related to the amount of gold the government has. You can no longer trade your dollars for gold at a bank.

Even though the gold standard is gone, the government still holds billions of dollars worth of gold in secure storage at Fort Knox, KY.

Outlining

An outline is a way to organize ideas or information into main ideas and sub-ideas (or supporting details). If you want to get set to improve as a student, it's a good idea to polish your outlining skills. An outline can be formal or informal. It can contain single words, phrases, or sentences, depending on its purpose. You will find outlining very helpful for many study situations.

You can use an outline to:

- organize ideas to prepare a speech
- organize ideas for a piece of writing
- plan a project
- record and review information from a textbook
- get ready to re-tell a story
- take notes in class
- take notes from a textbook assignment
- prepare to give or write a report
- write a story
- write a speech
- study a passage

I wrote this outline as I read a section from my history textbook. Doing the outline helped me find the main points in the assignment. Writing the outline also helped me process and remember the information.

The 1920s

I. America after the war
  A. Election of 1920
    1. 19th amendment (giving women the right to vote)
    2. large voter turnout
    3. victory of Harding
  B. Foreign policy
    1. 5-Power Naval Treaty
       (promised battleship constructions)
    2. Open Door Policy
       (9 nations assured rights to trade with China)
    3. Post-war isolationist mood
  C. Mood & Issues in the nation
    1. Wave of labor strikes
    2. Red Scare, Palmer Raids (fear of Communism)
    3. Revival of Ku Klux Klan, discrimination, race riots
    4. New immigration laws to slow flow of immigrants
       a. Emergency Quota Act
       b. National Origins Act
    5. Sacco-Vanzetti Case (result of xenophobia)
    6. Prohibition (18th Amendment)
    7. Growing fundamentalist movement
II. Roaring Twenties
  A. Jazz Age
  B. Cultural revitalization in Harlem
  C. Golden Age of Sports
  D. Rise in popularity of motion pictures
  E. Radio becomes giant industry
III. The automobile civilization
  A. Ford mass produces cars
  B. Rise of automobile leads to economic boom
  C. Expansion of road building and tourism
  D. Auto allows move to suburbs
  E. Increase in traffic and air pollution
  F. Rapid use of oil reserves

Better Grades & Higher Test Scores / SOCIAL STUDIES
Copyright ©2003 by Incentive Publications, Inc., Nashville, TN.

Taking Notes

A study skill of major importance is knowing how to take notes well and using them effectively. Good notes taken from classes and from reading are valuable resources to anyone trying to do well as a student. A lot of learning goes on while you're taking notes. You may not even realize it's happening!

When you take notes

1. . . . you naturally listen better. (You have to listen in order to get the information and write it down!)

2. . . . you listen differently, so you naturally learn and understand the material better. Taking notes forces you to focus on what's being said or read.

3. . . . you sort through the information and decide what to write. This means you naturally think about the material and process it—making it more likely that you'll remember it.

4. . . . the actual act of writing the notes fixes the information more firmly in your brain.

5. . . . you end up with good notes in your notebook. When you can actually look at written examples of definitions, facts, events, processes, or characteristics, you are way ahead in your efforts to review and remember important information.

1 Listen or read for a main idea, key formula, or important process. Write it down.

2 Write examples, problems, definitions, and details to support each key idea.

3 Review your notes as soon as possible after the class. This will help to fix the information in your brain.

Tips for Wise Note-Taking

. . . in class

- Have a notebook or a notebook section for social studies.
- When the class begins, write the topic for the day at the top of a clean page.
- Write the date at the top of the page.
- Use an erasable pen for clear notes, not a pencil.
- Write down examples of situations or problems.
- Write notes to yourself about explanations for different events or situations.
- Write neatly so you can read your notes later.
- Leave a big margin to the left of the outline. Use this space to mark important items or write key words.
- Leave a blank space after each main idea section.
- Pay close attention to the opening and closing remarks.
- Listen more than you write.
- ASK about anything you do not understand.

Get Set Tip # 5
When you take notes in class, be alert for signals from the teacher about important ideas. Write down anything the speaker (or teacher):

...writes on the board.

...gives as a definition.

...emphasizes with his or her voice.

...repeats.

...says is important.

. . . from a textbook assignment

- Skim through one section at a time to get the general idea. (Use the textbook divisions as a guide to separate sections, or read a few paragraphs at a time.)
- After skimming, go back and write down the main ideas.
- Write a few supporting details or examples for each main idea. If a social studies term, event, or concept is explained, write down a summary of the explanation or a correct example.
- Notice bold or emphasized words or phrases. Write these down with definitions.
- Read captions under pictures. Pay attention to facts, tables, charts, graphs, and pictures, and the explanations that go along with them. If information is very important, put it in your notes.
- Don't write too little. You won't have all the main points or enough examples.
- Don't write too much. You won't have time or interest in reviewing the notes.

Better Grades & Higher Test Scores / SOCIAL STUDIES
Copyright ©2003 by Incentive Publications, Inc., Nashville, TN.

Get Set: Study Skills

Preparing a Report

Reports are everywhere! Students are always being asked to do a report of some kind. When you hear the word, you might immediately think of a book report or a long written paper. But the world of reports is far broader than this. There are all kinds of reports. They can be papers, posters, demonstrations, speeches, audio or visual presentations, computer projects or art projects, to name a few. They can be assigned for any subject area to cover just about any topic.

Whatever the subject or the type of report, they all have some things in common. First, you need some raw material (facts and information) as the basis for the report. To get that, you need to do some research. Then, for any report, you must select and organize the information so that it can be communicated (or reported!) Finally, a report is presented. This means you need to find a way to share with someone else what you learned about the topic.

Here are some steps to follow for any report of any kind on any topic. Page 53 gives some suggestions for creative or out-of-the ordinary kinds of reports. This will get you thinking beyond the standard written report.

Step 1   Choose a topic.

Your topic might be assigned, but usually you Will have some choice. There are dozens of possibilities within any one subject or topic. When you do have a choice, follow these tips.

- Pick something that interests you.
- Make sure your topic is not too broad. If it is, there will be too much information to manage.
- Make sure your topic is not too narrow. If it is, you won't be able to find enough information to create a substantial report.

Step 2   Identify the subtopics.

- Make a list of the subtopics.
- Then, for each subtopic, note information you'll need to find that will support or explain that subtopic. *Ask:*

   What do I need to know about the topic?

   What categories are natural divisions for this topic?

- You might use a rough outline for this step.

DON'T CHOOSE A TOPIC THAT IS:
too broad: The History of All Transportation
too narrow: Facts About Red Cabooses

CHOOSE A TOPIC THAT IS JUST RIGHT:
The Growth of Railroads in the U.S.

Trains in America
I. *Early History*
   A. *Invention of trains*
   B. *The need for railroads in America*
   C. *The first railroads in America*
   D. *Development of railroad companies*
   E. *Trains and westward migration*
   F. *Trains and the economy*
II. *Recent History*
   A. *Passenger trains*
   B. *Trains transporting goods*
   C. *Railroad difficulties*
III. *Future of Trains*

I've chosen a topic that is one of my hobbies.

Step 3 Find information.

- Use as many resources as you can to find solid information on your topic. Don't limit yourself to just one source or one kind of source. (See pages 37-43.)

- As you observe, read, or listen to the sources, take notes. Write ideas, key words or phrases, and examples. Use a separate note card for each source and each major idea or fact you find. Use your subtopics as labels for the cards.

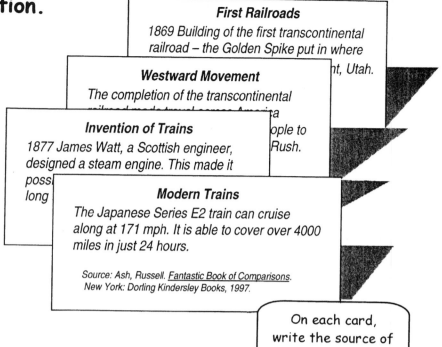

First Railroads
1869 Building of the first transcontinental railroad – the Golden Spike put in where [...]nt, Utah.

Westward Movement
The completion of the transcontinental [...] ople to [...] Rush.

Invention of Trains
1877 James Watt, a Scottish engineer, designed a steam engine. This made it possi[...] long [...]

Modern Trains
The Japanese Series E2 train can cruise along at 171 mph. It is able to cover over 4000 miles in just 24 hours.

Source: Ash, Russell. Fantastic Book of Comparisons. New York: Dorling Kindersley Books, 1997.

On each card, write the source of the information.

Step 4 Organize the information.

- Organize the information by grouping your cards into subtopics and placing them in a logical sequence. Decide what fits where.
- If you have too much information, or if some of your information doesn't quite fit, this is the time to eliminate some.
- If you have subtopics that are not well supported with examples or details, this is the time to do more research and collect more information.

Step 5 Decide on the format.

- If you've been asked to write a paper or give a speech, then the format is already decided.

- If you are free to choose a format or product, do this now.

- How will you show what you have learned? Will it be a paper, a speech, a demonstration, a dance, a musical production, a broadcast, an interview, a painting, a slide show, a mime?

- Decide now! The steps you follow from this point depend greatly on the format you choose.

Step 6 Begin to put the report together.

- If your report will be spoken or written, you'll begin writing sentences and paragraphs, making sure each paragraph covers a subtopic with supporting details.
- If your report follows a different format, you still need to decide how to communicate each idea and its supporting examples or details.

Get Set: Study Skills

Step 7 Review and edit your work.

- This is the time to look at your work. This is also a time to ask someone else to give a response. (Exactly how you review the work will depend on the format of the report.)

- Ask questions such as these about the "rough draft" of your report, whatever form it takes:

  Are the main ideas covered?
  Is the information clear?
  Is the information complete?
  Does the manner of presentation make sense?
  Does the report have a clear introduction and conclusion?
  Is there a logical order for the presentation?
  Is the material interesting? Is the presentation interesting?
  If written, does the piece flow along well?
  If written, are the mechanics and grammar correct?

- After you and another person (or persons) have reviewed it, make revisions that are necessary.

> **Get Set Tip # 6**
> Avoid these common problems with reports:
> - topic too broad
> - topic too narrow
> - missing some subtopics
> - not enough information on some subtopics
> - poor presentation of final product

Step 8 Put the final product together.

- Whatever the format, this is the time to prepare the final product. Add extra materials at this stage (drawings, diagrams, charts, maps, graphs, timelines, tables, surveys, music, etc).

Step 9 Present the report.

- How will you share the information? Turn it in? Hang it up? Sing it? Dance it? Show it? Read it? Perform it? Mail it? Publish it? This is the time to do it!

Creative Reporting

There are many ways a report can be structured and shared. It might take a little creativity (or a lot), but nearly any body of information can be presented in a number of different or unexpected ways. Here are just a few options for preparing and giving a report or presentation of your work and research.

Written or Spoken Reports

- clues to unravel a mystery
- phrases cut from magazines
- fictionalized account of an event
- book of crossword puzzles
- series of interview questions
- radio or TV broadcast
- series of riddles
- cause-effect account
- group of short poems
- series of emails

- viewpoint
- differing viewpoints
- one or more letters
- editorial
- diary entries
- narrative poem
- timeline
- protest
- dialogue
- argument

- The Fact Book About _____
- The ABC Book of _____
- Things You've Never Heard About_____
- A Top 10 List of _____
- 10 Facts & 10 Fables About _____
- A Day In the Life of _____
- The Truth About _____
- Myths About _____ Debunked
- 20 Questions & Answers About_____
- Strange & Amazing Facts About _____
- Future Predictions About _____

Reports That Combine Writing & Art

- children's picture book
- travel brochure
- time line
- book cover
- instructive poster
- illustrated guide book

- advertisement
- one or more maps
- original game
- music album cover
- How-To Handbook
- word & picture collage

- original CD
- cartoons
- original songs or an album
- slide presentation
- video presentation
- illustrated dictionary of terms

Other Reports:

- mime performance
- campaign speech
- demonstration
- scavenger hunt

- dance
- 3-D model
- drama
- sculpture

- drawings or paintings
- series of recipes
- plan for reality TV show
- rap performance

Get Set: Study Skills

How to Prepare for a Test

Good test preparation does not begin the night before the test. The time to get ready for a test starts long before this night. If you want to be a better test-taker, take the time to add some new habits to your life. They're not too hard; they just take some advance planning. These tips will help you get ready for a test weeks before the test and right up to test time.

1. Start your test preparation at the beginning of the year— or at least as soon as the material is first taught in the class.

The purpose of a test is to give a picture of what you are learning in the class. That learning doesn't start 12 hours before the test. It starts when you start attending the class. Think of test preparation this way, and you'll be less overwhelmed or anxious about an upcoming test.

- You'll be much better prepared for a test *(even one that is several days or weeks away)* if you . . .

  . . . pay attention in class.

  . . . take good notes and answer sample questions.

  . . . keep your notes and class handouts organized.

  . . . read all your assignments.

  . . . keep a good list of key events and definitions.

  . . . do your homework regularly.

  . . . make up any work you miss when you're absent.

  . . . ask questions in class about anything you don't understand.

  . . . review notes and handouts regularly.

2. Once you know the date of the test, make a study plan.

- Look over your schedule and plan time to start organizing and reviewing material.
- Allow plenty of time to go through all the material.
- Your brain will retain more if you review it a few times and spread the studying out over several days.

3. Get all the information you can about the test.

- Write down everything the teacher says about the test.
- Get clear about what material will be covered.
- If you can, find out about the format of the test.
- Make sure you get all study guides the teacher distributes.
- Make sure you listen well to any in-class reviews.

Is this Turkmenistan? Or, is it Uzbekistan? I should have studied those maps in my geography book!

4. Use your study time effectively.

Dos and Don'ts

- **DO** gather and organize all your notes and handouts.

- **DO** review your text; pay attention to bold words, bold statements, and examples of concepts, places, people, processes, or questions.

- **DO** identify the kinds of problems in the section being tested; practice solving a few of each kind.

- **DO** review the questions at the end of text sections; practice answering them.

- **DO** review your notes, using a highlighter to emphasize important points.

- **DO** review the study guides provided by the teacher.

- **DO** review any previous quizzes on the same material.

- **DO** predict the questions that may be asked and kinds of problems that will be included; think about how you would answer them.

- **DO** make study guides and aids for yourself.

- **DO** make sets of cards with key vocabulary words, terms and definitions, main concepts, events, or facts.

- **DO** ask someone (reliable) to quiz you on the main points and terms.

- **DON'T** spend your study time blankly staring your notebook or or mindlessly leafing through your textbook.

- **DON'T** study with someone else unless that person actually helps you learn the material better.

- **DON'T** study when you're hungry or tired.

- **DON'T** study so long at one time that you get tired, bored, or distracted.

5. Get yourself and your supplies ready.

Do these things the night before the test (not too late):
- Gather all the supplies you need for taking the test (good pencils with erasers, erasable pens, scratch paper, calculator with batteries).
- Put these supplies in your school bag.
- Gather your study guides, notes, and text into your school bag.
- Get a good night of rest.

In the morning on the day of the test:
- Eat a healthy breakfast.
- Look over your study guides and note card reminders.
- Relax and be confident that your preparation will pay off.

I'm eating my *brain* food.

55

How to Take a Test

The test:

I *think* it's B.

Government Test

X. The branch of the United Stat
government responsible
for declaring war is
A. the executive branch
B. the legislative branch
C. the judicial branch
2. The Secretary of State is part
of the
A. president's cabinet
B. court system
C. Department of Justice

Joe is not sure of the answer, so he makes a smart guess. He puts an X by the question so he will remember to come back to it later.

When he comes back to the question, he is still not sure, so he stays with his first answer.

I think I'll *keep* this answer.

Government Test

X1. The branch of the United Stat
government responsible
for declaring war is
A. the executive branch
B. the legislative branch
C. the judicial branch
2. The Secretary of State is part
of the
A. president's cabinet
B. court system
C. Department of Justice

Get Set Tip # 8
Research shows that your first answer is correct more often than not! So stick with it unless you are positive about another answer.

Before the test begins

- Get to class on time, or even a bit early, so you don't have to rush or feel extra stressed.

- Have supplies ready. Take sharpened pencils, scratch paper, pens, erasers, or any other supplies you need.

- Try to get a little exercise before class to help you relax.

- Go to the bathroom and get a drink.

- Get settled into your seat. Get your supplies out.

- If there's time, you might glance over your study guides while you wait.

- To relax, take some deep breaths; exhale slowly.

When you get the test

- Put your name on all pages.

- Before you write anything, scan over the test to see how long it is, what kinds of questions it has, and generally what it includes.

- Think about your time and quickly plan how much time you can spend on each section.

- Read each set of directions twice. Circle key words in the directions.

- Answer all the short-answer questions. Do not leave any blanks.

- If you are not sure of an answer, make a smart guess.

- Don't change an answer unless you are absolutely sure it is wrong.

Better Grades & Higher Test Scores / SOCIAL STUDIES

More Test-Taking Tips

Tips for Answering Multiple Choice Questions

Multiple choice questions give you several answers from which to choose.

- Read the question through twice.
- Before you look at the choices, close your eyes and answer the question. Then, look for that answer.
- Read all the choices through before you circle one.
- If you are not absolutely sure, cross out answers that are obviously incorrect.
- Choose the answer that is most complete or most accurate.
- If you're not absolutely sure, choose an answer that has not been ruled out.
- Do not change an answer unless you are absolutely sure of the correct answer.

Tips for Answering Matching Questions

Matching questions ask you to recognize facts or definitions in one column that match facts, definitions, answers, or descriptions in a second column.

- Read through both columns to familiarize yourself with the choices.
- Do the easy matches first.
- Cross off answers as you use them.
- Match the left-over items last.
- If you don't know the answer, make a smart guess.

Tips for Answering Fill-in-the Blank Questions

Fill-in-the-blank questions ask you to write a word that completes the sentence.

- Read through each question. Answer it the best you can.
- If you don't know an answer, **X** the question and go on to do the ones you know.
- Go back to the **X**'d questions. If you don't know the exact answer, write a similar word or definition—come as close as you can.
- If you have no idea of the answer, make a smart guess.

Tips for Answering True-False Questions

True-False questions ask you to tell whether a statement is true or false.

- Watch for words like *most, some,* and *often.* Usually statements with these words are TRUE.
- Watch for words like *all, always, only, never, none, nobody,* and *never.* Usually statements with these words are FALSE.
- If any part of a statement is false, then the item is FALSE.

Even More Test-Taking Tips

Tips for Answering Essay Questions

Essay questions ask you to write a short answer (usually a few paragraphs) about a subject.

- Make sure you are clear about what the question is asking.
- Think ahead to your answer. Sketch out a rough outline of the main points you will make and details supporting each point.
- Write an introduction which briefly states a summarized version of your answer.
- Write a body that states the main ideas clearly.
- Reinforce each main idea with details and examples.
- Write a summarizing sentence that restates the main idea.

Tips for Answering Reading Comprehension Tests

Reading comprehension tests ask you to read a piece of writing and answer questions about it.

- Read through the questions before you read the passage.
- Keep the questions in mind as you read the passage.
- Read each question carefully.
- Skim back through the passage to look for key words that are related to the question.
- Re-read that section carefully.
- Eliminate any answers that cannot be correct.
- Choose the correct answer.

GET SHARP →

on Culture & Society

Culture

Culture is the way of life of a group of people—a system of their values, beliefs, habits of conduct, and material goods. Every society is composed of one or more cultures. The term *nonmaterial culture* refers to the beliefs, values, and behaviors of a society. *Material culture* refers to the things that are created by a society.

Some Things to Know about Culture

- Culture is a set of learned behaviors. It is passed on to the younger generation by other members of the culture.
- Families, groups, and institutions play a part in passing on culture.
- Culture is expressed in many different ways. These expressions are called *traits.*
- Cultures differ from each other in many ways.
- Cultures are similar to each other in many ways.
- Cultures often cross political or national lines.
- Most nations include different cultural groups.
- Current expressions of culture are affected by the culture's history.
- Cultures borrow from, share with, and spread traits to other cultures.
- Cultures benefit from communication and interaction with different cultures.

Influences on Culture

These are some of the factors that affect the way a culture develops or changes:

- geography (things such as weather, climate, latitude, altitude, landforms, rivers and other water)
- availability of natural resources
- availability of food
- political boundaries
- natural disasters
- migrations
- neighboring countries
- wars or other conflicts
- technology and inventions
- past experiences of the society

Culture Cafe

May I take your order?

I'll have the cheese soufflé, pie a la mode, and two enchiladas.

Special of the Day - Mulligan Stew

I'll have the hamburger plate, but hold the beef.

The United States is a nation influenced by many cultures. Dozens of different languages are spoken in the country. The English language borrows many words from other languages.

In some cultures, people worship cows. In others, people eat them.

More Things to Know about Culture

Enculturation is the process by which members of a group learn the culture. As children grow up in a culture, they learn the cultural patterns and behaviors by watching, listening, and imitating.

Diffusion is the process by which cultural traits and patterns spread from one society to another.

Acculturation is the process that takes place when cultures that have contact with each other exchange or blend patterns of the two cultures.

Assimilation is the process by which people give up the ways of their culture and become part of a different culture.

Civilization generally refers to a culture or society that has advanced social systems such as political, economic, governmental, and educational systems.

A subculture is a group within a culture that holds to beliefs and behaviors that are a variation of the wider culture's beliefs and behaviors.

International culture describes a situation in which cultural traditions extend beyond the boundaries of one nation.

Multiculturalism describes a situation in which a society includes many different, distinct cultures.

Pop culture (popular culture) is the part of culture that is expressed in its current arts and entertainment. This includes such things as television, radio, sports, music, visual and performing arts, fashion, fads, hobbies, leisure activities, movies, and other media.

Cultural lag is the process that takes place when certain parts of a culture don't keep up with the changes in the rest of the culture.

Cultural relativism is the idea that one culture should not be judged by the rules of another culture.

Culture shock is the discomfort people feel when they come into contact with an unfamiliar culture.

Ethnocentrism is the attitude that one culture is superior to other cultures.

I'll have French Fries and a caviar burger with sauerkraut like I get back home in Moscow.

I'll choose the Belgian waffle with a side of salsa, and my son will have....

Dude, wassup? Just hit me with some fries, bro!

I'm really craving some Thai noodles with curry, and a bowl of oats for my horse.

Due to *cultural diffusion*, hungry Russians in a hurry can buy French fries from an American-style fast food restaurant in Moscow.

Emil's mom experiences *culture shock* every time she comes in contact with her son's *subculture*. She can't get used to his slang, music, and fashions.

Members of some Amish groups in the U.S. don't use motor-powered vehicles for transportation. This is an example of *cultural lag*.

Patterns & Expressions of Culture

There are thousands of different expressions of culture—endless varieties of behaviors.
These are some of the categories or traits which are examples of cultural behaviors or systems:

architecture
art
beliefs and values
celebrations
childcare practices
clothing for everyday life
clothing for special occasions
customs
dance, drama, and theater
economic systems
entertainment
fads
family structure
fashions
forms and uses of money
forms of entertainment
forms of power, rule, or authority
funeral and burial customs
hobbies
holidays
institutions and organizations
inventions
kinds of homes and shelter
kinds of technology
kinds of work
languages
laws and rules
leisure activities
music
patterns of movement
political systems
religious systems
rituals
rules and laws
symbols
taboos
traditions

ways of eating
ways of getting goods
ways of keeping safe
ways of learning and teaching
ways of preparing food
ways of providing services
ways of settling disputes
ways of travel
wedding customs
wedding ceremonies

Get Sharp Tip # 1

Anthropology is the study of human cultures.
Archaeology is the study of past cultures.

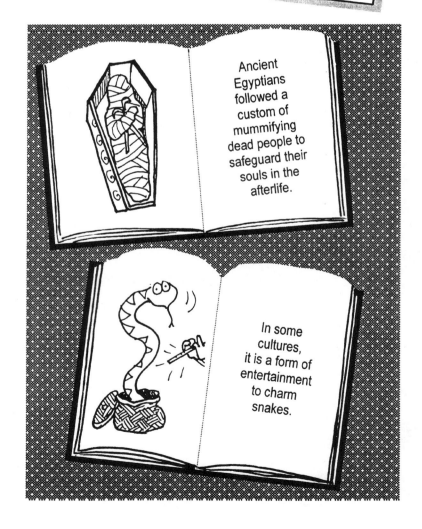

Ancient Egyptians followed a custom of mummifying dead people to safeguard their souls in the afterlife.

In some cultures, it is a form of entertainment to charm snakes.

All nations have a flag, which is a symbol for the country. Often the flag itself contains colors or icons which symbolize some value or characteristics of the country.

The flag of Australia includes a small version of Great Britain's flag, signifying the country's historical links to Great Britain. The large star, the Commonwealth Star, symbolizes the combined territories in the Commonwealth. The other five stars stand for the Southern Cross, a constellation that has long been associated with Australia.

Some Middle Eastern cultures have a taboo against women showing their faces or other parts of their bodies uncovered in public.

Hindus believe that the Ganges River is sacred. Many perform a ritual of bathing in the river because they believe it will purify their bodies and souls.

Some cultural patterns defined . . .

Symbol – an object that represents an idea, event, or concept important to a culture.

Customs – patterns of behavior that are common to a culture or society.

Mores – customs or patterns of behavior that are extremely strong or that result in strong punishment if they are violated.

Taboo – the prohibition of a certain behavior, under threat of serious punishment; an act or behavior that is strictly forbidden.

Totem – an object that is honored or revered by members of a group because it represents something sacred or special about the group.

The totem is often an animal or plant. A symbol of the totem is sometimes engraved or painted on a mask or totem pole, or tattooed on the body.

Rituals – are ceremonies and other events or behaviors that are significant to a culture.

Rituals are repeated regularly, generally according to some schedule. Rituals are often connected to religious beliefs or practices. They also are used to commemorate special events in the lives of the citizens. Birthdays, wedding ceremonies, religious confirmations, baby dedications, baptisms, and funerals are examples of rituals.

Rite of passage – a special ritual or ceremony that celebrates the transition from childhood to adulthood for members of the society.

Totem poles include many symbols. They are often created to symbolize the history, status, or rights of a family, tribe, or clan.

63

Cultural Interactions

The traits of a culture are shaped by many influences. Cultures are constantly changed and developed by interactions with the land, the climate, the past, new technological development, and exposure to other cultures. As a culture develops, it may also affect other cultures or bring changes to the land its people occupy. Here are a few examples of the ways cultures develop certain traits, change due to a particular influence, affect the environment, or influence other cultures.

Different cultures meet a need in similar ways.

Example:

All over the world, people carry babies in backpacks, front packs, and slings. Though the style and fabric may differ, parents of many cultures have found a similar answer to the need of carrying a small child while leaving their hands free to do other tasks.

A culture assimilates the ways of a new culture.

Example:

For centuries, arranged marriages have been a custom in some cultures of India. Many people of these cultures who live in America have relaxed these rules. This allows young people to choose their own mates, as is the usual custom in America.

A culture's need leads to the development of new technology.

Example:

People in the British Isles and on the European mainland across the English Channel had a need for transportation across the channel that was faster than boats. So they built the Chunnel, a tunnel beneath the English Channel. Using the Chunnel, a high speed **Eurostar** *train can take a passenger from Paris to London in just three hours.*

Different cultures develop different ways of meeting a need.

Example:

Some Australians greet each other affectionately by sticking out their tongues. In America or China, such a greeting would be considered rude, embarrassing, or insulting. In those cultures, people greet each other with other gestures, such as a bow, a kiss, a handshake, or a hug.

New technology changes the way of life in a culture.

Examples:

In recent years, lumber mills in the Pacific Northwest of the United States have become so automated that fewer people are needed to do the work which many mill workers used to do. As a result, many mill workers have lost their jobs.

Digital technology makes it possible to take a picture in China, scan and print it with a computer, and send it by the Internet to Argentina in a matter of seconds.

A culture develops customs or practices that honor its historical heritage.

Example:

There are two official languages in the Canadian province of Quebec: French and English. This honors the area's heritage, which was settled by people of both cultures.

A social situation sometimes leads a culture to develop a custom or set of behaviors.

Example:

In some African cultures, people stretch their lips by wearing a large disc inside the edge of the mouth. The practice is said to have developed to keep neighboring cultures from taking these people as slaves.

New technology can contribute to a culture in a harmful way.

Example:

An increasing number of auto accidents are occurring because people are using cell phones while they drive.

New technology can make positive contributions to a culture's development.

Example:

Since the invention of the jet airplane, people in different cultures living thousands of miles apart are able to visit and interact with one another with a relatively short travel time.

A culture meets some of its needs by making use of natural resources.

Example:

The tundra of Siberia is a natural habitat for reindeer. Because of this, the people of the area hitch sleds to reindeer for transportation. Reindeer meat and skin also provide clothing, food, and shelter for the people.

The natural resources of an area contribute to the culture's economy.

Example:

Beautiful opals are found in fields of Australia. The country's economy benefits from sale of these semi-precious stones throughout the world.

The physical geography of an area contributes to the culture's economy.

Example:

Thrill-seeking tourists come to Venezuela to parachute off the top of Angel Falls, the world's highest waterfall. These tourists spend money in the country, helping Venezuela's economy.

A culture develops behaviors in response to the geographic environment.

Examples:

In the high Andes Mountains, the geography is too rough for transporting goods with vehicles. Peruvian Indians have adapted to the problem by using llamas to carry goods and supplies around the rocky terrain.

In wet jungle areas of South America, some people build their riverside homes on stilts to protect them from rising water.

Many inhabitants of northern Africa wear long, loose clothing to keep cool and a head covering (called a kaffiyeh) to shield them from the hot desert sun.

A culture's economic needs or wants sometimes harm or deplete natural resources.

Examples:

For many years forests around the world have been cut for timber sales. People use the wood to build homes or other structures. As a result of the cutting, the natural habitat of some species such as the panda bear is shrinking. This loss of habitat even threatens the survival of some species.

Poaching (illegal hunting) is diminishing the number of tigers and other animals, such as orangutans. The poachers make money by selling young orangutans for pets or selling the tiger skins for decorations.

A culture's behavior can cause changes in the environment over a small or large area.

Example:

When rain forests are cut for lumber to build dwellings or to sell timber to other countries, the ecology of the area and of the entire globe changes. Erosion increases in the local area, causing loss of valuable soil and changing rivers and streams. Habitat is lost for many species of plants and animals. In addition, global temperatures are affected.

Societies & Social Groups

A *society* is a nation, community, or other broad group of people with common institutions and traditions. Every society has a number of smaller groupings within it. **Socialization** is the process by which one learns to adapt the behavior patterns of the surrounding society.

A *social group* is a number of individuals that have some sort of common relationship, purpose, or interest. In a social group, two or more people interact with each other and/or identify with each other. Members in most social groups share a common purpose that involves personal contact that will be repeated or ongoing. In other groups, there is a shared characteristic, but the group members do not necessarily even have contact with one another. There are literally thousands of different kinds of social groups within a society.

As you read these examples, think about what common relationship, purpose, or interest the group's members would have in common.

I see some purposes:
to help someone
to play a game together
to nurture children
to create a product
to get a job done

I see some relationships:
blood relatives
friends
members of the same team
co-workers
neighbors

I see some common interests:
soccer
bird watching
rap music
computers
SCUBA diving

A Few Social Groups

- members of the International Star Trek Fan Association
- member countries on the United Nations Security Council
- women attending a Mothers of Triplets Association meeting
- flute players in the San Francisco Symphony Orchestra
- members of the Sioux City Chamber of Commerce
- members of the Community Church in a town in Idaho
- members of the Boston College women's soccer team
- members of a particular rap singer's fan club
- members of the American Birding Association
- engineers in the design department at a car company
- the computer club at Walker Middle School
- the film crew on a movie
- competitors at a dance contest
- a neighborhood homeowners' association
- member countries in the United Nations
- fans of the Philadelphia Eagles football team
- a bridge club in Cape May, New Jersey
- people at a family reunion
- the staff in a doctor's office
- teachers at Winnetka High School
- South Dakota's state legislators
- the U.S. Olympic Committee
- your family
- a city police force's SWAT team
- Mr. Antoine's seventh grade history class
- the Gleason High School marching band
- members of a SCUBA diving class in Seattle

Social Roles

During each person's life, he or she will belong to many social groups. In every group, each individual plays or fills some kind of *role* or part in the group. Different roles serve different purposes in groups. There are numerous roles, and they vary from group to group. In many groups, there are differing levels of responsibility or power. Often one or more individuals fill some kind of leadership or authority role. At any one time in your life, you will probably be a member of several groups, filling several different roles.

Lucy

Lucy is a drummer and leader of her own band that she formed with four friends. She writes a lot of the music that the band plays. She is also a freshman at Jefferson High School, where she plays drums for a jazz group. After school twice a week, she tutors middle school kids in reading. Lucy is the youngest of five children in her family. Along with her sister and brothers, she visits her grandmother every weekend. Lucy plays the position of catcher on a city softball team during the spring. In the summer, she works as a counselor at a day camp where she helps handicapped kids learn to ride horses.

Juan

Juan works as an emergency technician for a large medical center. He also donates several hours a week to presenting health and emergency response lessons at a local school district. Juan has two teenage kids, and serves as chairman on the local school board. He takes meals to his aged mother at a nursing home five nights a week, and coaches his son's soccer team. He teaches a Sunday school class at the church he attends with his wife and family. Since Juan is a licensed EMT, he occasionally joins the county's search and rescue team when extra help is needed.

Hmmm...let's see...
My roles right now are...
  daughter
  sister
  granddaughter
  band leader
  drummer
  band member
  jazz group member
  student
  tutor
  volunteer
  team member
  catcher
  counselor
  teacher

Hmmmm...let's see...
My roles right now are...
  father
  son
  husband
  board member
  board chairman
  caretaker
  coach
  volunteer
  teacher
  church member
  team member
  EMT
  (Emergency Medical Technician)

Institutions

An *institution* is a particular set of organizations, patterns, customs, groups, or activities that meets the basic needs of a society. The social institutions of a society are some of its most important features. You might think of an institution as a school or a bank, but sociologists (scientists who study the patterns of human social interaction) describe institutions in a wider way. They have identified five basic categories of institutions that exist in all societies. The purpose of these institutions is to satisfy the basic functions and needs of the society.

The 5 Basic Social Institutions

The basic needs and functions in my life are satisfied by these five institutions.

Family   Religion   ECONOMY   Political Order   Education

A sampling of groups, patterns, and organizations that make up institutions:

- a church
- a temple
- a mosque
- Britain's monarchy
- a system of religious schools
- a national sports league
- a state's prison system
- a government's system of regulating businesses
- a nation's armed forces
- a university
- a banking system
- a school district
- a nation's court system
- a world court system
- a religious denomination
- a child care system
- a nation's railway system
- a nation's government
- political parties
- a county government
- a nation's economic practices
- a health care system
- a nation's emergency response program
- marriage

Institutions satisfy basic societal needs and functions such as these:

prepare workers for jobs
keep law and order
provide recreation
offer worship opportunities
provide transportation
pass on skills to individuals
settle disputes
support individuals
teach appropriate social behaviors
arrange to distribute goods
contribute to reproduction to ensure the continuation of the society

help people in emergencies
help needy citizens
nurture children
supervise and manage flow of money
keep people safe
teach religious values
provide justice
carry on traditions
arrange to produce goods
arrange to provide services
help people find answers to questions about life's meaning

Laws & Rules

Every society has rules and laws. Rules and laws serve some purpose for controlling, ordering, or protecting the people in the group, or for ensuring that the group functions to accomplish its purpose. Some rules and laws are written down, others are unwritten but understood by the society members. Most social groups also have rules or laws or both. In groups, many of the rules are unwritten. Generally, a law is more binding to an individual or group than a rule. However, societies and groups have ways of giving punishment to those who do not follow certain rules, as well as to those who break laws.

A law
is a rule that is established by an authority or society. In many cases, there are specific punishments given by a governmental authority to those who break a law.

A rule
is a direction, set of principles, or standard for behavior or conduct in a certain group or situation. Generally, a rule is less binding than a law.

I see some purposes for these laws and rules...
...to keep people safe
...to collect money for government services
...to keep order
...to keep the highways clean and safe

Examples of Laws:

8% state sales tax on all purchases in this state

NO LEFT TURN

Wage earners in the U.S. must file a yearly Income Tax Return.

No Trespassing on Federal Land

$300 Fine for Littering on State Highway

Speed Limit 70 mph

I realize that paying taxes is the law.

I understand that burping at the table is rude.

Examples of Rules:

Fireside Restaurant
Please wait to be seated.

No gum chewing allowed in this classroom.

Quiet
In the Library Shhhhhhhhh!

NO SWEARING IN THIS HOUSE

It is against the law in Pittsburgh, Pennsylvania to sleep on a refrigerator.

Some laws are really silly!

Peacocks have the right of way to cross the street in Arcadia, California.

Keeping a donkey in a bathtub is illegal in Georgia.

Authority & Power

Most social groups and institutions have an ***authority*** figure—someone who holds the most power in the group, or someone who is "in charge." In some cases, the authority rests in the hands of one person. In other groups, the authority is shared. Usually the authority serves some purpose such as leadership, keeping order, or seeing that proper rules are followed.

The Group	The Authority	The Purpose
tourists on a cruise ship	cruise director or captain	keep order and explain rules structure activities keep people safe
group of firefighters battling a fire	captain	keep firefighters safe get the job done
members of the United States Senate	president of the Senate	keep order see that work gets done set schedules
drivers on an Interstate Highway in California	state of California, California state police	keep people safe keep order on the highway
middle school soccer team	coach team captain	guide the practice keep order teach soccer skills
fans attending a high school basketball game	school officials	keep order keep people safe assure that rules are followed
group of travelers on a city bus	bus driver	ensure safety keep order get people to their destinations
school board	chairperson	keep order ensure that everyone gets a chance to speak get the board's work done
shoppers in a grocery store	store manager store security team	keep people safe help the shoppers make sure goods are not stolen

Political Systems

Some nations have a king or queen. Some have a sultan. Some countries have a prime minister or a president, while others have a shah. In some countries, a dictator is in charge. A political system is a power structure and a whole set of laws, practices, institutions, and organizations that accomplish the purpose of running the government. Here is an overview of some of the political systems throughout the world.

Get Sharp Tip # 2

To understand a political system well, ask questions such as these:

Who holds the power?
Who leads the government?
How is the leader selected?
How is the government structured?
Who makes the rules and laws?
How are laws enforced?
What rights do all citizens hold?

The United Arab Emirates is a group of seven Arab states that has formed a federation. Each state is ruled separately, but the federation manages foreign affairs and economic development.

Andorra is a co-principality. It is ruled jointly by the president of France and a bishop of Spain.

India has a parliamentary government. The government is headed by a prime minister. The lawmaking body is a parliament whose members are elected by the people.

Myanmar's government is a dictatorship. A military group controls the government. The senior general holds all the power and serves as the prime minister.

The country of Bhutan is ruled by a king who holds the highest power.

A parliamentary government is headed by an assembly of persons who make the laws of a nation. In some cases, the members of parliament are elected. In other cases, some or all of the members gain their positions by other means, such as appointment or family inheritance. In addition to the parliament, there may be an elected president or a prime minister.

A monarchy is a nation that is ruled by a sovereign such as a king, queen, or emperor whose power is inherited. The sovereign holds the highest power in some monarchies. In a *constitutional monarchy* (such as Great Britain), the sovereign is the head of state but holds no political power. The country is ruled by another form of government.

A republic is nation whose leaders are elected by the people for a specific length of time. The leaders are expected to represent the interests and wishes of the citizens. The head leader of a republic is generally a president.

A dictatorship is a system controlled by a person who has absolute power. The dictator position is not inherited. Sometimes a dictator takes power by force or gains power because he or she controls the armed forces of the nation.

A federation is a joint federal government formed by a group of independent states. A federation is formed to meet needs (such as foreign affairs or national defense) that can be managed more successfully by a larger group

A territory is a country that is not under its own rule, but is owned and governed by another nation.

A co-principality is a country that is ruled jointly by two other countries or authorities.

I want to hold the highest power!

How could I get to be the queen of Bhutan?

Religions

A *religion* is a belief in or worship of some sort of higher power or principle outside the human. Some cultures worship one God. Others worship many gods. For some religions, there is no god. Some cultures believe that animals or trees are sacred. Statues and icons are a part of worship in some cultures. The people of the world have many different beliefs and ways to worship. In all cases, religious beliefs help people make sense of the world around them. Religion helps people answer questions about the meaning of life, the purpose for living, and the mysteries of death. About six billion people in the world follow some type of organized religion. Here is a description of some of the world's major religions.

Get Sharp Tip # 3

Monotheism is a belief in one God. Polytheism is a belief in many gods.

Buddhism

Number of believers: approximately 325 million

Beginnings: Siddhartha Gautama, known as the Buddha, founded Buddhism around 525 B.C..

Beliefs: Buddhists believe that the life of all beings includes suffering. They believe that suffering occurs because of desire, and that to escape suffering, believers must give up attachment to worldly life and belongings. This release, they believe, comes through leading a disciplined life of self denial that can bring a person to *nirvana*, or perfect peace.

Holy writings or teachings: the sacred teachings of Buddha, known as the *Tripitaka*.

Christianity

Number of believers: approximately 2 billion

Beginnings: Jesus, a Jew born in about 7 B.C., and his followers founded Christianity.

Beliefs: Christianity is a monotheistic religion. Its followers believe that Jesus Christ is the Son of God, and that he was sent by God to live among humans and offer them a way to be forgiven of their sins and join the kingdom of God. Jesus Christ was executed by crucifixion on a cross. Christians believe that he rose from the dead, and that belief in him and his resurrection is a way to gain salvation. Its believers spread Christianity across the globe. There are three major divisions of Christianity. The Roman Catholics follow the authority of the Pope. Protestantism began when reformers broke away from the Roman Catholic Church in the mid-1500s. There are many different sects or denominations of Protestantism. Protestants reject the idea that a pope or priest or other higher person must speak to God for them. Orthodox Christians follow most of the teachings of the Roman Catholics, but follow a patriarch rather than the Pope.

Holy writings or teachings: the Old Testament and the New Testament of the *Bible*.

Hinduism

Number of believers: approximately 780 million

Beginnings: The Hindu religion has no founder. It is considered to be the oldest religion in the world, and dates back as far as prehistoric times.

Beliefs: Hinduism is the major religion of India. There is no one belief that is held by all Hindus. There is freedom to believe in one god, many gods, or no god. The central belief is that a divine intelligence, called *Brahman*, is in all beings. Hinduism is based on the idea of reincarnation—the concept that all living beings are in a cycle of death and rebirth, and that human beings are reborn several times in different forms or bodies. For Hindus, the goal of life is to escape the cycle and become a part of the *Brahman*. Hindus believe that, to achieve this goal, one must lead a pure life. The practice of Hinduism includes many rituals and ceremonies for purification.

Holy writings or teachings: the *Vedas* and many other religious writings and poems

Judaisim

Number of believers: approximately 14 million

Beginnings: It is believed that Abraham was the first Jew. He lived in the 1300s B.C.

Beliefs: Judaism is the oldest of the monotheistic religions. It centers on the existence of one god, Yahweh, who created the universe and rules it. The Jews believe that Yahweh entered into a covenant with them, promising to be present with them throughout their history. Followers of Judaism believe that they are "God's Chosen People." They also believe they should keep God's commandments and worship God faithfully.

Holy writings or teachings: the *Torah*, which is the first five books of the Old Testament of the *Bible*.

Islam

Number of believers: approximately 1 billion

Beginnings: Muhammad founded the religion in Arabia in 610 A.D. The followers of Islam are called Muslims. They refer to Muhammad as the Prophet.

Beliefs:
Islam is a monotheistic religion. They worship the God, Allah, whom they believe determines the fate of humans, and follow the teachings of Muhammad, whom they believe is the one true prophet of Allah. Beliefs include the duties of praying five times a day, giving money to the poor and to their church (mosque), fasting during the day in the month of Ramadan, and making a pilgrimage to Mecca once in their lifetime if it is possible.

Holy writings or teachings: the *Koran*

Sikhism

Number of believers: approximately 19 million

Beginnings: Sikhism began under guru Nanak around 1500 A.D. but was influenced by other gurus who have shaped the religion since.

Beliefs: The Sikhs accept the Hindu concept of the cycle of birth, death, and rebirth, but reject the idea of many gods. They pursue *moksha*, which is release form the cycle. They believe that *moksha* can only be attained with the help of a spiritual teacher, or guru, and that it can be gained by ritual spiritual devotions of singing, praising, and repeating God's name. For Sikhs, following a strict ethical code is part of the process of attaining this release.

Holy writings or teachings: the *Adi Granth*, a book of teachings about the Sikh faith and practice

Celebrations

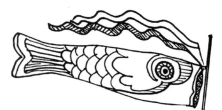

All over the world, people celebrate! It's one of the wonderful things humans have in common. No matter what the culture, time in history, geographical setting, language, political system, religion, or economic system, all people seem to find ways to commemorate and rejoice in special occasions. Everyone loves to dance and sing, parade and feast, and take part in the traditions and rituals that are meaningful to them. Births, deaths, marriages, religious anniversaries, the seasons, the harvest, and so many other human events are all good reason to celebrate—and we do!

Maligawa Tusker is the elephant who carries a replica of Buddha's sacred tooth in a golden casket on its back.

The *dance* is a very important part of the *N'cwala* festivities. The warrior dance has very specific steps that the boys do with joy and exuberance.

St. Lucia's crown is made of evergreen lingoberry leaves and candles, and symbolizes the promise of rebirth after the long winter season.

Carp kites symbolize energy and determination for Japanese boys. The kites come in different sizes, but the largest always represents the father and flies on top.

Esala Perahera
The August festival of Esala Perahera in Sri Lanka includes ten days and nights of singing, dancing, and feasting. It ends on the night of the full moon wit a parade of a hundred elephants in honor of Buddha.

N'cwala
The Zambian festival of N'cwala celebrates the end of harvest time in February. A dance is a central part of the celebration. In the traditional ritual, the best dancers are singled out by the Ngoni chieftain as great warriors.

The Feast of St. Lucia
On the darkest day of winter in December, the people of Sweden celebrate the festival of St. Lucia, the patron saint of light. Each community chooses a young girl to represent St. Lucia in a procession of candlelight and carol-singing.

Kodomono-Hi
This Japanese Children's Day Festival takes place on May 5. Young boys display colorful fish kites and streamers on poles in their gardens and on their rooftops. The boys bathe with iris leaves to protect them from evil influences, and eat tiny rice cakes called *chimaki*. Girls have their own holiday, Hina Matusun—a day when they float special dolls in boats on the river.

Eid ul-Fitr

During the month of the Islamic religious holiday called Ramadan, Muslims do not eat or drink between sunrise and sunset. To mark the end of Ramadan, they have a 3-day feast called *Eid ul-Fitr*. They also exchange presents and give food to the poor.

Carnival

Before the beginning of Lent (the season of penance before Easter), a great carnival takes place in Rio de Janeiro, Brazil. Everyone takes part, even the children. People wear magnificent costumes, ride on fancy floats, dance the samba, and feast. Everyone enjoys taking advantage of this last change to feast before Lent begins.

Cinco de Mayo

In Mexico, and among Mexican people around the world, May 5th is the day for a grand celebration. It marks the victory of the Mexican Army over the French at the Battle of Puebla.

Muslim children eat a special cookie called a *ma'moul*. The cookies are made of flour, dates and pistachio nuts, and are pressed into molds to make them more decorative.

The word *carnival* means "good-bye to meat" and refers to the 40 days of fasting that Brazilians practice during Lent.

A *piñata* is a papier-mache toy smashed by blind-folded children to get the candy inside.

The *menorah* is the candelabra that represents the eight days of Hanukkah.

The Chinese Dragon is called *Gum Loong*, or Golden Dragon. He comes at the end of the parade to wish everyone good luck, prosperity, and peace.

Christian children often take part in Christmas plays that re-enact the *Nativity*.

Christmas

Many countries, including America, celebrate Christmas on the 25th of December to remember the birth of Christ. It evolved into a holiday that celebrates both the religious tradition and a secular tradition of giving gifts. Today, children wait for Santa Claus to come on Christmas Eve and fill their stockings with presents and candy. Many families put up Christmas trees and share presents with family and friends.

Hanukkah

Hanukkah is a Jewish holiday meaning the festival of lights. It commemorates the time when the Temple of Jerusalem was recaptured in 164 B.C. Each of eight candles is lit from the central candle which symbolizes the drop of oil used to light the reclaimed temple. Families celebrate with feasting, gifts, and games.

Chinese New Year

This is one of the most spectacular and colorful of the world's celebrations. The Chinese New Year festival begins on the first day of the Chinese calendar, and lasts for 15 days. This occurs near the beginning of February. The celebrations include parades with colorful costumes, banners, and wonderful long dragons.

75

Languages

There are thousands of different ways to say "Hello," "Happy Holidays," or "Merry Christmas." About 6500 different languages are spoken in the world today. Two-thirds of those languages have more than 1000 native speakers.

> The most popular language spoken in the world is Mandarin Chinese. There are 885 million people in China and over one billion worldwide who speak that language.

> And my Grandma Hsu is one of them! She's teaching me her language, too.

The Top 15 Spoken Languages in the World

What's the language?	How many speak it? (approximate number of speakers for whom the language is their native, or first, first language)	Where is it spoken?
1 Mandarin Chinese	1 billion	China, Taiwan
2 English	350 million	Britain, U.S., Canada, Australia
3 Spanish	250 million	Spain, Central America, South America, U.S.
4 Hindi	200 million	India
5 Arabic	150 million	Arabian Peninsula, Iraq, Syria, Jordan, Lebanon, northern Africa, Ethiopia
6 Bengali	150 million	Bangladesh
7 Russian	150 million	Russia and other countries that were part of the former Soviet Union
8 Portuguese	135 million	Portugal, Brazil
9 Japanese	120 million	Japan
10 German	100 million	Germany, Austria, Switzerland
11 French	70 million	France, Belgium, Switzerland, Canada
12 Panjabi	70 million	Afghanistan, Bangladesh, India, Iran, Nepal, Pakistan, Sri Lanka
13 Javanese	65 million	Java
14 Bihari	65 million	India, Nepal
15 Italian	60 million	Italy, San Marino

GET SHARP →

on Globes & Maps

Using Globes & Maps

You have probably never stopped to count the number of times you use a map in a week or month or year. **Globes** and **maps**, which are visual representations of some part of the world or universe, are more a part of life than we often realize. It's a good thing, too! Without maps, we'd be at a loss for finding our way around a lot of places such as stores, parks, malls, museums, subway systems, cities, countries, or continents. Without maps, we'd be missing a great deal of information about our world. As our cities, towns, and world get more complicated, we rely more and more on maps. If you need to get to a library across the city this afternoon, you can log onto the Internet and get a custom-made bus route just for you. It will tell you when to leave, what buses to catch, and how long your trip will take!

Globe

Physical Map

Political Map

The United States of America

Weather Map

Atlas

Better Grades & Higher Test Scores / SOCIAL STUDIES
Copyright ©2003 by Incentive Publications, Inc., Nashville, TN.

Relative Location Maps

Distribution Map

Grid Map

Floor Plan

Cultural Map

Contour Map

3-D Map

Better Grades & Higher Test Scores / SOCIAL STUDIES
Copyright ©2003 by Incentive Publications, Inc., Nashville, TN.

Get Sharp: Globes & Maps

Globes

Northern Hemisphere

Southern Hemisphere

Eastern Hemisphere

Western Hemisphere

Earth, like all other planets, is shaped like a sphere. A photograph or other flat representation of Earth can only show half (a *hemisphere*) of Earth's surface at any one time. A *globe* is a sphere which represents the Earth, so a globe is useful to show the whole Earth at once. Globes show the land masses and bodies of water on Earth's surface. Some globes also show other features, such as land elevations, ocean depths, the political divisions (counties) of the world, ocean currents, or major cities.

The ancient Greeks made the first globes to show relative locations of things on Earth. They divided the globe into the 360 equal segments that are used to measure circles (called *degrees*). They used vertical and horizontal lines to mark off each of the 360 segments from north to south and east to west. These lines became known as the lines of *longitude* and *latitude.*

Longitude & Latitude

Longitude

The *lines of longitude*, imaginary lines called *meridians*, run north and south from the North Pole to the South Pole. The first meridian, or *prime meridian*, is at 0° longitude. It passes through the Royal Naval Observatory in Greenwich, England. The *longitude location* of a place is the distance measured east or west of this line. 180°E longitude and 180°W longitude are the same location, exactly halfway around the Earth from the prime meridian. The 180° meridian is known as the *International Date Line.*

Latitude

The *lines of latitude*, imaginary lines called *parallels,* run east and west around the Earth. The line at 0° latitude is the *equator.* The *latitude location* of a place is the distance in degrees north or south of the equator. These are other specific lines of latitude:

• the *Tropic of Cancer* at 23°27'N latitude
• the *Tropic of Capricorn* at 23°27'S latitude
• the *Arctic Circle* at 66°31'N latitude
• the *Antarctic Circle* at 66°30'S latitude
• the *North Pole* at 90°N latitude
• the *South Pole* at 90°S latitude

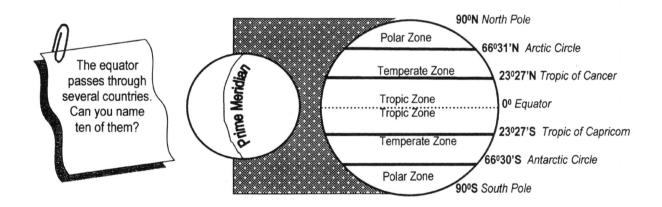

The equator passes through several countries. Can you name ten of them?

90°N *North Pole*
Polar Zone
66°31'N *Arctic Circle*
Temperate Zone
23°27'N *Tropic of Cancer*
Tropic Zone
0° *Equator*
Tropic Zone
23°27'S *Tropic of Capricorn*
Temperate Zone
66°30'S *Antarctic Circle*
Polar Zone
90°S *South Pole*

Climate Zones

The latitude of a region is related to its climate, because the Sun's rays do not fall at the same angle at all locations north or south of the equator.

The tropical zone of the Earth lies between the Tropic of Cancer and the Tropic of Capricorn. This area receives the most direct rays of the Sun.

The temperate zones of the Earth lie between the Tropic of Cancer and the Arctic Circle in the Northern Hemisphere and the Tropic of Capricorn and the Antarctic Circle in the Southern Hemisphere. Since the Sun's rays are less direct in these zones than in the tropical zone, climates are cooler.

The polar regions of the Earth lie north of the Arctic Circle and south of the Antarctic Circle. Polar regions receive the most indirect rays of the Sun, and are therefore the coldest areas on Earth.

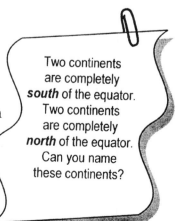

Two continents are completely **south** of the equator. Two continents are completely **north** of the equator. Can you name these continents?

Latitude

This map shows the major lines of latitude running through North America, South America, and part of Antarctica. From looking at this map, you can learn some things such as:

- No part of the North American continent reaches the North Pole.
- Fort Yukon, Alaska, is on the Arctic Circle.
- All of the continental United States lies between the Tropic of Cancer and the Arctic Circle.
- The southern tip of South America has a latitude similar to the southern tip of Greenland.
- The city of Houston is close to 30°N latitude.
- Most of Antarctica is south of the Antarctic Circle.
- Most of Greenland is north of the Arctic Circle.
- The equator crosses South America.
- Mexico is not on the equator.
- Quito, Ecuador is on the equator.

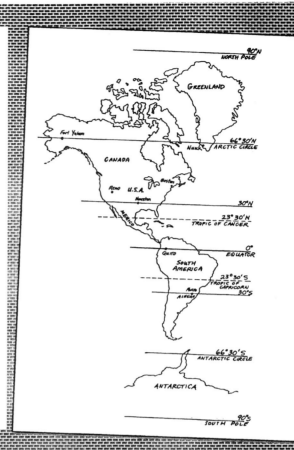

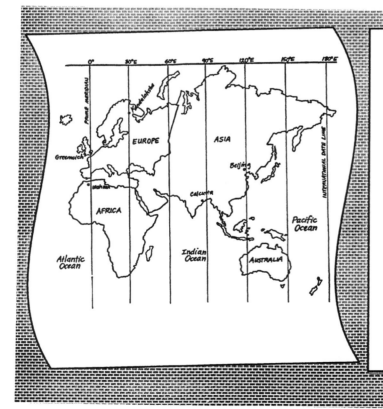

Longitude

This map shows lines of longitude through four continents. By reading the map, you can learn some things such as:

- The prime meridian passes through the continent of Africa.
- Some locations in Africa are east longitude; others are west longitude.
- Most of Australia lies between 120°E and 150°E longitude.
- Europe stretches from about 10°W to 65°E longitude.
- Beijing and Calcutta are about 30° apart in longitude.
- The International Date Line crosses the continent of Asia.

Earth's Grid

The lines of longitude and latitude form a ***global grid*** (system of parallel and perpendicular lines). This grid is very helpful in locating points on Earth's surface. You can find any place on Earth if you know its latitude and longitude. The location of St. Petersburg, Russia, for instance, is 59°N, 30°E. To find St. Petersburg, place your finger on the spot where the equator and the prime meridian meet. This is 0°,0° on the global grid. Move your finger north and stop just below the 60° parallel (line of latitude). Now move your finger east to the 30° meridian (line of longitude).

Get Sharp Tip # 4

The first number in a location is its latitude and the second number is its longitude. (77°N, 15°E reads 77° north latitude, 15° east longitude.)

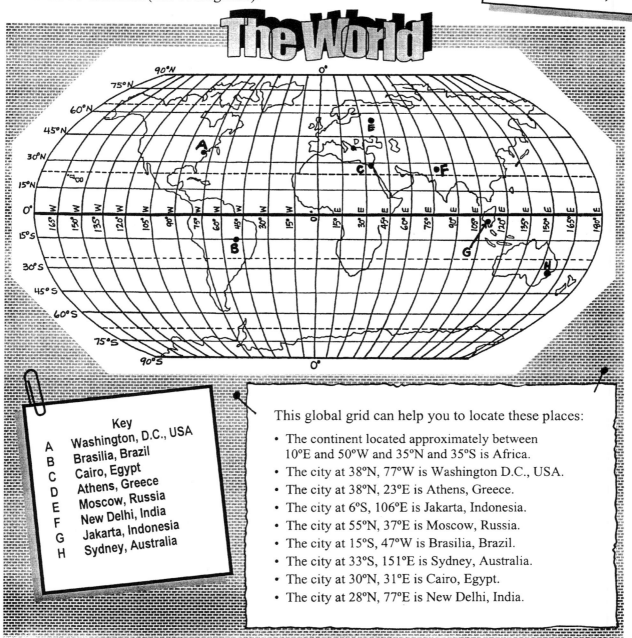

Key

A Washington, D.C., USA
B Brasilia, Brazil
C Cairo, Egypt
D Athens, Greece
E Moscow, Russia
F New Delhi, India
G Jakarta, Indonesia
H Sydney, Australia

This global grid can help you to locate these places:

- The continent located approximately between 10°E and 50°W and 35°N and 35°S is Africa.
- The city at 38°N, 77°W is Washington D.C., USA.
- The city at 38°N, 23°E is Athens, Greece.
- The city at 6°S, 106°E is Jakarta, Indonesia.
- The city at 55°N, 37°E is Moscow, Russia.
- The city at 15°S, 47°W is Brasilia, Brazil.
- The city at 33°S, 151°E is Sydney, Australia.
- The city at 30°N, 31°E is Cairo, Egypt.
- The city at 28°N, 77°E is New Delhi, India.

Get Sharp: Globes & Maps

Maps

A *map* is a representation of a place on Earth presented on a flat surface. Maps can also be made of places beyond Earth. A map can represent something as simple as the top of your desk or the arrangement of food on a plate, or a map can represent something as complex as the entire world or a piece of the solar system.

Maps are grouped according to the kinds of information they provide. Most maps fall into one of the three groups: Physical, political, or cultural.

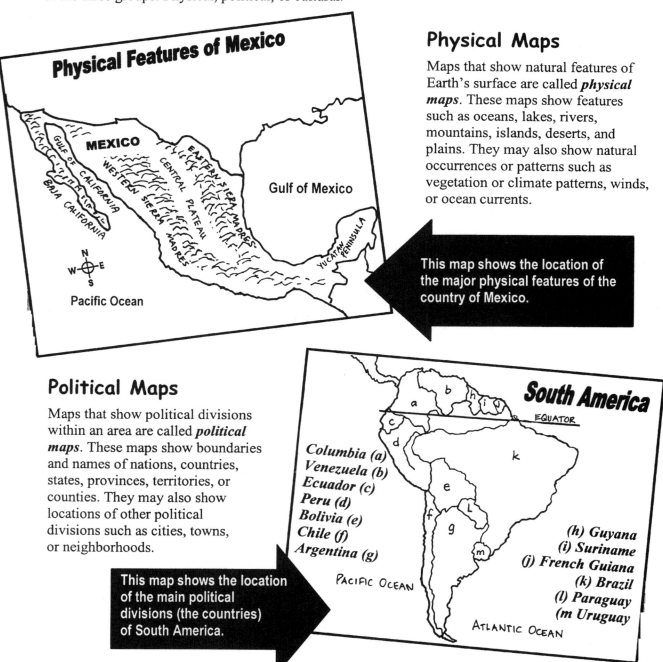

Physical Maps

Maps that show natural features of Earth's surface are called *physical maps*. These maps show features such as oceans, lakes, rivers, mountains, islands, deserts, and plains. They may also show natural occurrences or patterns such as vegetation or climate patterns, winds, or ocean currents.

This map shows the location of the major physical features of the country of Mexico.

Political Maps

Maps that show political divisions within an area are called *political maps*. These maps show boundaries and names of nations, countries, states, provinces, territories, or counties. They may also show locations of other political divisions such as cities, towns, or neighborhoods.

This map shows the location of the main political divisions (the countries) of South America.

84

Better Grades & Higher Test Scores / SOCIAL STUDIES
Copyright ©2003 by Incentive Publications, Inc., Nashville, TN.

Cultural Maps

Maps that show human features within an area are called ***cultural maps***. These maps show such things as population, language, customs, or economic activity. They may also show locations of particular cultural features that humans have added to the world.

Native American Populations in the United States in the Year 2000

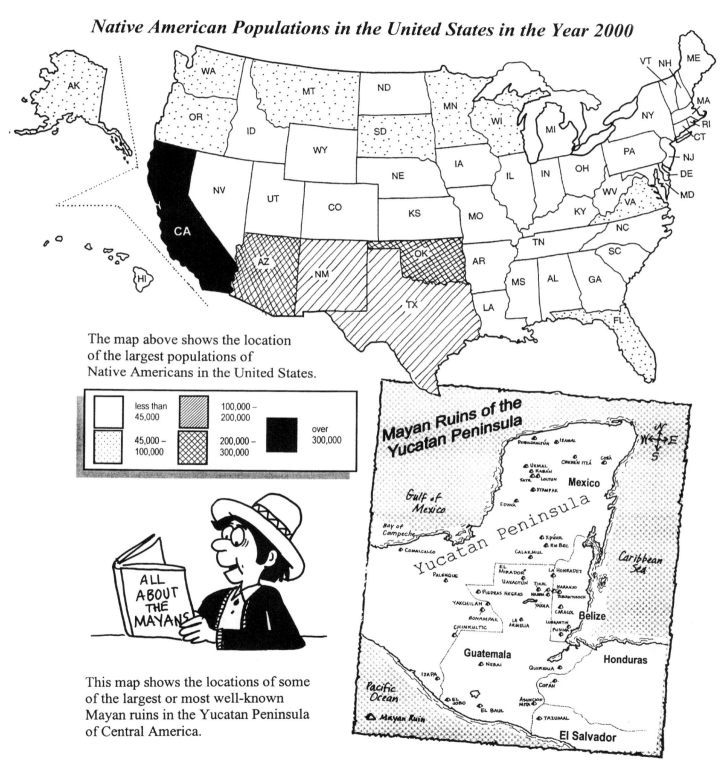

The map above shows the location of the largest populations of Native Americans in the United States.

	less than 45,000		100,000 – 200,000		
	45,000 – 100,000		200,000 – 300,000		over 300,000

This map shows the locations of some of the largest or most well-known Mayan ruins in the Yucatan Peninsula of Central America.

Mayan Ruins of the Yucatan Peninsula

Mexico

Gulf of Mexico

Bay of Campeche

Yucatan Peninsula

Caribbean Sea

Belize

Guatemala

Honduras

Pacific Ocean

El Salvador

85

Parts of a Map

In order to use maps effectively, it is important to know how to "read" them. A map has several parts, made up of words, symbols, pictures, lines, or photographs. All these parts help to present information to the map-reader.

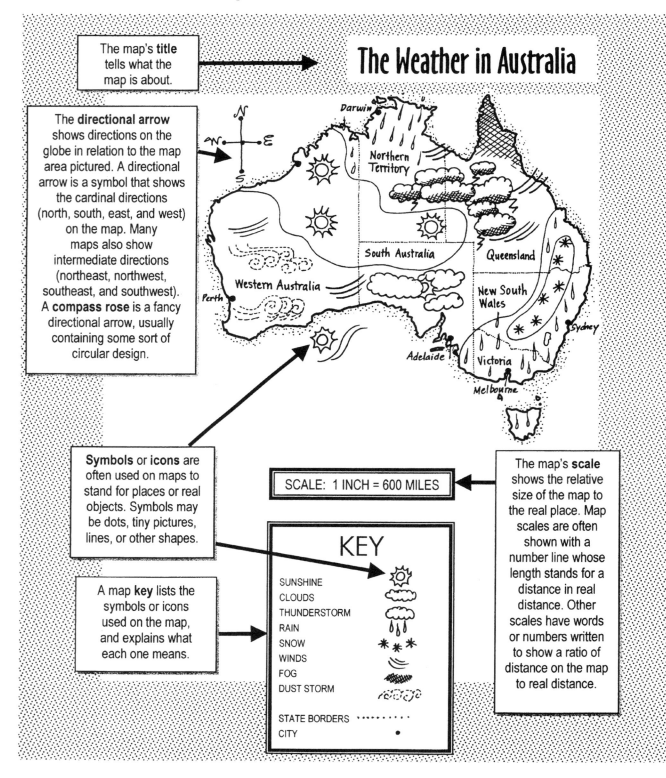

The map's **title** tells what the map is about.

The Weather in Australia

The **directional arrow** shows directions on the globe in relation to the map area pictured. A directional arrow is a symbol that shows the cardinal directions (north, south, east, and west) on the map. Many maps also show intermediate directions (northeast, northwest, southeast, and southwest). A **compass rose** is a fancy directional arrow, usually containing some sort of circular design.

Symbols or **icons** are often used on maps to stand for places or real objects. Symbols may be dots, tiny pictures, lines, or other shapes.

A map **key** lists the symbols or icons used on the map, and explains what each one means.

SCALE: 1 INCH = 600 MILES

The map's **scale** shows the relative size of the map to the real place. Map scales are often shown with a number line whose length stands for a distance in real distance. Other scales have words or numbers written to show a ratio of distance on the map to real distance.

KEY

SUNSHINE
CLOUDS
THUNDERSTORM
RAIN
SNOW
WINDS
FOG
DUST STORM

STATE BORDERS
CITY

Special Purpose Maps

Maps that give information about specific subjects or are designed for a unique purpose can be called *special-purpose maps*. There are literally hundreds of different kinds of maps created for giving specialized information or helping people find various locations. This page and pages 88-92 will give you examples of some special purpose maps.

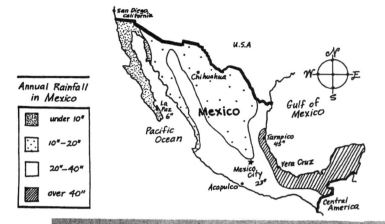

Weather or Climate Maps

Weather or *climate* maps give information about the climate or weather patterns of an area.

This map shows the average annual rainfall of Mexico.

Elevation Maps

Elevation maps are physical maps that show how the surface varies from place to place. (These are sometimes called *landform maps*.) Differences in elevation can be shown on a map with color, shading, pictures, or lines. A *contour map* uses a series of lines to show change in elevation. A *contour line* on the map is a line that connects areas of the same elevation.

This contour map shows the elevation on these small islands. When you see several lines close together on a contour map, you can assume the land has a sudden elevation increase. This alerts you to a hill, mountain, or cliff on the land.

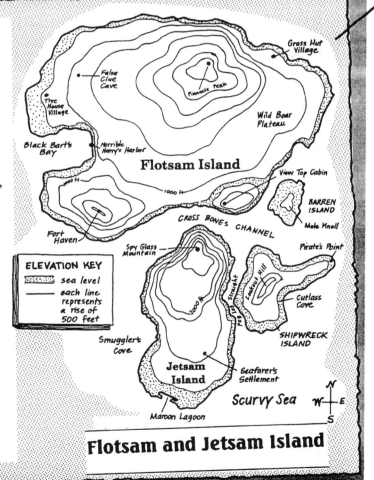

Flotsam and Jetsam Island

Grid Maps

A **grid map** is a map that has lines drawn over it to form a grid. The purpose of the grid is to make it easier to find the locations of places or items on the map. You read the map grid by looking at the letters or numbers in the margins of the map. Generally, letters run along one edge of the map and numbers run along another side. You identify a location by a combination of a letter and a number.

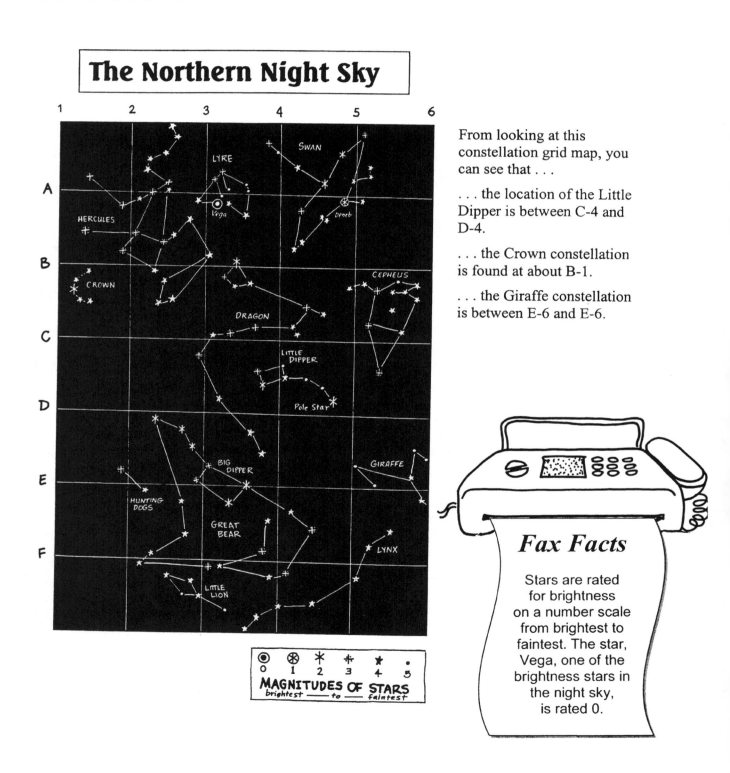

The Northern Night Sky

From looking at this constellation grid map, you can see that . . .

. . . the location of the Little Dipper is between C-4 and D-4.

. . . the Crown constellation is found at about B-1.

. . . the Giraffe constellation is between E-6 and E-6.

MAGNITUDES OF STARS
brightest —— to —— faintest

Fax Facts

Stars are rated for brightness on a number scale from brightest to faintest. The star, Vega, one of the brightness stars in the night sky, is rated 0.

Road or Route Maps

Road maps or *route maps* help people find their way to and from many places.

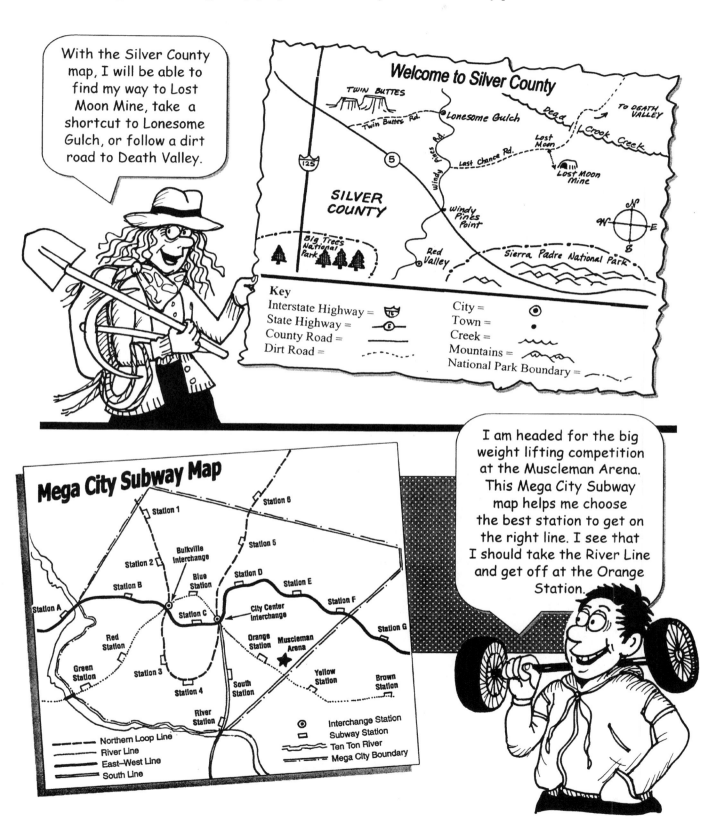

Floor Maps

A *floor map* or *floor plan* is a map that shows the way around a room, building, shopping center, or other structure. This kind of a map uses lines, shapes, and sometimes color or shading to show such things as the layout of the structure, the position of the rooms or furniture, the halls or walkways, the doors, and the windows.

The floor plan of this yacht shows a visitor the features and layout of the yacht. The map shows the layout of places and spaces on three different decks.

Better Grades & Higher Test Scores / SOCIAL STUDIES
Copyright ©2003 by Incentive Publications, Inc., Nashville, TN.

Relative Location Maps

A *relative location map* shows the position of a person, place, or object in relation to the surroundings. You can find relative location maps at most shopping centers, malls, museums, and other large public places. These maps help people figure out exactly where they are and where a specific spot or item is located.

Distribution Maps

Some maps show how a cultural or physical feature is distributed in different parts of the world, country, or other area. Maps that show how something is spread out across an area are called ***distribution maps***. This kind of a map could use symbols, icons, or colors to show the locations of bus stations throughout a city, where diamond mines are in a country, how population is distributed on a continent, what kind of vegetation grows around the world, or all the places in a county where someone can donate blood.

This is an example of a distribution map that a researcher made after traveling around the northern U.S. and southern Canada to investigate sightings of Bigfoot.

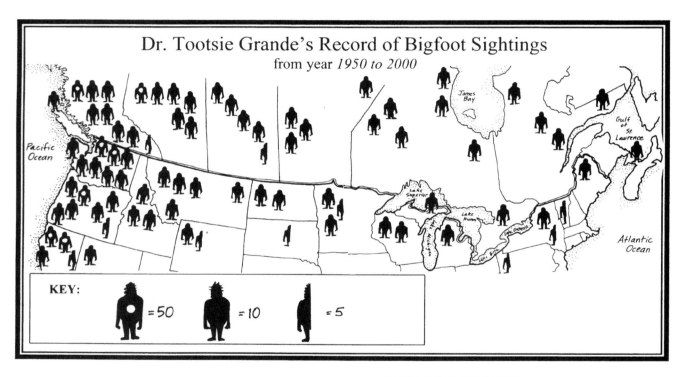

GET SHARP →

on World Geography

Five Themes of Geography

Geography is such a broad subject that it is often divided into two parts. **Physical geography** is the study of the kinds of land and water that make up Earth's surface. **Cultural geography** is the study of the people who live on Earth—their ways of life, how they have used and changed the Earth, and how the physical geography has affected their ways of life. The study of geography examines different themes, known as the **Five Fundamental Themes of Geography**.

Get Sharp Tip # 5

Geography is not just about the land, water, and weather. Geography is also human. It includes a study of the world's people and how they interact with the places they live.

What is geography?

Geography is the study of the world and everything on it.

The word **geography** has Greek roots. **Geo** means "earth." **Graph** means "writing."

1. PLACE

No one place on Earth is exactly like any other place. To describe any one place, you need to show its uniqueness. Geographers look at the specific physical characteristics of a place, such as shape of the land, kinds of landforms, elevations, variations in elevation, bodies of water, plant and animal life, natural resources, climate, and soil. They also look at the human characteristics of a place: where the people live, how close together they live, how they make a living, their social and cultural practices and traditions, their languages, their political systems, and their relationships with the land and their neighbors.

2. LOCATION

Location is the specific spot where something can be found.

Absolute location is the exact spot on the Earth. Geographers make use of maps, globes, and cardinal directions (north, south, east, and west) to describe the absolute location of a place. The lines of latitude and longitude allow anyone to give a very precise description of the absolute location.

Relative location is the relationship of one place, person, or thing in comparison to some other spot. Knowing or finding relative location helps us find our way around parts of the world dozens of times a day. Relative location allows you to explain that you live 300 miles from the Pacific Ocean, 6 blocks from school, 9 miles from the zoo, or 40° north of the equator.

3. HUMAN and ENVIRONMENT INTERACTION

The physical environment affects the way people live and the way cultures develop. It affects many (if not most) of the human activities of an area. The activities of humans, in turn, have effects on the natural environment. Geographers are interested in knowing how these two factors interact with one another. There are thousands of examples of these interactions. People in Africa may build homes from stones because there are no trees to provide wood. In the islands of the southern Pacific Ocean, many people earn a living from fishing because fish are plentiful. Herds of buffalo used to roam the Great Plains in the center of the United States, but humans have turned so much of this land into farms that there is no longer room for the large herds.

4. HUMAN MOVEMENT

Patterns of movement affect the way human cultures develop. Movement of large groups of people is of great interest to geographers. These movements, called *migrations*, have been caused by many factors such as natural disasters (floods, volcanoes, earthquakes, droughts), famine, war, or displacement by a government (such as the relocation of American Indian tribes to reservations). There are other kinds of movement that geographers study: Movement of individual people or families, movement of goods, movement of ideas, or movement of information.

5. REGIONS

A *region* is an area that has some common features which set it apart from other areas. These features might be physical, cultural, or a combination of both. Separating parts of the world into regions allows geographers to study areas more closely and understand them better. For purposes of studying world geography, the world is often divided into these physical-cultural regions: North America, Latin America, Western Europe, Eastern Europe, the Middle East and North Africa, Sub-Saharan Africa, Southern and Eastern Asia, and the South Pacific (which includes Australia and Oceania—the islands of the South Pacific Ocean).

GPS, the Global Positioning System, is a great way to find a location. It's a system that can show the exact position on Earth of any person or object, any time, anywhere, in any weather. 24 GPS satellites, orbiting above the Earth, transmit radio signals that can be detected by anyone with a GPS receiver.

ROAD MAP

I need to get one of those receivers for my dad. He's always getting lost!

Get Sharp: Geography

The World's Land & Water

Earth's surface is made up of land and water. The largest bodies of land are called **continents**. There are seven continents on Earth: North America, South America, Europe, Asia, Africa, Australia, and Antarctica. Europe and Asia share the same land mass. Large bodies of water, called **oceans**, separate the continents. Most of the large bodies of water are connected, but this huge covering of water is divided into four oceans: the Atlantic Ocean, the Pacific Ocean, the Indian Ocean, and the Arctic Ocean.

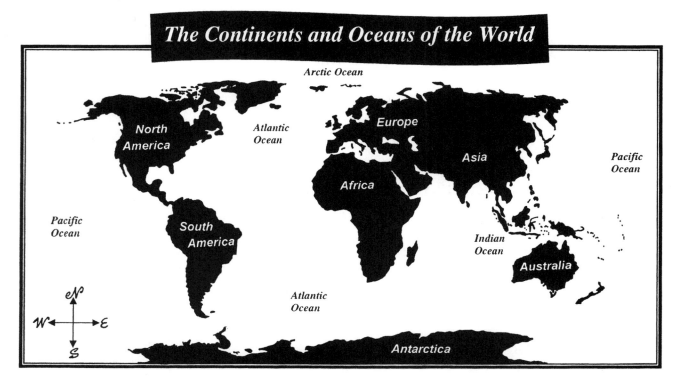

The Continents and Oceans of the World

You might want to know . . .

- The world has more water than land. Almost two-thirds of Earth's surface is covered with water.

- About 98% of Earth's water is in the sea. Most of the rest is locked up in ice in the Arctic and Antarctica. A fraction of a percent is in groundwater, lakes, rivers, and the atmosphere.

- The Pacific Ocean is the largest body of water. It covers 64,200,000 square miles and has an average depth of 12,900 feet.

- The Atlantic Ocean is saltier than the Pacific Ocean.

- Together, Europe and Asia cover about 20,800,000 square miles.

- The lowest point of dry land, Death Valley in California, USA, is 282 feet below sea level.

- The highest point of land, Mt. Everest in Nepal and Tibet, is 29,035 feet above sea level.

There is only one continent that has no snakes. There are no reptiles of **any** kind on Antarctica!

The Physical World

The physical world is an amazing collection of ups and downs.

Here is an overview of the major physical features of the world.

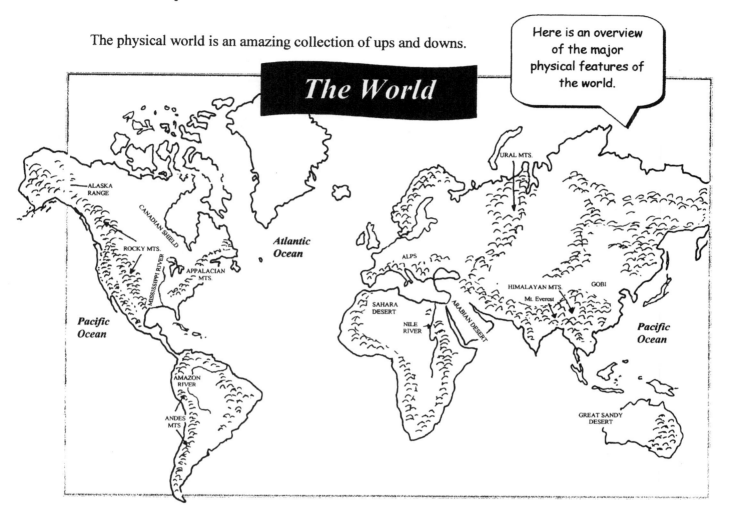

The World's Longest Rivers

River	Length in Miles	Continent	River	Length in Miles	Continent
Nile	4160	Africa	Yenisey	2540	Asia
Amazon	4000	South America	Parana	2480	South America
Yangtze	3960	Asia	Mississippi	2340	North America
Huang Ho	3400	Asia	Missouri	2320	North America
Ob-Irtish	3360	Asia	Volga	2290	Europe
Amur	2740	Asia	Purus	2100	South America
Lena	2730	Asia	Madeira	2010	South America
Congo	2720	Africa	Yukon	1980	North America
Mackenzie	2640	North America	Rio Grande	1900	North America
Mekong	2600	Asia	Darling	1750	Australia
Niger	2590	Africa	Zambezi	1700	Africa

Get Sharp: World Geography

Earth's Amazing Surface

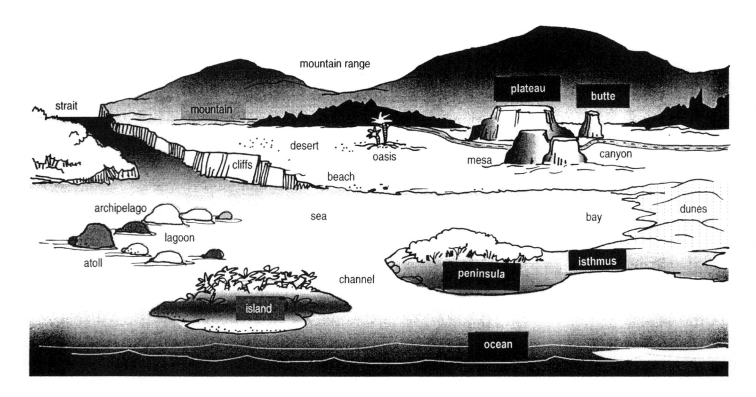

The surface of Earth is a wonderful collection of peaks and troughs, dry lands and wet lands, rippling streams and wild seas, breathtaking panoramas and curious formations. Here's a brief, illustrated overview of landforms and water forms that spread across Earth's surface.

archipelago – large group or chain of islands

atoll – ring-shaped coral island or string of islands, usually surrounding a lagoon

bay – part of a large body of water that extends into the land

beach – gently sloping shore of ocean or other water body

butte – flat-topped hill; smaller than a mesa

canal – waterway built to connect two other bodies of water

canyon – deep, narrow valley with steep sides

cape –coastline that projects into the water

channel – narrow strip of water between two land bodies

cliff – steep rock face

delta – land formed by deposits at the mouth of the river

dune – mound, hill, or ridge of sand heaped by wind

fjord – deep narrow inlet of the sea between steep cliffs

foothills – hilly area at the base of a mountain range

glacier – large sheet of ice that moves slowly over a land surface

gulf – part of an ocean or sea that extends into the land; larger than a bay

hill – rounded, raised landform; lower than a mountain

island – body of land completely surrounded by water

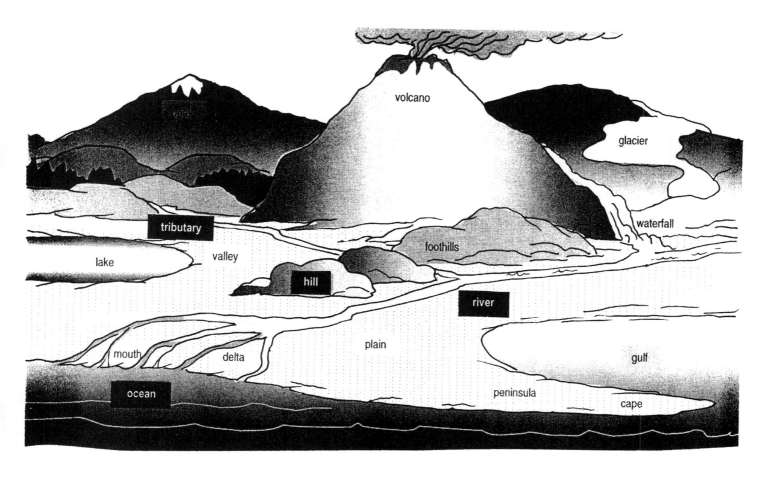

isthmus – narrow strip of land (bordered by water) joining two larger bodies of land

lake – body of water completely surrounded by land

lagoon – shallow water area enclosed within an atoll or cut off from sea by a strip of land

mesa – high, flat landform rising steeply above surrounding land; smaller than a plateau

mountain – high, rounded or pointed landform with steep sides

mountain range – row or chain of mountains

mouth – place where a river empties into a body of water

oasis – a place in a desert where a supply of water makes the land fertile

ocean – one of Earth's four largest bodies of water

peak – pointed top of a mountain or hill

peninsula – body of land nearly surrounded by water

plain – large area of level or gently rolling land

plateau – area of high, flat land; larger than a mesa

river – large stream of water that flows across land and empties into a larger water body

sea – large bay of water partly or entirely surrounded by land

strait – narrow waterway or channel connecting two bodies of water

tributary – river or stream that flows into a larger river or stream

valley – V-shaped depression between mountains or hills

volcano – mountain created by volcanic action

waterfall – flow of water falling from a high place to a low place

99

World Extremes

The extremes on Earth's surface make geography especially fascinating. Around the world, there are breath-taking highs, lows, depths, and widths. Some of them are easily seen; others are too high or deep beneath water to view easily. Here's a list of some of the most spectacular record-holding extremes in the world.

HIGHEST

Highest mountain – Mount Everest in Nepal and Tibet: 29,035 feet.

Highest active volcano – Guallatiri in Chile: 19,882 feet

Highest waterfalls – Angel Falls in Venezuela: 3212 feet

Highest wave (aside from a tsunami) – Recorded in 1933 in the Pacific Ocean: 112 feet

Highest tsunami (tidal wave) – Recorded in 1968 in Lituya Bay, Alaska: 1700 feet

DEEPEST

Deepest ocean – Pacific Ocean: 35,937 feet (water at deepest point)

Deepest sea – Caribbean Sea: 22,788 feet

Deepest lake – Lake Baikal in Russia: 1.02 miles

Deepest ocean trench – Marianas Trench in the Pacific Ocean: 35,840 feet (That's almost 7 miles deep!)

Deepest cave – Lamprechtsofen-Vogelschacht in Austria: 5354 feet

Deepest canyon – Kings Canyon in California: 8199 feet

LOWEST

Lowest point of dry land – Death Valley in California, USA: 282 feet below sea level

BIGGEST

Biggest sea – Arabian Sea: 1,492,000 square miles

Biggest lake – Caspian Sea in Europe and Asia: 143,244 square miles

Biggest freshwater lake – Lake Superior in North America: 31,761 square miles

Biggest river delta – Ganges River and Brahmaputra River delta: 30,000 square miles

Biggest island – Greenland in the North Atlantic Ocean: 840,000 square miles

Biggest island in fresh water – Marajo, in the mouth of the Amazon River in Brazil: 18,500 square miles

Biggest desert – Sahara Desert in Africa: 3,500,000 square miles

Biggest glacier – Lambert-Fischer Glacier in Antarctica: 320 miles long

Biggest area of glaciers – Antarctica: 4,610,610 square miles of ice

Biggest iceberg – North Atlantic Ocean in 1987: 208 miles long and 60 miles wide

Biggest ocean – Pacific Ocean: 64,200,000 square miles

Biggest meteorite crater – Sudbury Crater in Ontario, Canada: 87 miles wide

LONGEST

Longest underwater mountain range – Mid-Atlantic Range: 7022 miles

Longest above water mountain range – The Andes Mountains in South America: 4500 miles

Longest cave system – Mammoth Cave System in Kentucky, USA: 352 miles

Longest canyon – Grand Canyon in Arizona: 277 miles

Longest reef – Great Barrier Reef in waters off Australia: 1260 miles

Longest fjord – Nordvest Fjord in Greenland: 194 miles

Longest river – The Nile River in Egypt and Sudan: 4160 miles

TALLEST

Tallest mountain that rises out of the ocean – Mauna Kea: 33,480 feet from the floor of the Pacific Ocean (Mauna Kea forms the island of Hawaii.)

Tallest underwater mountain – The Great Meteor Tablemount, North Atlantic Ocean: 13,123 feet

Tallest sand dunes – Found in the Sahara Desert in Africa: as tall as 1500 feet

Tallest iceberg – 550 feet, seen off Greenland in 1958

OTHER EXTREMES

Greatest outflow of any river – Amazon in Brazil, discharges 2.5 cubic miles of water a minute

Saltiest sea – Dead Sea (in the Middle East, west of Israel)

Oldest lake – Lake Baikal in Russia: 25 million years old

Fastest-moving glacier – Quarayaq Glacier in Greenland: flows up to 70-80 feet a day

Windiest spot ever recorded – Port Martin, Antarctica: 65 mph for a month

Sunniest place – Eastern Sahara Desert: Sun shines 97% of the time

Least sunny place – North Pole: 182 days a year with no sunshine

Wettest spot in the world – Mt. Waialeale on the island of Kauai, Hawaii: about 500 inches a year, falling 350 or more days a year

Driest spot – Atacama Desert in Chile: about 0.02 inches of rain a year

The coldest temperature ever recorded – Vostok, Antarctica: –128.6 F

The highest temperature ever recorded in the shade – Aziziyah, Libya: 136 F

Lake Baikal, in Siberia, holds one-fifth of the world's fresh water.

The water in the Great Salt Lake of Utah, USA, is four times saltier than the water in any ocean.

Get Sharp: World Geography

World Time Zones

If the time were the same around the world, there would be sunlight at noon in some places and darkness at noon in other places. Earth makes a complete 360° turn every 24 hours; therefore different parts of Earth are facing the Sun at different times in the day. To keep the time in an area related to the position of the Sun, Earth is divided into 24 time zones, each of them 15° in size. A *time zone* is an area within which the time is the same at a given moment. The base location for determining time is the prime meridian, which runs through Greenwich, England, at 0° longitude.

WORLD TIME ZONES

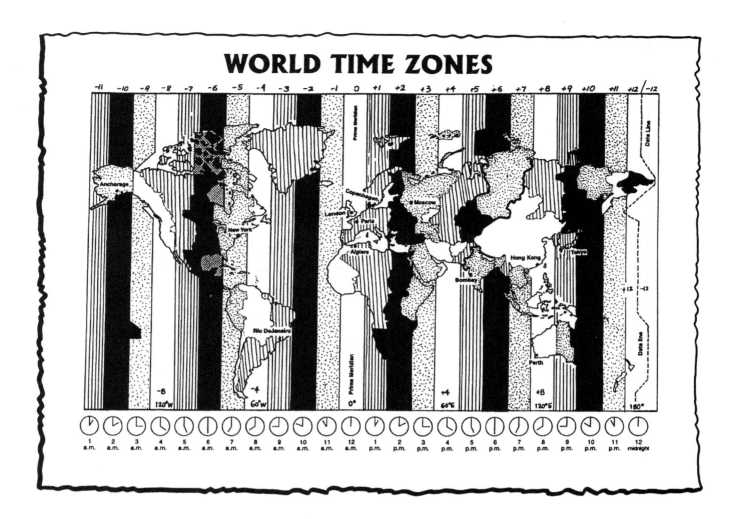

Some Time Zone Challenges

Find the right answer on the checkerboard.

1. It's 6:00 AM on Friday in Perth, Australia. Joe calls his cousin in Rio de Janeiro, Brazil, to wish her happy birthday. What time is it right now in Rio?	**4:00 PM, Saturday** / **18 hours** / **7:00 AM, Thursday**
2. A bear on loan to a New York zoo from Moscow, Russia is shipped from Moscow Saturday at 9:30 AM. She travels 14 hours. What time does the bear arrive in New York?	**7:00 PM, Thursday** / **22 hours** / **4:40 PM, Saturday**
3. Zelda left Anchorage, Alaska, at noon on Monday for a trip to London, England. She arrives on Tuesday at 2:30 PM. How long was the trip?	**17 hours** / **8:00 AM, Sunday** / **7:00 PM, Friday**

The World's Nations

The world is divided into different political areas. Some of these are independent countries or nations. Others are territories or other areas governed by another nation. This list shows the name of each of the world's 193 self-governing nations, along with its location, size, population (in 2001), and the capital city. Maps showing these nations can be found on pages 114-119.

Bangladesh is mostly surrounded by India. The country has suffered repeated problems and damage from famine, monsoons, floods, and cyclones.

Nation	Location	Area in square miles	Population	Capital City
Afghanistan	Southern Asia	250,00	27,755,775	Kabul
Albania	Eastern Europe	11,100	3,544,841	Tirane
Algeria	Northern Africa	919,600	32,277,942	Algiers
Andorra	Western Europe	174	68,403	Andorra La Vella
Angola	Southern Africa	481,400	10,593,171	Luanda
Antigua & Barbuda	In the Caribbean Sea, east of Puerto Rico	174	67,448	St. John's
Argentina	South America	1,068,300	37,812,817	Buenos Aires
Armenia	Western Asia	11,500	3,330,099	Yerevan
Australia	In the South Pacific Ocean, south of Asia	2,967,910	19,546,792	Canberra
Austria	Central Europe	32,380	8,169,929	Vienna
Azerbaijan	Western Asia	33,440	7,798,497	Baku
The Bahamas	In the Atlantic Ocean, east of Florida	5,380	330,529	Nassau
Bahrain	In the Persian Gulf, east of Qatar	240	656,397	Manama
Bangladesh	Southern Asia	56,000	133,376,684	Dhaka
Barbados	In the Atlantic Ocean, east of Puerto Rico	165	276,607	Bridgetown
Belarus	Eastern Europe	80,200	10,335,382	Minsk
Belgium	Western Europe	11,780	10,272,595	Brussels
Belize	Central America	8,860	262,999	Belmopan

The tiny island country of Barbados is famous for its 5000 green monkeys.

> Canada has the longest coastline in the world. It is 155,000 miles long - long enough to wrap around the world more than six times.

> The lush Amazon Rainforest in Brazil is home to almost half of the animal and plant species on Earth.

> China has the most neighbors of any country. It shares borders with 15 countries. Look on the map, and see if you can name them all!

Nation	Location	Area in square miles	Population	Capital City
Benin	Western Africa	43,480	6,787,625	Porto-Novo
Bhutan	South-Central Asia	18,000	2,094,176	Thimphu
Bolivia	South America	424,160	8,445,134	La Paz
Bosnia & Herzegovina	Southern Europe	19,740	3,964,388	Sarajevo
Botswana	Southern Africa	231,800	1,591,232	Gaborone
Brazil	South America	3,286,490	176,029,560	Brasilia
Brunei	In the southern Pacific Ocean on the island of Borneo	2,230	350,898	Bandar Seri Begawan
Bulgaria	Eastern Europe	42,820	7,621,337	Sofia
Burkina Faso	Western Africa	105,900	12,603,185	Ouagadougou
Burundi	Central Africa	10,750	6,373,002	Bujumbura
Cambodia	Southeastern Asia	69,900	12,775,324	Phnom Penh
Cameroon	Central Africa	183,570	16,184,748	Yaounde
Canada	North America	3,851,810	31,902,268	Ottawa
Cape Verde	In the Atlantic Ocean, west of the tip of Africa	1,560	408,760	Praia
Central African Republic	Central Africa	240,530	3,642,739	Bangui
Chad	Northern Africa	496,000	8,997,237	N'Djamena
Chile	South America	292,260	15,498,930	Santiago
People's Republic of China	Eastern Asia	3,705,410	1,284,303,705	Beijing
Columbia	South America	439,740	41,008,227	Bogata
Comoros	In the Indian Ocean, east of Mozambique, Africa	860	614,382	Moroni

Timor declared independence from Portugal in 1975. Nine days later it was invaded by Indonesia. After much war and bloodshed, East Timor was recognized as an independent state in 2002.

A village in Denmark has a very short name. The village is A. This name is even shorter than the Scottish town, Ae.

The Galapagos Islands of Ecuador have only non-human residents. It is a refuge to thousands of birds, seals, giant turtles, and iguanas.

Nation	Location	Area in square miles	Population	Capital City
Democratic Republic of the Congo	Central Africa	905,570	55,225,578	Kinshasa
Republic of the Congo	Central Africa	132,000	2,958,448	Brazzaville
Costa Rica	Central America	19,700	3,834,934	San Jose
Cote d'Ivoire (Ivory Coast)	Western Africa	124,500	16,804,784	Yamoussoukro
Croatia	Southern Europe	21,830	4,390,751	Zagreb
Cuba	In the Caribbean Sea, south of Florida	42,800	11,224,321	Havana
Cyprus	In the Mediterranean Sea, west of Turkey	3,570	767,314	Nicosia
Czech Republic	Central Europe	31,350	10,256,760	Prague
Denmark	Northern Europe	16,640	5,368,854	Copenhagen
Djibouti	Northern Africa	8,500	472,810	Djibouti
Dominica	In the Caribbean Sea, east of Puerto Rico	290	70,158	Roseau
Dominican Republic	Shares an island with Haiti in the Caribbean Sea, east of Cuba	18,810	8,721,594	Santo Domingo
East Timor	In the southern Pacific Ocean, north of Australia	5,740	871,000	Dili
Ecuador	South America	109,480	13,447,494	Quito
Egypt	Northeastern Africa	386,660	70,712,345	Cairo
El Salvador	Central America	8,120	6,353,681	San Salvador
Equatorial Guinea	West Africa	10,830	498,114	Malabo
Eritrea	Northeastern Africa	46,840	4,465,651	Asmara
Estonia	Northern Europe	17,460	1,415,681	Tallinn
Ethiopia	Eastern Africa	435,190	67,673,031	Addis Ababa
Fiji	In the southern Pacific Ocean, east of Australia	7,050	856,346	Suva

The World's Nations, continued

Indonesia is made up of more than 13,000 islands. If you count the water between the islands, the country spans about 2 million square miles.

The people of India watch a lot of movies. Almost 3 billion movie tickets are sold each year!

France leads the world in garlic production – with 138,000 tons a day.

Nation	Location	Area in square miles	Population	Capital City
Finland	Northern Europe	130,130	5,183,545	Helsinki
France	Western Europe	211,210	59,765,983	Paris
Gabon	Central Africa	103,350	1,233,353	Libreville
The Gambia	Western Africa	4,400	1,455,842	Banjul
Georgia	Western Asia	26,900	4,960,951	Tbilisi
Germany	Central Europe	167,890	83,251,851	Berlin
Ghana	Western Africa	92,100	20,244,154	Accra
Greece	Southern Europe	50,940	10,645,343	Athens
Grenada	In the Caribbean Sea, north of Venezuela	130	89,211	Saint George's
Guatemala	Central America	42,040	13,314,079	Guatemala City
Guinea	Western Africa	94,930	7,775,065	Conakry
Guinea-Bissau	Western Africa	13,950	1,345,479	Bissau
Guyana	South America	83,000	698,209	Georgetown
Haiti	Shares an island with the Dominican Republic in the Caribbean Sea, east of Cuba	10,710	7,063,722	Port-au-Prince
Honduras	Central America	43,280	6,560,608	Tegucigalpa
Hungary	Central Europe	35,920	10,075,030	Budapest
Iceland	In the northern Atlantic Ocean, west of northern Europe	40,000	279,384	Reykjavik
India	Southern Asia	1,269,350	1,045,845,266	New Delhi
Indonesia	In the southern Pacific and Indian Oceans, south of Asia	705,190	232,073,071	Jakarta
Iran	Southwestern Asia	636,000	66,662,704	Tehran

Get Sharp: World Nations

Nation	Location	Area *in square miles*	Population	Capital City
Iraq	Southwestern Asia	168,750	24,001,816	Baghdad
Ireland	In the Atlantic Ocean, west of Great Britain	27,140	3,883,159	Dublin
Israel	Middle East	8,020	6,029,529	Jerusalem
Italy	Southern Europe	116,310	57,715,625	Rome
Jamaica	In the Caribbean Sea, south of Cuba	4,240	2,680,029	Kingston
Japan	in the Pacific Ocean, east of Asia	145,880	126,974,628	Tokyo
Jordan	Middle East	35,300	5,307,470	Amman
Kazakhstan	Central Asia	1,049,200	16,741,519	Astana
Kenya	Eastern Africa	224,960	3,138,735	Nairobi
Kiribati	In the mid-Pacific Ocean, northeast of Australia	280	96,335	Tarawa
Kuwait	Southwestern Asia	6,880	2,111,651	Kuwait City
Kyrgyzstan	Western Asia	76,600	4,822,166	Bishkek
Laos	Southeastern Asia	91,400	5,777,180	Vientiane
Latvia	Central Europe	24,900	2,366,515	Riga
Lebanon	Middle East	4,000	3,677,780	Beirut
Lesotho	Southern Africa	11,720	2,207,954	Maseru
Liberia	Western Africa	43,000	3,288,198	Monrovia
Libya	Northern Africa	679,360	5,368,585	Tripoli
Liechtenstein	Southern Europe	60	32,842	Vaduz
Lithuania	Northern Europe	25,200	3,601,138	Vilnius

People in Japan eat over 27 tons of fish every day.

The tallest chimney in the world is at the Ekibastuz Power Station in Kazakhstan. It is 1,377 feet high.

Liberia is home to the pygmy hippopotamus. It is a miniature version (about half the size) of a usual hippo.

Nation	Location	Area in square miles	Population	Capital City
Luxembourg	Western Europe	1,000	448,569	Luxembourg
Macedonia	Southern Europe	9,780	2,054,800	Skopje
Madagascar	In the Indian Ocean, east of Africa	226,600	16,473,477	Antananarivo
Malawi	Southern Africa	45,750	10,701,824	Lilongwe
Malaysia	Southwestern Asia and the South China Sea on the Island of Borneo	127,320	22,662,365	Kuala Lumpur
Maldives	In the Indian Ocean, south of India	115	320,165	Male
Mali	Western Africa	480,000	11,340,480	Bamako
Malta	In the Mediterranean Sea, south of Italy	120	397,499	Valetta
Marshall Islands	In the Pacific Ocean, northeast of Australia	70	73,630	Majuro
Mauritania	Western Africa	398,000	2,828,858	Mouakchott
Mauritius	In the Indian Ocean, east of Africa	720	1,200,206	Port Louis
Mexico	North America	761,610	103,400,165	Mexico City
Micronesia	In the Pacific Ocean, northeast of Australia	270	135,689	Palikir
Moldova	Eastern Europe	13,000	4,434,547	Chisinau
Monaco	Western Europe	0.75	31,987	Monaco
Mongolia	Central Asia	604,000	2,649,432	Ulaanbaatar
Morocco	Northwestern Africa	172,410	31,167,783	Rabat
Mozambique	Southern Africa	309,500	19,607,519	Maputo
Myanmar (Burma)	Southern Asia	262,000	42,238,224	Yangon
Namibia	Southern Africa	318,700	1,820,916	Windhoek
Nauru	In the western Pacific Ocean, northeast of Australia	8	12,329	Yaren district

The biggest of the 1000 Maldives islands is only about 5 square miles.

A citizen of Tangiers, Morocco, is called a Tangerine.

Mongolia is the world's least densely-populated country.

Monaco is The most densely-populated country.

The capital of Mexico is sinking because it is built on an underground water reservoir. Since water is being drawn out rapidly, Mexico City is sinking at a rate of about 6 inches a year.

The World's Nations, continued

Nation	Location	Area in square miles	Population	Capital City
Nepal	Central Asia	54,000	25,873,917	Kathmandu
Netherlands	Northern Europe	16,060	16,067,754	Amsterdam
New Zealand	In the southern Pacific Ocean, east of Australia	103,740	3,908,037	Wellington
Nicaragua	Central America	50,000	5,023,818	Managua
Niger	Northern Africa	489,000	10,639,744	Niamey
Nigeria	Western Africa	356,670	129,934,911	Abjua
North Korea	Eastern Asia	46,540	22,224,195	Pyongyang
Norway	Northern Europe	125,180	4,525,116	Oslo
Oman	Southwestern Asia	82,030	2,713,462	Muscat
Pakistan	Southwestern Asia	310,400	147,663,429	Islamabad
Palau	In the northern Pacific Ocean, southeast of the Philippines	180	19,409	Koror
Panama	Central America	30,200	2,882,329	Panama City
Papua New Guinea	Shares an island in the southern Pacific Ocean with Indonesia, northeast of Australia	178,700	5,172,633	Port Moresby
Paraguay	South America	157,050	5,884,491	Asuncion
Peru	South America	496,230	27,949,639	Lima
Philippines	In the northwestern Pacific Ocean, east of southeastern Asia	115,830	84,525,639	Manila
Poland	Central Europe	120,730	38,625,478	Warsaw
Portugal	Southern Europe	35,670	10,084,245	Lisbon
Qatar	Middle East	4,420	793,341	Doha
Romania	Southern Europe	91,700	22,317,730	Bucharest
Russia	Spans from eastern Europe across the whole of northern Asia	4,420	1,415,681	Moscow

In Paraguay, it is legal to duel as long as both parties are registered blood donors.

The population of Nigeria is growing by about 8000 people each day.

The Netherlands grow and sell more flowers each year than any other country in the world.

Nation	Location	Area in square miles	Population	Capital City
Rwanda	Central Africa	10,170	7,398,074	Kigali
Saint Kitts and Nevis	In the Caribbean Sea, east of Puerto Rico	100	38,736	Basseterre
Saint Lucia	In the Caribbean Sea, north of Venezuela	240	160,145	Castries
Saint Vincent	In the Caribbean Sea, north of Venezuela	150	116,394	Kingstown
Samoa	In the southern Pacific Ocean, east of Australia	1,100	178,63	Nicosia
San Marino	Southern Europe	23	27,730	San Marino
Sao Tome and Principe	In the Atlantic Ocean, west of central Africa	390	170,371	Sao Tome
Saudi Arabia	Western Asia	756,990	23,513,330	Riyadh
Senegal	Western Africa	75,750	10,589,571	Dakar
Seychelles	In the Indian Ocean, east of Africa	180	80,098	Victoria
Sierra Leone	Western Africa	27,700	5,614,743	Freetown
Singapore	In the southern Pacific Ocean, off the tip of southeastern Asia	250	4,452,732	Singapore
Slovakia	Eastern Europe	18,860	5,422,366	Bratislava
Slovenia	Eastern Europe	7,820	1,932,917	Ljubljana
Solomon Islands	In the western Pacific Ocean, northeast of Australia	10,980	494,786	Honiara
Somalia	Eastern Africa	246,200	7,753,310	Mogadishu

Singapore means "City of Lions." A lion has never been seen in Singapore.

Volcanoes National Park in northwestern Rwanda is home to half of the remaining mountain gorillas in the world.

Some of the fiercest battles of World War II were fought on the Solomon Islands. The islands became an independent state in 1976.

Nation	Location	Area *in square miles*	Population	Capital City
South Africa	Africa	471,010	43,647,458	Pretoria and Cape Town
South Korea	Eastern Asia	46,540	22,224,195	Seoul
Spain	Western Europe	194,890	40,077,100	Madrid
Sri Lanka	In the Indian Ocean, southeast of India	25,330	19,576,783	Colombo
Sudan	Northern Africa	967,500	37,090,298	Khartoum
Suriname	South America	63,040	436,494	Paramaribo
Swaziland	Southern Africa	6,700	1,123,605	Mbabane
Sweden	Northern Europe	173,730	8,876,744	Stockholm
Switzerland	Central Europe	15,940	7,301,994	Bern and Lausanne
Syria	Northwestern Asia	71,500	17,155,814	Damascus
Taiwan	In East China Sea-Pacific Ocean, east of China	13,890	22,548,009	Taipei
Tajikistan	Western Asia	55,300	6,719,567	Dushanbe
Tanzania	Eastern Africa	364,900	31,187,939	Dar-es-Salaam
Thailand	Southeastern Asia	198,000	62,354,402	Bangkok
Togo	Western Africa	21,930	5,285,501	Lome
Tonga	In the southern Pacific Ocean	290	106,137	Nuku'alofa
Trinidad and Tobago	In the Caribbean Sea, north of Venezuela, South America	1,980	1,163,724	Port-of-Spain
Tunisia	Northern Africa	63,170	9,815,644	Tunis
Turkey	Eastern Europe and partly in western Asia	301,380	67,308,928	Ankara
Turkmenistan	Western Asia	188,500	4,688,963	Ashgabat
Tuvalu	In the southern Pacific Ocean, east of Australia	10	11,146	Funafuti Atoll
Uganda	Eastern Africa	91,140	24,699,073	Kampala
Ukraine	Eastern Europe	233,100	48,396,470	Kiev
United Arab Emirates	Middle East	32,000	2,445,989	Abu Dhabi

More sugar is eaten per person in Swaziland than in any other country – 448 pounds a year!

About 10 million people in the world live in places that are not independent. These places are dependent territories ruled by the UK, Denmark, France, Portugal, Norway, Australia, or New Zealand.

Sri Lanka is the home to one of the most poisonous snakes in the world, the carpet viper. On the average, two people are killed in the country each day by poisonous snakes.

The Vatican City is the smallest independent state. Its birthrate is zero because the citizens are Roman Catholic priests who are not allowed to marry.

The United States produces more vehicles than any other country – about 32,000 a day!

South Africa leads the way in digging up gold. Almost two tons a day are mined there.

Zimbabwe is a new name for that country. Before 1980, the country was named Southern Rhodesia.

Tanzania is home to the Serengeti – a $3\frac{1}{2}$ million acre park that is home to thousands of wild animals.

Nation	Location	Area in square miles	Population	Capital City
United Kingdom (Great Britain)	In the Atlantic Ocean, west of the European mainland	94,530	59,778,002	London
United States	North America	3,717,810	280,562,489	Washington, D.C.
Uruguay	South America	68.040	3,386,575	Montevideo
Uzbekistan	Central Asia	172,740	25,56,441	Tashkent
Vanuatu	In the southern Pacific Ocean, east of Australia	5,700	196,178	Port-Vila
Vatican City	Within the city of Rome, Italy	0.2	870	no capital
Venezuela	South America	352,140	24,287,670	Caracas
Vietnam	Southeastern Asia	127,240	89,018,416	Hanoi
Yemen	Southwestern Asia	203,850	18,701,257	Sanaa
Yugoslavia	Eastern Europe	39,520	10,262,087	Belgrade, Podgorica
Zambia	Southern Africa	290,580	9,959,037	Lusaka
Zimbabwe	Southern Africa	150,800	11,376,676	Harare

North America – Political Divisions

North America is a vast continent that includes 3 large countries and 20 smaller ones, some of them tiny islands.

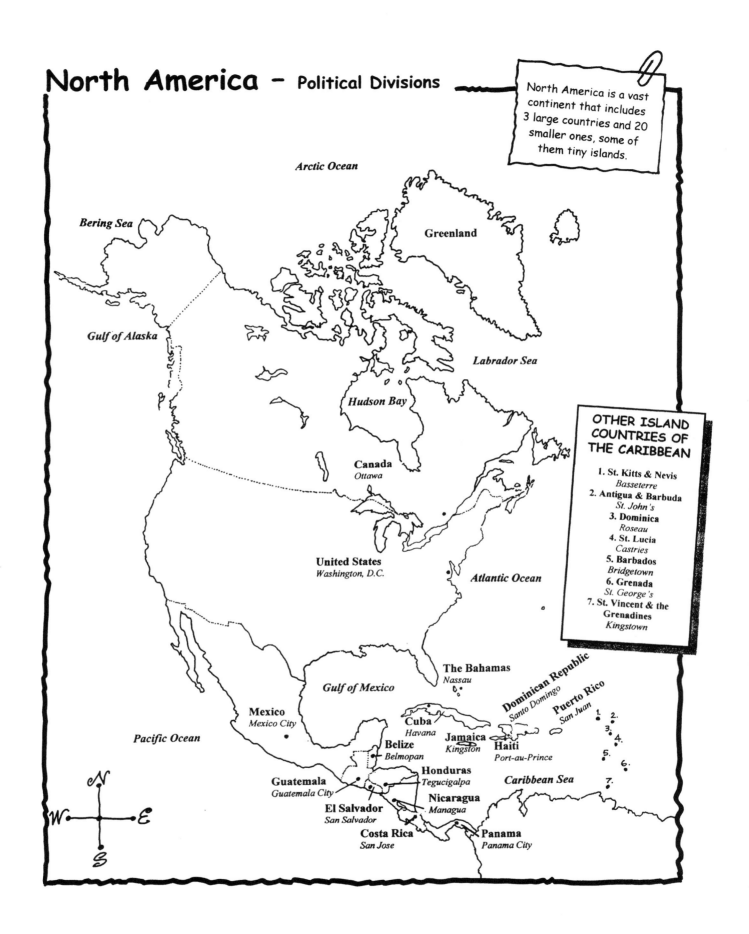

OTHER ISLAND COUNTRIES OF THE CARIBBEAN

1. **St. Kitts & Nevis**
   Basseterre
2. **Antigua & Barbuda**
   St. John's
3. **Dominica**
   Roseau
4. **St. Lucia**
   Castries
5. **Barbados**
   Bridgetown
6. **Grenada**
   St. George's
7. **St. Vincent & the Grenadines**
   Kingstown

Arctic Ocean
Bering Sea
Greenland
Gulf of Alaska
Labrador Sea
Hudson Bay
Canada
Ottawa
United States
Washington, D.C.
Atlantic Ocean
Pacific Ocean
Mexico
Mexico City
Gulf of Mexico
The Bahamas
Nassau
Dominican Republic
Santo Domingo
Puerto Rico
San Juan
Cuba
Havana
Jamaica
Kingston
Belize
Belmopan
Haiti
Port-au-Prince
Guatemala
Guatemala City
Honduras
Tegucigalpa
Caribbean Sea
El Salvador
San Salvador
Nicaragua
Managua
Costa Rica
San Jose
Panama
Panama City

N
W E
S

South America – Political Divisions

Trinidad and Tobago
Port of Spain

Venezuela
Caracas

Guyana
Georgetown

Suriname
Paramaribo

French Guiana (Fr.)
Cayenne

Atlantic Ocean

Colombia
Bogota

Ecuador
Quito

Peru
Lima

Brazil
Brasilia

Bolivia
La Paz

Pacific Ocean

Paraguay
Asuncion

Atlantic Ocean

Chile

Santiago

Argentina
Buenos Aires

Uruguay
Montevideo

N
W E
S

South America was colonized by Spanish conquerors except for the land that is now Brazil, which was settled by the Portuguese. As a result, most of the countries are Spanish-speaking, but Portuguese is the main language in Brazil.

Get Sharp Tip # 6
Antarctica is the only continent with no political divisions. Since it has no permanent residents, there is no governmental unit on the continent.

115

Europe – Political Divisions

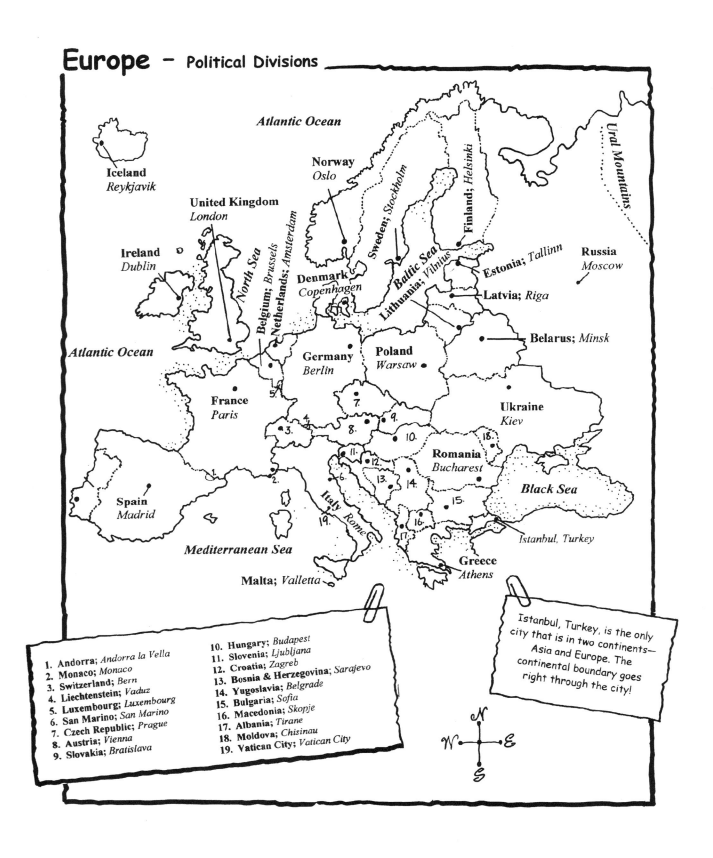

Atlantic Ocean

Iceland
Reykjavik

Norway
Oslo

United Kingdom
London

Ireland
Dublin

Finland; Helsinki

Sweden; Stockholm

Ural Mountains

North Sea

Atlantic Ocean

Belgium; Brussels
Netherlands; Amsterdam

Denmark
Copenhagen

Baltic Sea

Lithuania; Vilnius

Estonia; Tallinn

Russia
Moscow

Latvia; *Riga*

Belarus; *Minsk*

Germany
Berlin

Poland
Warsaw

France
Paris

5
7.
4
3. 8.
9.
10.
18.

Ukraine
Kiev

11.
12.
6.
13.
14.

Romania
Bucharest

Black Sea

Spain
Madrid

Italy Rome

19.

15.

16.

17.

Mediterranean Sea

Istanbul, Turkey

Greece
Athens

Malta; *Valletta*

1. **Andorra;** *Andorra la Vella*
2. **Monaco;** *Monaco*
3. **Switzerland;** *Bern*
4. **Liechtenstein;** *Vaduz*
5. **Luxembourg;** *Luxembourg*
6. **San Marino;** *San Marino*
7. **Czech Republic;** *Prague*
8. **Austria;** *Vienna*
9. **Slovakia;** *Bratislava*

10. **Hungary;** *Budapest*
11. **Slovenia;** *Ljubljana*
12. **Croatia;** *Zagreb*
13. **Bosnia & Herzegovina;** *Sarajevo*
14. **Yugoslavia;** *Belgrade*
15. **Bulgaria;** *Sofia*
16. **Macedonia;** *Skopje*
17. **Albania;** *Tirane*
18. **Moldova;** *Chisinau*
19. **Vatican City;** *Vatican City*

Istanbul, Turkey, is the only city that is in two continents— Asia and Europe. The continental boundary goes right through the city!

N
NW E
S

Asia – Political Divisions

1. Lebanon
Beirut

2. Israel
Jerusalem

3. Jordan
Amman

4. Syria
Damascus

5. Georgia
Tbilisi

6. Azerbaijan
Baku

7. Armenia
Yerevan

Arctic Ocean

Europe

Ural Mts.

Russia
Moscow

Kazakhstan
Astana

Mongolia
Ulaanbaatar

N. Korea
Pyongyang

Japan
Tokyo

Turkey
Ankara

Cyprus
Nicosia

Iraq
Baghdad

Uzbekistan
Tashkent

Turkmenistan
Ashgabat

Kyrgyzstan
Bishkek

China
Beijing

S. Korea
Seoul

Kuwait
Kuwait City

Iran
Tehran

Afghanistan
Kabul

Tajikistan
Dushanbe

Saudi Arabia
Riyadh

Bahrain
Manama

Pakistan
Islamabad

Bhutan
Thimphu

Taiwan
Taipei

Qatar
Doha

India
New Delhi

Laos
Vientiane

Yemen
Sanaa

Oman
Muscat

Arabian Sea

United Arab Emirates
Abu Dhabi

Bangladesh
Dhaka

Myanmar (Burma)
Yangon

Thailand
Bangkok

Vietnam
Hanoi

Philippines
Manila

Brunei
Bandar Seri Begawan

Pacific Ocean

Maldives
Male

Indian Ocean

Sri Lanka
Colombo

Cambodia
Phnom Penh

Singapore
Singapore

Malaysia
Kuala Lumpur

Java
Jakarta

Indonesia
Jakarta

East Timor
Dili

Asia is the largest continent. It is home to the ten highest mountain peaks, the lowest place on Earth (the Dead Sea), and over 65% of the world's people.

N W E S

Africa – Political Divisions

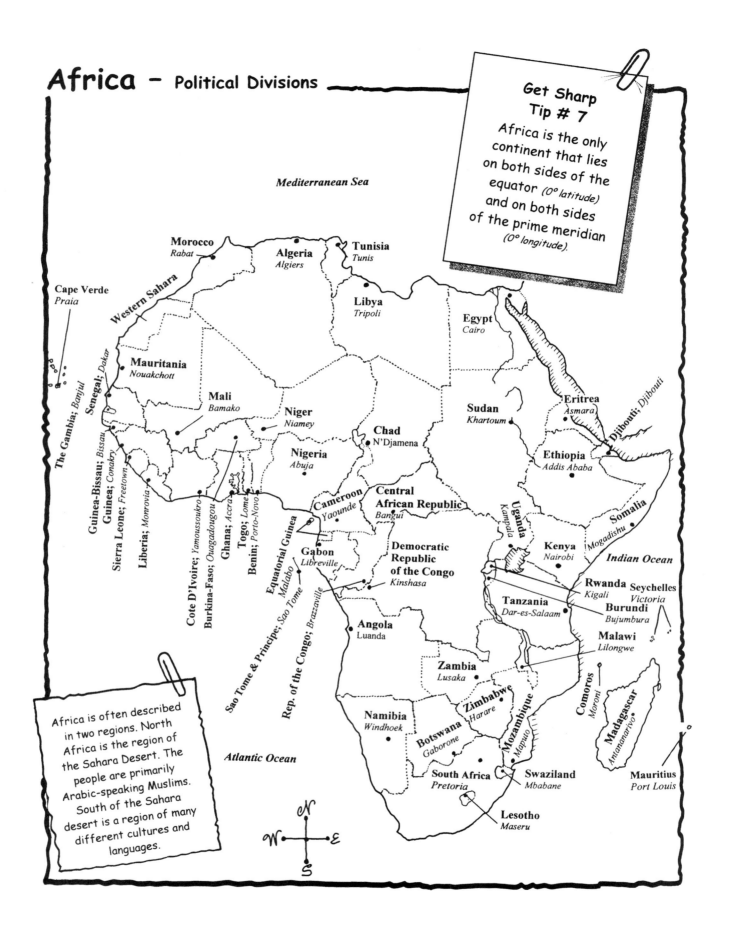

Get Sharp Tip # 7

Africa is the only continent that lies on both sides of the equator *(0° latitude)* and on both sides of the prime meridian *(0° longitude)*.

Mediterranean Sea

Morocco
Rabat

Algeria
Algiers

Tunisia
Tunis

Cape Verde
Praia

Western Sahara

Libya
Tripoli

Egypt
Cairo

Mauritania
Nouakchott

The Gambia; Banjul

Senegal; Dakar

Guinea-Bissau; Bissau

Guinea; Conakry

Sierra Leone; Freetown

Liberia; Monrovia

Mali
Bamako

Niger
Niamey

Chad
N'Djamena

Nigeria
Abuja

Sudan
Khartoum

Eritrea
Asmara

Djibouti; Djibouti

Ethiopia
Addis Ababa

Cote D'Ivoire; Yamoussoukro

Burkina-Faso; Ouagadougou

Ghana; Accra

Togo; Lome

Benin; Porto-Novo

Cameroon
Yaounde

Central African Republic
Bangui

Uganda
Kampala

Somalia
Mogadishu

Kenya
Nairobi

Indian Ocean

Equatorial Guinea; Malabo

Gabon
Libreville

Democratic Republic of the Congo
Kinshasa

Sao Tome & Principe; Sao Tome

Rep. of the Congo; Brazzaville

Rwanda
Kigali

Seychelles
Victoria

Tanzania
Dar-es-Salaam

Burundi
Bujumbura

Angola
Luanda

Malawi
Lilongwe

Zambia
Lusaka

Comoros
Moroni

Namibia
Windhoek

Zimbabwe
Harare

Mozambique
Maputo

Madagascar
Antananarivo

Botswana
Gaborone

Mauritius
Port Louis

Atlantic Ocean

South Africa
Pretoria

Swaziland
Mbabane

Lesotho
Maseru

Africa is often described in two regions. North Africa is the region of the Sahara Desert. The people are primarily Arabic-speaking Muslims. South of the Sahara desert is a region of many different cultures and languages.

118

Australia & Oceania – Political Divisions

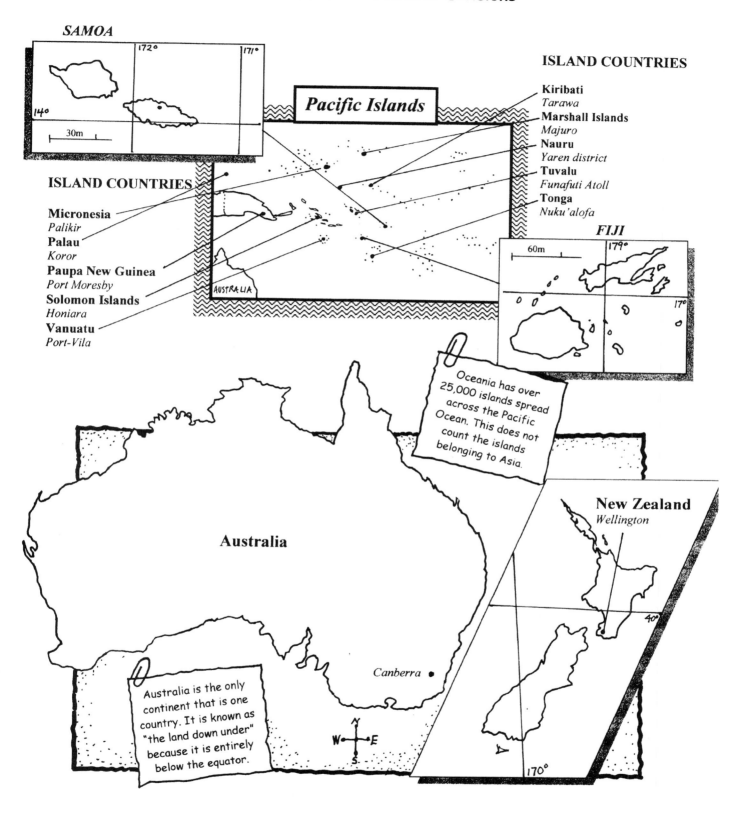

SAMOA

172°   171°

14°

30m

ISLAND COUNTRIES

Micronesia
Palikir
Palau
Koror
Paupa New Guinea
Port Moresby
Solomon Islands
Honiara
Vanuatu
Port-Vila

Pacific Islands

AUSTRALIA

ISLAND COUNTRIES

Kiribati
Tarawa
Marshall Islands
Majuro
Nauru
Yaren district
Tuvalu
Funafuti Atoll
Tonga
Nuku'alofa

FIJI

60m   179°

0   0   17°

Oceania has over 25,000 islands spread across the Pacific Ocean. This does not count the islands belonging to Asia.

New Zealand
Wellington

40°

Australia

Canberra

170°

W   N   E
S

Australia is the only continent that is one country. It is known as "the land down under" because it is entirely below the equator.

Better Grades & Higher Test Scores / SOCIAL STUDIES
Copyright ©2003 by Incentive Publications, Inc., Nashville, TN.

Get Sharp: World Nations

World Population

Population is the number of people in a given area. *Population density* describes how close together people live. An area with high population density is very crowded.

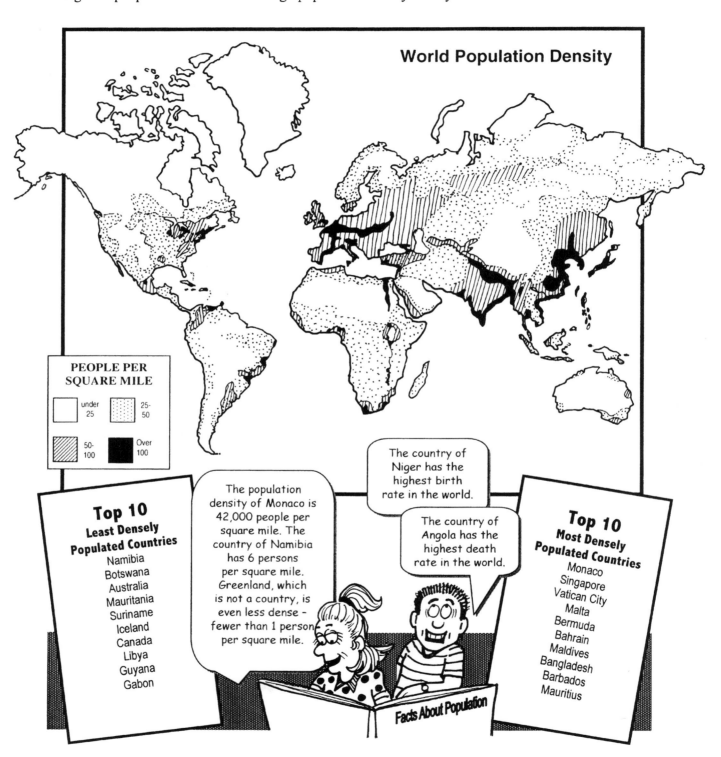

World Population Density

PEOPLE PER SQUARE MILE

- under 25
- 25-50
- 50-100
- Over 100

Top 10 Least Densely Populated Countries
Namibia
Botswana
Australia
Mauritania
Suriname
Iceland
Canada
Libya
Guyana
Gabon

The population density of Monaco is 42,000 people per square mile. The country of Namibia has 6 persons per square mile. Greenland, which is not a country, is even less dense – fewer than 1 person per square mile.

The country of Niger has the highest birth rate in the world.

The country of Angola has the highest death rate in the world.

Facts About Population

Top 10 Most Densely Populated Countries
Monaco
Singapore
Vatican City
Malta
Bermuda
Bahrain
Maldives
Bangladesh
Barbados
Mauritius

World Population Tops 6 Billion

According to the U.S. Census Bureau, the world population reached 6 billion in July, 1999. The same source estimates that the world population will almost double by 2040.

Top 10 Populations of Countries
(Countries with Most People in 2002)

		Population to nearest 1000
1.	China	1,204,384,000
2.	India	1,045,845,000
3.	United States	287,041,000
4.	Indonesia	232,073,000
5.	Brazil	176,030,000
6.	Pakistan	147,663,000
7.	Russia	144,979,000
8.	Bangladesh	133,377,000
9.	Nigeria	129,935,000
10.	Japan	126,975,000

The people of the United Kingdom are the world's top consumers of baked beans.

The people of Lebanon eat the most vegetables per person.

Top 10 Populations of Cities
(Cities with Most People in 2002)

		Population to nearest 1000
1.	Tokyo, Japan	26,444,000
2.	Mexico City, Mexico	18,131,000
3.	Bombay India	18,066,000
4.	Sao Paulo, Brazil	17,755,000
5.	New York City, US	16,640,000
6.	Lagos, Nigeria	13,427,000
7.	Los Angeles, US	13,140,000
8.	Calcutta, India	12,918,000
9.	Shanghai, China	12,887,000
10.	Buenos Aires, Argentina	12,560,000

The Swiss people are the world's top consumers of chocolate, eating an average of 26 pounds a year each.

The top butter consumers in the world are the people in New Zealand.

The people of Somalia are the most undernourished in the world.

The people of Finland drink more coffee per person than anywhere else in the world.

How World Population Has Changed

World Population . . .

in 1950	2,556,000,053
in 1960	3,039,451,023
in 1970	3,706,618,163
in 1980	4,453,831,714
in 1990	5,278,639,789
in 2000	6,082,966,429
in 2002	6,157,400,560

The French are the world's top consumers of fat.

World Connections

The distance around Earth is thousands of miles, and the world's peoples are from hundreds of different cultures. Yet, today, the world seems small. A traveler can speed from one continent to another in a few hours. In just seconds, you can communicate by Internet with a friend halfway around the world. In addition, the issues, needs, problems, and lives of people all over the world are connected by the fact that we all share the same home—planet Earth. Here are some of the kinds of connections that bring us together.

Big Problems

All humans on Earth share in problems such as these things— they affect us all, and affect the world we share.

global warming

pollution

deforestation

poor air quality

terrorism

natural disasters

poverty

shrinking resources

food shortages

population increases

wars

political conflicts

hunger

Cultural

Geographical borders do not confine cultures. Many cultures have spread all over the world. Cultures have shared and exchanged ideas with one another. The world is a multicultural habitat for humans.

Religious

Geographical borders do not confine religion. Ideas from most religions have spread all over the world. Wherever a person lives, the understanding and tolerance of many religious ideas is a part of life as a world citizen.

Economic

In today's modern world, economic systems, patterns, and institutions tie nations and cultures together. Any country's economic policies are affected by the economic status and practices of other countries.

Travel & Communication

Technology has caused the world to "shrink." Jet airplanes, fast trains, telephones, computers, and the Internet have made it possible to visit or connect with someone else just about anywhere in the world. It is possible to get a message to someone at the top of Mt. Everest, on a subway underground, deep in a cave, or in the Amazon rainforest.

Human Needs or Wants

All humans have similar needs for things such as food, shelter, safety, space, and relationships. Humans have wants, too, although these differ among people and cultures. Meeting needs and satisfying wants for people in one part of the world affects people in other parts of the world. This happens because Earth's resources are limited. Filling wants and needs uses resources, and often leaves some sort of impact on the world's environment (air, water, or land).

Environmental Needs

All the world's people share the Earth's environment. A healthy environment or an unhealthy environment eventually affects us all. Deforestation in South America affects the climate worldwide. Air pollution in China is carried across oceans by winds. Depletion of coal and oil supplies in North America puts extra demand on those resource supplies elsewhere in the world.

World Organizations

Many organizations have sprung up to meet needs the world or a part of the world. These organizations have the support and cooperation of more than one nation and fill a variety of needs: social, political, military, economic, or humanitarian.

These are a few of the organizations in which several nations cooperate to meet some kind of need that crosses national borders.

AL Arab League

Purpose: to promote better relations among members of several Middle Eastern and African nations and the PLO

CIS Commonwealth of Independent States

Purpose: an agreement among nations that were once a part of the Soviet Union, formed to help the new countries work together

Commonwealth Commonwealth of Nations

Purpose: an organization of countries that have been under British rule, formed to cooperate in economic and foreign affairs

EU European Union

Purpose: an agreement of several European countries to cooperate in many economic and political areas

IAEA International Atomic Energy Agency

Purpose: to work for peaceful and safe uses of atomic energy

ICSW International Council on Social Welfare

Purpose: to advance social welfare, social justice, and social development in many nations

ILO International Labor Organization

Purpose: to promote the welfare of workers worldwide

IMF International Monetary Fund

Purpose: to help nations cooperate on financial matters that affect the world's nations

IMO International Maritime Organization

Purpose: to promote marine safety, prevent pollution from ships, and set high standards for shipping

NATO North Atlantic Treaty Organization

Purpose: a military alliance of U.S., Canada, and many European countries, formed to keep peace in Europe and protect one another

OAS Organization of American States

Purpose: for a group of North American and South American countries to work together for peace, self-defense, and cooperation

OPEC Organization of Petroleum Exporting Countries

Purpose: to increase revenue from the sale of oil

UN United Nations

Purpose: an organization of most of the world's nations, formed to work for world peace and security and the bettering of humans
(See page 124 for more on the UN.)

UNESCO United Nations Educational, Scientific, and Cultural Organization

Purpose: to promote education and cultural development across the world

UNICEF United Nations Children's Fund

Purpose: to help children get the care and stimulation they need; to reduce illness and death in children; to protect children in war or natural disasters

WHO World Health Organization

Purpose: to promote health and health education

WTO World Trade Organization

Purpose: to oversee international trade

The United Nations

The United Nations (UN) is a community of nations joined together to work toward making the world a better place. The UN began in 1945 at the end of World War II. Representatives of 50 nations gathered in San Francisco, California, and wrote an agreement called the *UN Charter*. By the year 2000, the UN had 189 member nations. The UN headquarters is in New York City, New York. The World Court is located at The Hague, Netherlands.

UN Day is celebrated on October 24 each year with concerts, speeches, parades, and other events around the world.

The Purposes of the United Nations

- to maintain international peace
- to develop friendly relations among nations
- to cooperate in solving international problems
- to promote respect for human rights and basic human freedoms
- to help countries achieve their goals for meeting these purposes

The Structure of the United Nations

The General Assembly includes all members of the UN, with each country having one vote. The assembly discusses world problems, appoints the secretary-general, agrees on the budget, and admits new members.

The Security Council has five permanent members (China, France, Great Britain, Russia, and the U.S.) and ten members elected by the General Assembly for 2-year terms. The council discusses and votes on matters of world peace and security.

The Economic and Social Council has 54 members, each elected for a term of 3 years. The council discusses and acts on issues related to economic development, trade, and a variety of social issues such as health, human rights, children, education, food, and population.

The International Court of Justice (World Court) has 15 judges, each elected for a 9-year term. The judges are all from different countries. The court settled disputes between countries.

The Secretariat is a part of the organization that operates the day-to-day business of the UN. This organ of the UN is headed by the secretary-general, who is appointed by the General Assembly.

UN Agencies & Programs

The UN operates several agencies and programs to deal with a long list of world concerns and problems. The organization is active in working on issues, problems, and concerns such as:

peacekeeping
humanitarian needs
human rights
needs of children
environmental protection
disease prevention
treatment of diseases
poverty
consumer protection
safe travel
stopping terrorism
stopping drug trafficking
clearing land minds
helping refugees
fighting against AIDS

Remarkable Creations

Humans have made some amazing additions to the world's landscape. These are just a few of the astounding, creative cultural landmarks that have been designed and built over the course of human history on Earth. See pages 126-127 for the locations of the structures.

The Eiffel Tower is a steel and iron tower built in Paris for the World's Fair of 1889.

The Panama Canal, completed in 1914, is a waterway built across the Isthmus of Panama. It allows ships to pass between the Atlantic and Pacific Oceans.

The Sydney Opera House, in Sydney, Australia, is a huge performance center of unusual architecture. It has a roof of overlapping shells that look like two huge sails.

The Gateway Arch is a 630-foot arch overlooking the Mississippi River in St. Louis, Missouri. It was built to honor the Louisiana Purchase.

The Tower of London is a group of buildings along the Thames River in London. The buildings have been a prison and a castle. It is now an arsenal and a museum, holding the British crown jewels.

The Great Wall of China is the longest human-built structure, stretching 4500 miles across China.

Stonehenge is a mysterious stone circle built in ancient times in southwestern England.

The Taj Mahal is a huge white marble structure built as a tomb for the wife of Shah Jahan.

The Great Sphinx, a great monument with the head of a human and the body of a lion, sits near the great pyramids in Egypt.

Christ the Redeemer is a tall statue of Christ that overlooks the harbor in Rio de Janeiro, Brazil.

I'm going to fly from Panama to Peru, then straight on to Brazil and Paris. Let's see . . . where could I borrow some money?

Mt. Rushmore, in South Dakota, holds the faces of several American presidents carved into the rock.

The Statue of Liberty is a tall statue of a lady standing in the harbor of New York City, welcoming visitors to a free land.

Chichen Itza, the ruins of a powerful city of the ancient Mayan empire, is found in eastern Mexico.

The Space Needle looks like a needle. It was the centerpiece of the 1962 Seattle World's Fair.

Notre Dame is a famous and beautiful two-towered cathedral in Paris. Its name means, "Our Lady."

The Leaning Tower of Piza is an Italian bell tower in the town of Pisa. Because it was built on unstable soil, the tower is leaning about 14 feet out of alignment.

St. Basil's Cathedral is a beautiful Russian Orthodox church built at the southern end of the Red Square in Moscow, Russia.

Machu Picchu is known as the "Lost City of the Incas." It is a collection of ruins of an ancient Incan city, found high in the Andes Mountains of Peru.

The Parthenon is an ancient Greek temple overlooking the city of Athens, Greece. It sits on top of a hill called the "Acropolis."

The Mona Lisa, completed in 1506 by Leonardo da Vinci, is probably the most famous painting in the world. It hangs in the Louvre Museum in Paris, France.

The Egyptian Pyramids are large stone tombs built for Egyptian pharaohs. Ruins of 35 pyramids are still standing along the Nile River.

Remarkable Creations

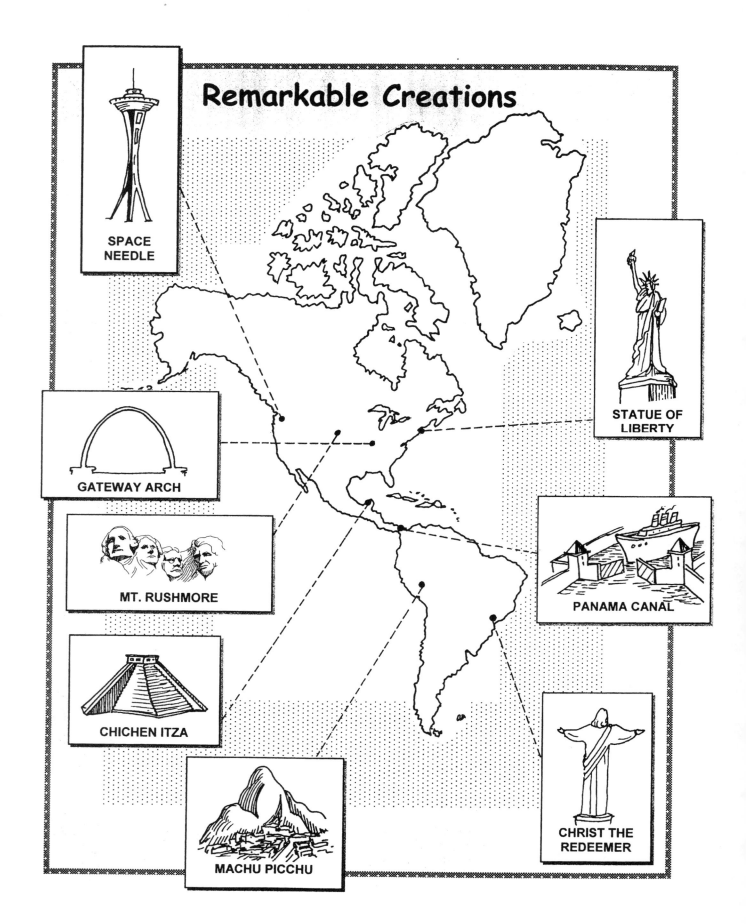

SPACE NEEDLE

GATEWAY ARCH

MT. RUSHMORE

CHICHEN ITZA

MACHU PICCHU

STATUE OF LIBERTY

PANAMA CANAL

CHRIST THE REDEEMER

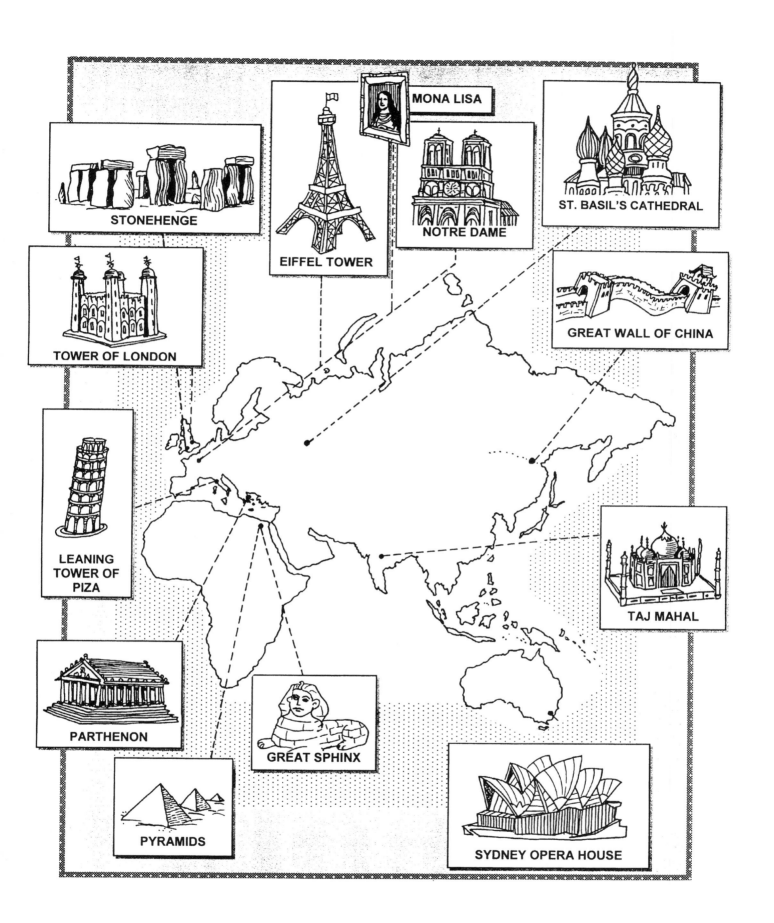

STONEHENGE

MONA LISA

EIFFEL TOWER

NOTRE DAME

ST. BASIL'S CATHEDRAL

TOWER OF LONDON

GREAT WALL OF CHINA

LEANING TOWER OF PIZA

TAJ MAHAL

PARTHENON

PYRAMIDS

GREAT SPHINX

SYDNEY OPERA HOUSE

Get Sharp: Remarkable Creations

Record-Setting Creations

It seems that humans are always building structures bigger, longer, deeper, or taller. These are some of the remarkable cultural creations whose incredible measurements set world records.

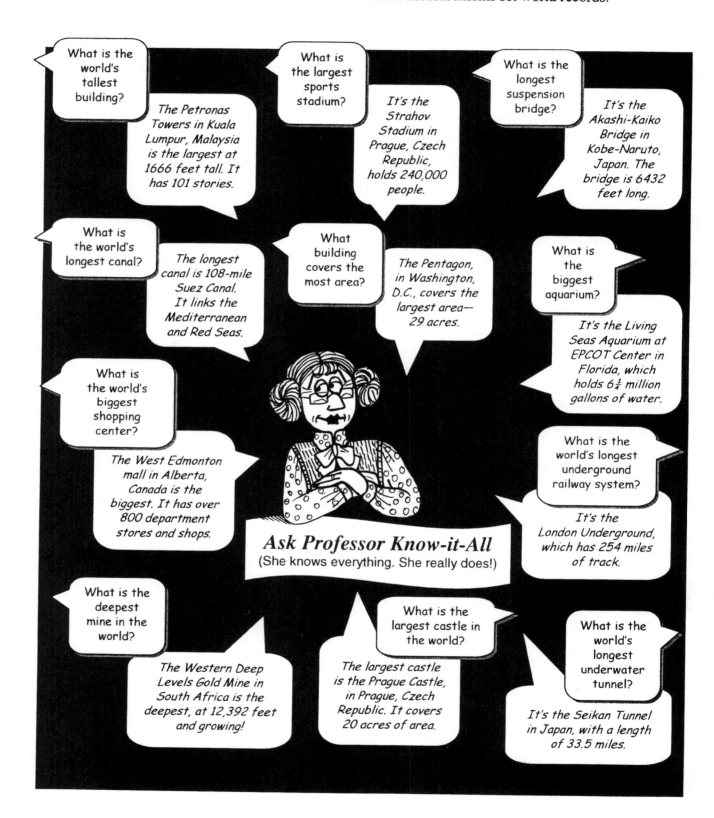

What is the world's tallest building?

The Petronas Towers in Kuala Lumpur, Malaysia is the largest at 1666 feet tall. It has 101 stories.

What is the largest sports stadium?

It's the Strahov Stadium in Prague, Czech Republic, holds 240,000 people.

What is the longest suspension bridge?

It's the Akashi-Kaiko Bridge in Kobe-Naruto, Japan. The bridge is 6432 feet long.

What is the world's longest canal?

The longest canal is 108-mile Suez Canal. It links the Mediterranean and Red Seas.

What building covers the most area?

The Pentagon, in Washington, D.C., covers the largest area— 29 acres.

What is the biggest aquarium?

It's the Living Seas Aquarium at EPCOT Center in Florida, which holds $6\frac{1}{4}$ million gallons of water.

What is the world's biggest shopping center?

The West Edmonton mall in Alberta, Canada is the biggest. It has over 800 department stores and shops.

Ask Professor Know-it-All
(She knows everything. She really does!)

What is the world's longest underground railway system?

It's the London Underground, which has 254 miles of track.

What is the deepest mine in the world?

The Western Deep Levels Gold Mine in South Africa is the deepest, at 12,392 feet and growing!

What is the largest castle in the world?

The largest castle is the Prague Castle, in Prague, Czech Republic. It covers 20 acres of area.

What is the world's longest underwater tunnel?

It's the Seikan Tunnel in Japan, with a length of 33.5 miles.

GET SHARP →

on United States Geography

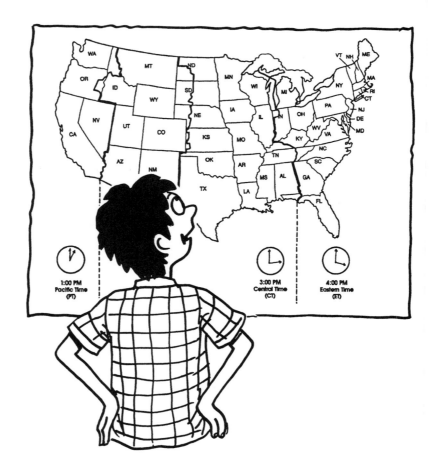

U.S. Land and Water

This map shows some of the major physical features of the United States.

Alaska Range
Mt. McKinley

Coastal Mts.
Columbia River
Rocky Mountains
Missouri River
Missouri River
The Great Plains
Crater Lake
Mt. Shasta
Snake River
Sierra Nevadas
Central Valley
The Great Salt Lake
Great Basin
Rocky Mountains
Mt. Whitney
Colorado River
Arkansas River
Mojave Desert
The Grand Canyon
Rio Grande
Red River
Pacific Ocean
Gulf of Mexico

The United States is a land of great variety in physical features. If you travel around the country, you'll see an amazing, breathtaking assortment of tall mountains, rolling hills, flat plains, rushing rivers, vast forests, deep canyons, high plateaus, wide valleys, rocky cliffs, long beaches, and lakes of all sizes.

Top Dry Spots

Highest Spot:
Mt. McKinley (Denali) in Alaska – 20,320 feet

Lowest Dry Land Spot:
Death Valley, California – 282 feet below sea level

Deepest Canyon:
The Grand Canyon, Arizona – 1 mile deep

Top Wet Spots

Largest Lakes: the Great Lakes – combined area almost 95,000 square miles

Deepest Lake: Crater Lake, Oregon – 1932 feet

Longest River: Mississippi-Missouri-Red Rock River system – 3710 miles

131

U.S.A. - Vital Statistics

Capital: Washington, D.C.

Size: 3,717,796 square miles (3,536,278 land and 181,518 water)

Relative size: the 4th largest country in area

Location: North America, between Canada and Mexico, with one state northwest of Canada and another state in the central Pacific Ocean

Latitude range: 19°N – 71°N

Longitude range: 67°W – 172°E

Span: stretches from the Atlantic Ocean to the Pacific Ocean across the whole of the North American continent

Northernmost point: Point Barrow, Alaska

Southernmost point: Ka Lae, Hawaii

Easternmost point: West Quoddy Head, Maine

Westernmost point: Cape Wrangell, Alaska

Geographic center of the 50 states: Butte County, South Dakota

Length of coastline: 12,380 miles

Natural resources: forests, coal, natural gas, oil, minerals, salt, silver, gold, and many others

Average temperatures: range from 10° below zero in parts of Alaska to almost 80° above zero in Death Valley, California

Precipitation levels: range from less than 2 inches a year in Death Valley to over 450 inches a year on Mt. Waialeale, Hawaii

Climate: mostly moderate, with considerable variation in temperatures and precipitation, except for Alaska which has cool summers and long cold winters and Hawaii, where it is warm most of the time with high levels of precipitation

This is a quick overview of some basic facts about the United States – its land, location, and people.

Political divisions: 50 states and several territories

Economy: a free enterprise system

Economic output: highest production of goods and services in the world; one of the highest standards of living in the world

Products: a wide variety of agricultural goods, timber, power, domesticated farm animals, electronic equipment, and other manufactured goods, along with many services

Get Sharp Tip # 8

In addition to the 50 states, the United States governs several territories and outlying areas. These are mostly located in the Pacific Ocean and the Caribbean Sea:

Puerto Rico
Guam
U.S. Virgin Islands
Northern Mariana Islands
American Samoa
Midway Islands
Wake Island
Johnston Atoll
Baker Islands
Howland Islands
Jarvis Islands
Kingman Reef
Navassa Island
Palmyra Atoll

Population: 281,421,906 *(2000 census)*

Relative population: world's 3rd largest country

Male/female population ratio: 49.1% male; 50.9% female

Population density: 79.6 persons per square mile

Number of families: 71,787,347

Average family size: 3.14 persons

Median age: 35.3 years

Population under 18 years old: 72,293,812

Population 85 years and older: 4,239,587

Life expectancy: average 76.9 years (men: 74.1, women: 79.5)

Way of life: 0.3% urban; 19.7% rural

Number of people age 3 and older enrolled in school: 76,632,927

Number of universities: 5758

Households with no telephone service: 2,570,705

Major religions practiced: Protestant Christian, Roman Catholic, Christian Orthodox, Judaism, Islam, Buddhism, Anglicanism, and Hinduism

Main languages spoken: English, Spanish, French, German, Italian, and Chinese

Number of persons who speak a language other than English at home: 46,851,595

Most populated state: California, population 33,871,648

Least populated state: Wyoming, population 493,782

Most densely populated state: New Jersey, 1124 persons per square mile

Least densely populated state: Alaska, 1.1 persons per square mile

Most populated city: New York City, population 8,008,278

The border between the U.S. and Canada is the longest border between any two countries in the world. It is 3987 miles long.

U.S. residents are the world's top consumers of cocoa, meat, and soft drinks.

The U.S.A. was named after Amerigo Vespucci, one of the earliest European explorers to visit the North American continent.

The U.S. population increased 13.1% between 1990 and 2000.

80.4% of Americans over the age of 25 have completed a high school education.

I've lived here all my life and I never knew that!

Very interesting!

— 133 —

The 50 States

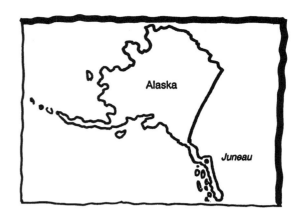

THE UNITED STATES

The largest state:
Alaska, 591,004 square miles

The smallest state:
Rhode Island, 1212 square miles

The United States of America is divided into fifty states and the capital, Washington, D.C., which is a city that is not within any state. The first state to enter the union was Delaware. It became a state on December 7, 1787. The last state, Hawaii, entered the union on August 21, 1959.

Northernmost city: Barrow, Alaska, 71°17' N
Southernmost city: Hilo, Hawaii, 19°43' N
Easternmost city: Eastport, Maine, 66°59' W
Westernmost city: West Unalaska, Alaska, 63°32' W

I notice that more states begin with **N** than any other letter!

I notice that more capitals begin with **C** and **S**.

The States – Vital Statistics

Here you have it – some important facts about all the 50 states!

Get Sharp Tip # 9
Washington, D.C., the nation's capital, is not a state. It is a city that covers 69 square miles and has a population of 529,000.

State *postal abbreviation and nickname*	Capital	Some Other Large Cities	Neighbors *bordering states*	Area *in square miles*	Population *2000 census*
Alabama - AL *The Heart of Dixie* *Cotton State* *Yellowhammer State*	Montgomery	Birmingham, Huntsville, Mobile	Florida, Georgia, Tennessee, Mississippi	52,237	4,447,100
Alaska - AK *The Last Frontier*	Juneau	Anchorage Fairbanks	Canada	615,230	626,932
Arizona - AZ *Grand Canyon State*	Phoenix	Tucson Mesa Glendale Scottsdale	California, Nevada, Utah, Colorado, New Mexico	114,006	5,130,632
Arkansas - AR *Razorback State* *Natural State*	Little Rock	Fort Smith North Little Rock	Oklahoma, Missouri, Tennessee Mississippi, Texas, Louisiana	53,182	2,673,400
California - CA *Golden State*	Sacramento	Los Angeles San Diego San Jose San Francisco	Arizona, Nevada Oregon	158,869	33,871,648
Colorado - CO *Centennial State*	Denver	Colorado Springs Aurora Lakewood	Utah, Wyoming Nebraska, Kansas Oklahoma, Arizona New Mexico	104,100	4,301,261
Connecticut - CT *Constitution State* *Nutmeg State*	Hartford	Bridgeport New Haven Hartford Stamford	New York Massachusetts Rhode Island	5544	3,405,565
Delaware - DE *First State* *Peach State*	Dover	Wilmington Newark	Maryland New Jersey Pennsylvania	2396	783,600

Visitors can keep the diamonds they find at a mine in Crater of the Diamonds State Park near Murfreesboro, Arkansas.

The U.S. bought Alaska from Russia in 1867 for about 2 cents an acre. Some people thought it was a waste of money.

State *postal abbreviation and nickname*	Capital	Some Other Large Cities	Neighbors *bordering states*	Area *in square miles*	Population *2000 census*
Florida - FL *Sunshine Sate*	Tallahassee	Jacksonville Miami Tampa St. Petersburg	Georgia, Alabama	59,928	15,982,378
Georgia - GA *Peach State*	Atlanta	Augusta Columbus Savannah	Florida, Alabama, North Carolina, South Carolina, Tennessee	58,977	8,186,453
Hawaii - HI *Aloha State*	Honolulu	Hilo Kailua Kaneohe	none	6459	1,211,537
Idaho - ID *Gem State*	Boise	Nampa Pocatello	Washington, Oregon, Nevada, Utah, Wyoming, Montana	83,574	1,293,593
Illinois - AL *Prairie State*	Springfield	Chicago Rockford Aurora Peoria	Wisconsin, Iowa, Missouri, Kentucky, Indiana	57,918	12,419,294
Indiana - IN *Hoosier State*	Indianapolis	Fort Wayne Evansville South Bend Gary	Illinois, Ohio, Michigan, Kentucky	36,420	6,080,485
Iowa - IA *Hawkeye State*	Des Moines	Cedar Rapids Davenport Sioux City	Nebraska, Missouri, Minnesota, Illinois, South Dakota, Wisconsin	56,276	2,926,324
Kansas - KS *Sunflower State*	Topeka	Wichita Kansas City Overland Park	Colorado, Nebraska, Missouri, Oklahoma	82,282	2,688,418
Kentucky - KY *Bluegrass Sate*	Frankfort	Lexington Louisville	Tennessee, Missouri, Indiana, Illinois, West Virginia, Virginia, Ohio	40,411	4,041,769

Hawaii was the last state admitted to the United States. It gained statehood in 1959.

Louisville, Kentucky is home to the nation's most famous horse race, the Kentucky Derby.

The everglades Swamp in Florida is a huge swamp covering 1½ million acres - but that's only a fifth of the swamp's size before it was drained to gain land for development.

State *postal abbreviation and nickname*	Capital	Some Other Large Cities	Neighbors *bordering states*	Area *in square miles*	Population *2000 census*
Louisiana - LA *Pelican State*	Baton Rouge	New Orleans Shreveport	Texas, Arkansas, Mississippi	49,651	4,468,976
Maine - ME *Pine Tree State* *Chickadee State*	Augusta	Portland Lewiston Bangor	New Hampshire	33,741	1,274,923
Maryland - MD *Free State* *Old Line State*	Annapolis	Baltimore Frederick Gaithersburg	Delaware, Virginia, West Virginia, Pennsylvania	12,297	5,296,496
Massachusetts - MA *Bay State*	Boston	Springfield Lowell Worcester	New Hampshire, Vermont, Maine, New York, Connecticut, Rhode Island	9241	6,349,097
Michigan - MI *Great Lakes State* *Wolverine State*	Lansing	Detroit Flint Grand Rapids Warren	Ohio, Indiana, Wisconsin	58,216	9,938,444
Minnesota - MN *North Star State*	St. Paul	Minneapolis	North Dakota, South Dakota, Iowa, Wisconsin	86,943	4,919,479
Mississippi - MS *Magnolia State*	Jackson	Gulfport Biloxi	Alabama, Tennessee, Arkansas, Louisiana	48,286	2,844,648
Missouri - MO *Show Me State*	Jefferson City	Kansas City St. Louis Springfield	Arkansas, Iowa, Tennessee, Kentucky, Illinois, Kansas, Nebraska, Oklahoma	69,709	5,595,211

Missouri and Tennessee have the most neighbors. They each are bordered by eight states.

Michigan is the only state with two geographical parts. It is made of two peninsulas. Both parts are surrounded by Great Lakes on three sides.

The oldest high school in the U.S. is in West Roxbury, Massachusetts. The school began in 1645.

138

State *postal abbreviation and nickname*	Capital	Some Other Large Cities	Neighbors *bordering states*	Area *in square miles*	Population *2000 census*
Montana - MT *Magnolia Sate*	Helena	Billings Missoula Great Falls	Idaho, Wyoming, North Dakota, South Dakota	147,046	902,105
Nebraska - NE *Cornhusker State*	Lincoln	Omaha	Wyoming, South Dakota, Iowa, Missouri, Kansas, Colorado	77,358	1,711,263
Nevada - NV *Sagebrush State*	Carson City	Las Vegas Reno	California, Arizona, Utah, Idaho, Oregon	110,567	1,998,257
New Hampshire - HN *Granite State*	Concord	Manchester Nashua	Vermont, Maine, Massachusetts	9283	1,235,786
New Jersey - NJ *Garden State*	Trenton	Newark Jersey City Paterson	Delaware, Pennsylvania, New York	8125	8,414,350
New Mexico - NM *Cactus State*	Santa Fe	Albuquerque Las Cruces	Arizona, Texas, Oklahoma, Utah, Colorado	121,598	1,819,040
New York - NY *Empire State*	Albany	New York Buffalo Rochester	Vermont, New Jersey, Massachusetts, Connecticut, Pennsylvania	53,989	18,976,457
North Carolina - NC *Tar Heel State*	Raleigh	Charlotte Greensboro Durham Winston-Salem	South Carolina, Virginia, Tennessee	52,672	4,012,012

Nevada is a Spanish word meaning "snow-clad."

North Carolina got its nickname from a Civil War story. Supposedly, many Confederate soldiers ran away during a tough battle and left Carolina soldiers to fight alone. So they threatened to put "tar" on the heels of those soldiers in the next battle so they would "stick" to the fight.

New York City has 162 skyscrapers. That's more than any other city in the world.

The States – Vital Statistics, continued

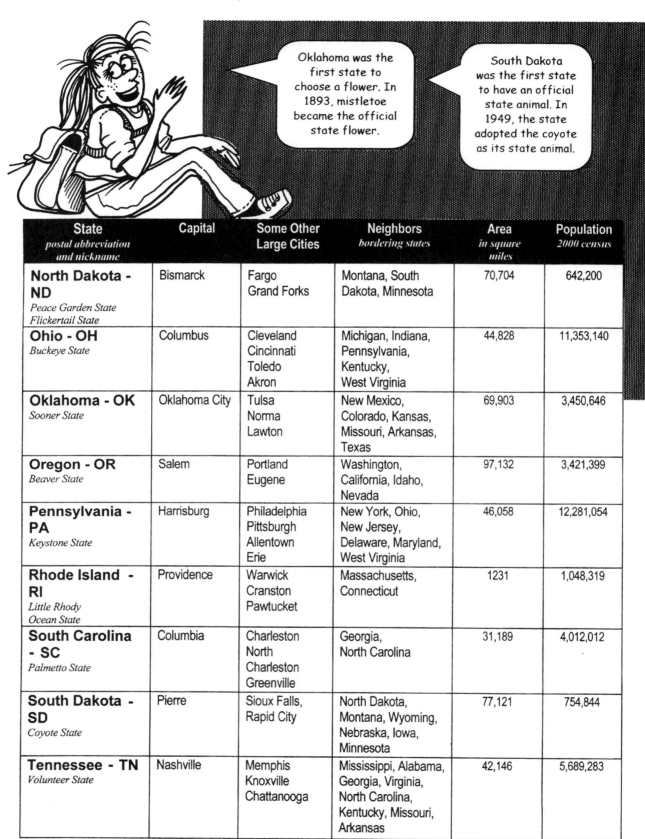

Oklahoma was the first state to choose a flower. In 1893, mistletoe became the official state flower.

South Dakota was the first state to have an official state animal. In 1949, the state adopted the coyote as its state animal.

State *postal abbreviation and nickname*	Capital	Some Other Large Cities	Neighbors *bordering states*	Area *in square miles*	Population *2000 census*
North Dakota - ND *Peace Garden State* *Flickertail State*	Bismarck	Fargo Grand Forks	Montana, South Dakota, Minnesota	70,704	642,200
Ohio - OH *Buckeye State*	Columbus	Cleveland Cincinnati Toledo Akron	Michigan, Indiana, Pennsylvania, Kentucky, West Virginia	44,828	11,353,140
Oklahoma - OK *Sooner State*	Oklahoma City	Tulsa Norma Lawton	New Mexico, Colorado, Kansas, Missouri, Arkansas, Texas	69,903	3,450,646
Oregon - OR *Beaver State*	Salem	Portland Eugene	Washington, California, Idaho, Nevada	97,132	3,421,399
Pennsylvania - PA *Keystone State*	Harrisburg	Philadelphia Pittsburgh Allentown Erie	New York, Ohio, New Jersey, Delaware, Maryland, West Virginia	46,058	12,281,054
Rhode Island - RI *Little Rhody* *Ocean State*	Providence	Warwick Cranston Pawtucket	Massachusetts, Connecticut	1231	1,048,319
South Carolina - SC *Palmetto State*	Columbia	Charleston North Charleston Greenville	Georgia, North Carolina	31,189	4,012,012
South Dakota - SD *Coyote State*	Pierre	Sioux Falls, Rapid City	North Dakota, Montana, Wyoming, Nebraska, Iowa, Minnesota	77,121	754,844
Tennessee - TN *Volunteer State*	Nashville	Memphis Knoxville Chattanooga	Mississippi, Alabama, Georgia, Virginia, North Carolina, Kentucky, Missouri, Arkansas	42,146	5,689,283

Washington has the greatest high school graduation rate in the country. 92% of residents over age 25 have a high school education.

The Great Salt Lake in Utah is the largest natural lake in the U.S. outside of the Great Lakes. Its water is saltier than any ocean.

Cody, Wyoming, is known as "The Rodeo Capital of the World." The Cody Nite Rodeo puts on an event every night from June 1 – August 31.

State *postal abbreviation and nickname*	Capital	Some Other Large Cities	Neighbors *bordering states*	Area *in square miles*	Population *2000 census*
Texas - TX *Lone Star State*	Austin	Houston Dallas San Antonio El Paso Fort Worth	New Mexico, Oklahoma, Arkansas, Louisiana	267,277	20,851,820
Utah - UT *Beehive State*	Salt Lake City	West Valley City Provo	Nevada, Idaho, Wyoming, Colorado, New Mexico, Nevada	84,904	2,333,169
Vermont - VT *Green Mountain State*	Montpelier	Burlington Essex	New Hampshire, New York, Massachusetts	9615	608,827
Virginia - VA *Old Dominion*	Richmond	Virginia Beach Norfolk Chesapeake Richmond	Maryland, West Virginia, Kentucky, Tennessee, North Carolina	42,326	7,078,515
Washington - WA *Evergreen State*	Olympia	Seattle Spokane Tacoma	Oregon, Idaho	70,637	5,894,121
West Virginia - WV *Mountain State*	Charleston	Huntington Wheeling	Pennsylvania, Ohio, Kentucky, Virginia, Maryland	24,231	1,808,344
Wisconsin - WI *Badger State*	Madison	Green Bay Kenosha Racine	Minnesota, Iowa, Illinois	65,499	5,363,675
Wyoming - WY *Cowboy State*	Cheyenne	Casper Laramie	Idaho, Utah, Montana, North Dakota, South Dakota, Colorado	97,818	493,782

U.S. Regions

The New England region is famous for its maple syrup and beautiful autumn leaves.

The United States is such a large country that its land, climate, and resources vary widely. In order to learn about the country, it is helpful to divide it into areas smaller than the whole span of thousands of miles. The continental United States can be divided into eight different regions. The states that make up each region of the United States share similar landforms, natural resources, and climate.

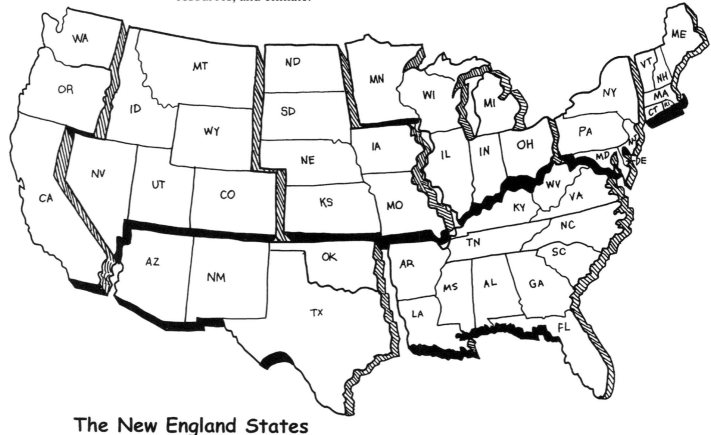

The New England States

This small region in the northeast corner of the country has a rural landscape, small villages, rugged ocean coastlines, sandy beaches, and beautiful scenery. Its land is too rocky and hilly for much agriculture, but the region produces many dairy and poultry products. The climate is cold in the winter, with frequent snow or rain. The summers are warm and humid.

States in the region:

Maine	New Hampshire
Massachusetts	Vermont
Connecticut	Rhode Island

In Devon, Connecticut, it is illegal to walk backwards after sunset.

Largest cities: Boston, Hartford, Providence

Economic activities:

industry	manufacturing
dairy farming	poultry farming
fishing	tourism

Get Sharp Tip # 10

A *region* is a large area that has common features.

The Mid-Atlantic States

This is the most densely populated region in the country; it's home to several large cities. The many harbors make it a worldwide trade center. There is coal mining in the Appalachian Mountain region. These mountains also attract hikers and vacationers. The region is filled with farms, lakes, scenic forests, and sandy beaches along its Atlantic coast. The big cities, historic sites, and ocean beaches attract many tourists. The winters are cool or cold and wet. Summers are humid and warm or hot.

States in the region:

New York	New Jersey	Maryland
Pennsylvania	Delaware	

Largest cities:

New York	Newark	Philadelphia
Pittsburgh	Buffalo	Baltimore

Economic activities:

manufacturing	mining	banking
farming	fishing	service industries
shipping	tourism	mining

The Southern States

This region has been a major agricultural area for the country. The tourist business is also healthy because of the rolling hills, beautiful mountains, and Atlantic and Gulf beaches. Its warm climate makes the region an attractive place to live, do business, and vacation. Winters are mild; springs and summers are hot and humid.

States in the region:

Kentucky	Tennessee	West Virginia
Georgia	Virginia	Alabama
North Carolina	Mississippi	South Carolina
Arkansas	Louisiana	Florida

Largest cities:

New Orleans	Nashville
Miami	Atlanta

Economic activities:

agriculture
dairy farming
mining
industry
tourism

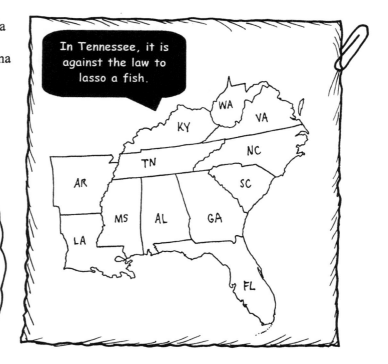

Get Sharp: U.S. Regions

The Great Lakes States

Every state in this region touches one of the Great Lakes. The water affects the climate and economy of the whole region. The Great Lakes are a part of an extensive water transportation system. Thanks to a series of locks, canals, and rivers, ships can travel from the region to the Atlantic Ocean or the Gulf of Mexico. Many ports and harbors are found in the region, allowing ships to carry away the products of mining and manufacturing. This area also has many dairy farms. The climate is cold in the winter with rain and snow. The summers are warm or hot with moderate rain.

States in the region:

Minnesota	Wisconsin	Michigan
Ohio	Illinois	Indiana

Largest cities:

Chicago	Detroit	Minneapolis

Economic activities:

mining	shipping	dairy farming
industry	agriculture	

> In Wisconsin, it is illegal to kiss on a train.

> The Great Lakes hold almost one-fourth of all the fresh water in the world.

The Midwestern States

This region is primarily a plains region that covers much of the central part of the country. With its rich soil, this is a main region for producing wheat, corn, and livestock. It is a major corn and wheat producing area. The winters are cold in the northern plains, and mild in the southern parts of the region. Summers are hot and dry, with some thunderstorms.

States in the region:

Iowa	Missouri	North Dakota
Kansas	Nebraska	South Dakota

Largest cities:

Kansas City
St. Louis   Omaha

Economic activities:
agriculture
(corn, soybeans, wheat)

> Burping during a church service is illegal in Omaha.

The Rocky Mountain States

The Rocky Mountains are the centerpiece of this region. The region also has plains, plateaus, forests, and deserts. It is a rich ranching and mining area. Its beauty attracts many tourists. It is the home to the Colorado River.

States in the region:

Colorado	Nevada	Montana
Wyoming	Utah	Idaho

Largest cities:
Denver   Salt Lake City

Economic activities:
mining
ranching
farming
tourism

> It's against the law to grow dandelions in Boulder, Colorado.

144

The Southwestern States

This is a region of large cattle ranches and fields of crops (such as cotton), which spread over vast areas. The plentiful oil and natural gas beneath its surface has made the region wealthy. The southwest is also a region of pleasant weather that attracts tourists and permanent residents alike. Winters are mild and dry. Summers are hot and dry. It is the home to the Grand Canyon and other areas of great beauty.

States in the region:
Arizona   New Mexico
Texas   Oklahoma

Largest cities:
Phoenix   Dallas
Houston   Oklahoma City

Economic activities:
ranching
oil drilling
oil refineries
tourism
mining

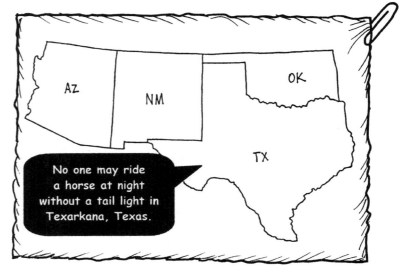

Cowboys wearing 10-gallon hats are a symbol of Texas.

No one may ride a horse at night without a tail light in Texarkana, Texas.

The Pacific Coast States

This region borders the Pacific Ocean. It has a long, beautiful coastline, dense forests and mountains. The coasts supply fish; the forests supply timber; and the valleys produce fruits, wine, and vegetables. It is also a region of manufacturing and technological development, with a computer and electronics industry that has grown rapidly in recent years. Due to the effects of the ocean, the climate is mild. Irrigation and a long growing season allow for plentiful agriculture in the long coastal valleys and valleys between mountain ranges.

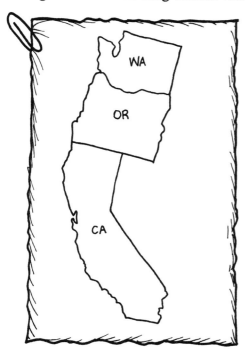

States in the region:
Oregon   California   Washington

Largest cities:
Los Angeles   San Francisco   Seattle

Economic activities:
timber industry
high technology production
tourism
entertainment industry
agriculture
mining
fishing

It is against the law in Washington to buy a mattress on Sunday.

Washington is home to Mt. St. Helen's, the most recent volcano to erupt in the continental U.S. (1980)

145

See the U.S.A.

The Empire State Building

The Empire State Building in New York City is 70 years old. It has 102 stories, and with its spire, reaches a height of 1250 feet!

Niagara Falls!

Niagara Falls is a spectacular double falls on the New York-Canadian border. Horseshoe Falls is 2600 feet wide, and the American Falls is 1000 feet wide.

Come tour the U.S.A.! From north to south, and from east to west, it's full of fascinating sites to see!

TRAVEL LORE, INC.

I want to see the **Grand Canyon!**

The Grand Canyon was gouged out of rock by the Colorado River. It is a mile deep at its deepest spot.

And while I'm in the Southwest, I want to see the famous **Anasazi cliff dwellings**, built in about AD 1200. These ancient dwellings are found in the Four Corners area – where Arizona, Utah, Colorado, and New Mexico meet.

The **Carlsbad Caverns** in New Mexico are some of the biggest underground limestone caves in the world. The largest cave is called the *Big Room*. It is 1800 feet long, with a 225 foot ceiling.

I'd love to see the **Cowboy Hall of Fame** in Oklahoma City, Oklahoma. I hear they have a life-size replica of an early cowboy. And then...

...I *have* to see the **Crazy Horse Memorial**, a huge sculpture being carved into a mountain-side in South Dakota. The monument honors a brave Lakota Indian Chief.

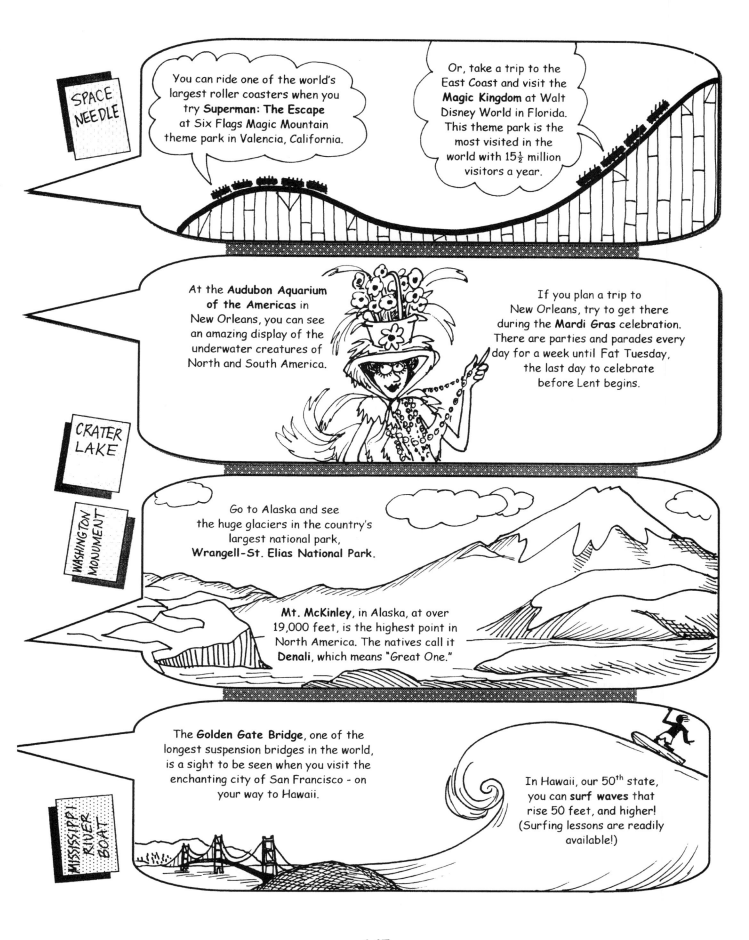

SPACE NEEDLE

You can ride one of the world's largest roller coasters when you try **Superman: The Escape** at Six Flags Magic Mountain theme park in Valencia, California.

Or, take a trip to the East Coast and visit the **Magic Kingdom** at Walt Disney World in Florida. This theme park is the most visited in the world with 15½ million visitors a year.

At the **Audubon Aquarium of the Americas** in New Orleans, you can see an amazing display of the underwater creatures of North and South America.

If you plan a trip to New Orleans, try to get there during the **Mardi Gras** celebration. There are parties and parades every day for a week until Fat Tuesday, the last day to celebrate before Lent begins.

CRATER LAKE

WASHINGTON MONUMENT

Go to Alaska and see the huge glaciers in the country's largest national park, **Wrangell-St. Elias National Park.**

Mt. McKinley, in Alaska, at over 19,000 feet, is the highest point in North America. The natives call it **Denali**, which means "Great One."

The **Golden Gate Bridge**, one of the longest suspension bridges in the world, is a sight to be seen when you visit the enchanting city of San Francisco - on your way to Hawaii.

MISSISSIPPI RIVER BOAT

In Hawaii, our 50th state, you can **surf waves** that rise 50 feet, and higher! (Surfing lessons are readily available!)

147

Record-Setting Wonders

Here are a few of the highest, longest, biggest, deepest, tallest, lowest, and otherwise most spectacular natural and human-created features of the United States.

Tallest

Tallest active volcano: Mt. Mauna Loa, Hawaii – 13,681 feet above sea level *(32,000 feet from its base on the Floor of the Pacific Ocean)*

Tallest building: Sears Tower, Chicago – 1454 feet tall *(with spires: 1707 feet)*

Tallest structure: a television tower in Blanchard, North Dakota – 2063 feet

Tallest statue: Chief Crazy Horse, Black Hills of South Dakota – 563 feet

Tallest monument: Gateway Arch, St. Louis, Missouri – 630 feet

Tallest active geyser: Steamboat Geyser, Yellowstone National Park – more than 300 feet

Most

State with the most tribal land: Arizona – 20,087,538 acres

State most visited by U.S. tourists: Florida – over 6 million a year

State with most lakes: Alaska – over 3 million lakes

State with the most geysers: Wyoming – over 300

Most spectacular geyser: Old Faithful, Yellowstone National Park – erupts every 30 seconds

Most damaging hurricane: Hurricane Andrew in 1992 – $25 billion damage

Most visited city: New York City – 5½ million a year

Most common U.S. city name: Fairview

Highest, Lowest, & Deepest

Highest mountain: Mt. McKinley (Denali), Alaska – 20,320 feet

Highest island: Akutan, Alaska – 13,698 feet

Highest waterfalls: Yosemite Falls, California – 2425 feet

Highest town: Climax, Colorado – 11,560 feet

Highest bridge: Royal Gorge, Colorado – 1053 feet above water

Lowest town: Calipatria, California – 185 feet below sea level

Lowest point: Death Valley, California – 282 feet below sea level

Deepest cave: Lechuguilla Cave in Carlsbad Caverns, New Mexico – 1521 feet

Deepest lake: Crater Lake, Oregon – 1,932 feet

Deepest gorge: Hell's Canyon, Snake River, Idaho – 7,900 feet

Longest

Longest river: Mississippi-Missouri-Red Rock River system – 3710 miles

Longest cave: Mammoth Cave System – 352 miles

Longest suspension bridge: Verrazano Narrows, New York – 4250 feet

Longest steel arch bridge: New River Gorge, Fayetteville, Virginia – 1700 feet

Longest cantilever bridge: Commodore Barry, Pennsylvania – 1644 feet

State with longest shoreline: Alaska – 33,904 miles

Biggest

Biggest waterfalls: Niagara Falls – two falls, total of 3600 feet wide

Biggest lake: Lake Superior – 31,820 sq. mi.

Biggest island: Hawaii – 4037 sq. mi.

Biggest island in a lake: Isle Royal, Lake Superior – 209 sq. mi.

Biggest city: New York City – population 8,008,278

Biggest canyon: Grand Canyon, Arizona – 277 miles long, 1 mile deep at deepest point

Biggest Native American Reservation: Navajo, in Utah-Arizona-New Mexico – 230,000 population

Biggest meteorite found: Canyon Diablo, Arizona – 30 tons

Biggest university: University of California – 157,400 students

Biggest library: Library of Congress, Washington DC – 24,000,000 books

Other Record-Setters

Oldest city in the 50 states: St. Petersburg, Florida – settled in 1513

Oldest U.S. city: San Juan, Puerto Rico – settled in 1508

Coldest city: International Falls, Minnesota – average temperature, 36.8° F

Hottest city: Key West, Florida – average temperature, 77.8° F

Hottest temperature: 134° F, recorded in Death Valley, California

Coldest temperature: –80° F, recorded in Prospect Creek, Alaska

Wettest spot: Mt. Waialeale, Hawaii – 460 to 500 inches annually

Driest spot: Yuma, Arizona – 2.17 inches annually

Oldest national park: Yellowstone National Park – established in 1872

Smallest park: Mills End Park, Portland, Oregon – a circle 2 feet in diameter

Busiest airport: JFK International, New York – 17,378,000 passengers per year

Busiest seaport: South Louisiana Port, New Orleans, Louisiana – 245 million tons of cargo in the year 2000

Busiest underground railway: New York Subway – over 1 trillion passengers per year

Why is New York City called the *Big Apple*?

The phrase was first used in a book, *The Wayfarer in New York*, in 1909. The author, Edward S. Martin, explained that New York was one fruit of a tree that spread across all of America—but New York seemed to get a larger share of the tree's sap (meaning the national wealth), making it the ***Big Apple***.

149

U.S. Time Zones

When you travel across the United States, you need to keep track of the time! That's because the country is so wide that it crosses five time zones. Get to know the U.S. time zones, so you can always be sure what time it is where!

Time Zone Challenges – The Family Reunion

Before the reunion—

> I just remembered! I have to call my mother in Alaska about the family reunion. It's midnight here in Virginia. What time is it in Alaska?

> Go ahead and call her now. It's four hours earlier out there— only 8:00 PM!

After the reunion—

> Oh, no! Mom changed planes in Baltimore and mistakenly boarded a flight that left there at 8:00 PM Eastern Time headed for Hawaii! The flight is nine hours long. I want to leave a message for her at the Honolulu Airport. What time will she arrive there?

> She'll get to Hawaii at midnight Hawaii time.

The day of the reunion—

> Hello, son. This is your mother speaking. I just arrived in Massachusetts from Alaska. I left Alaska at 6:45 on Tuesday, and now it's 1:15 AM, Wednesday, Eastern Time here. How long did my trip take?

> Let's see, Mom. Your trip took you through four time zones, and that adds up to 14½ hours! The problem is— the family reunion is in Virginia.

> Lucky duck!

Time Zones in the U.S.A.

12:00 PM
Alaska Time

11:00 AM
Hawaii Time

1:00 PM
Pacific Time
(PT)

2:00 PM
Mountain Time
(MT)

3:00 PM
Central Time
(CT)

4:00 PM
Eastern Time
(ET)

GET SHARP →

on World History

Prehistory

People have lived on Earth for thousands, perhaps millions, of years. Some scientists believe that archeological evidence shows human existence may stretch back as far as the Pleistocene geologic epoch, beginning about two million years ago. Archaeologists have learned about early history by studying things that were left behind: tools, bones, utensils, weapons, fossils, ruins of buildings or other structures, and artwork. Such things left behind by a culture or group of people are called ***artifacts***.

The earliest periods of human history are divided into two segments: the ***Old Stone Age*** (or Paleolithic period) and the ***New Stone Age*** (or Neolithic period).

The Old Stone Age

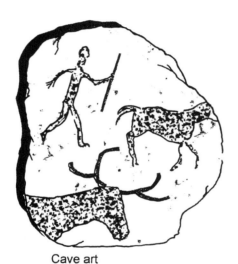

Cave art

The Old Stone Age dates from approximately two million years ago to about 10,000 years ago. The outstanding feature of the Old period is the appearance of humans, perhaps around 35,000 to 40,000 B.C. These prehistoric people were believed to have lived mainly in Europe, Africa, and Asia. They lived by gathering food and hunting prehistoric animals, made crude implements and tools of stone and bones, and used the skins and furs of animals to make clothing. Artifacts show that more humans began to live in communities in the later years of the Old Stone Age. As they joined in groups, new cultures grew. They built shelters, made tools that were more effective, developed belief systems centered around the supernatural created jewelry, and left simple drawings on cave walls. Artifacts also suggest that some cultures expanded their activities to fishing and hunting reindeer.

The New Stone Age

The New Stone Age, dating from about 10,000 B.C., is characterized by the use of stone tools, the existence of settlements dependent on farming and domestication of animals, and the presence of arts or crafts. Because people found ways to produce food without wandering to follow herds of wild animals, they were able to settle down into villages. The earliest known settlement was in southwestern Asia about 8000 B.C. Scientists have found evidence of primitive, independent farming communities in the Tigris and Euphrates River Valleys, the Nile River Valley, the Indus Valley, and the Huang He Valley in China. By 2000–1500 B.C., groups were cultivating crops and domesticating animals in southeast Asia, Mexico, and South America.

Seeds and grains

Early Civilizations

**Get Sharp
Tip # 12**

Periods of history are usually described in years **before the birth of Christ** (B.C.) and **after Christ's death** (A.D.)

Another description uses the term

common era (C.E.), beginning in A.D. 0-6, and **before common era** (B.C.E.)

Civilization generally refers to a culture or society that has advanced social systems such as political, economic, governmental, and educational systems. Agriculture changed the lives of early people. Once they were able to grow food, they no longer needed to wander in order to find food. As the nomadic life ended, people settled into one area and formed permanent settlements, usually in areas where land was fertile. Civilizations developed quickly. With a settled life, cultures were able to become more complex. About 3500 B.C., the first traces of writing appeared. From that point on, humans could keep records that told their own story of their cultures and their histories. These are some of the early civilizations that developed in Asia, the Middle East, Africa, Europe, and the Americas.

Sumer

One of the earliest civilizations grew up in an area of fertile land that stretched from the Eastern shores of the Mediterranean Sea between the Tigris and Euphrates Rivers to the Persian Gulf. The crescent-shaped area had very rich soil, so it was known as the *Fertile Crescent*. Cultures developed from about 4000 B.C. in the area of Mesopotamia (meaning *land between the rivers*). The Sumerian culture in southern Mesopotamia grew rapidly from about 3500 to 2000 B.C. Here, the people farmed, raised cattle, developed trade, and created crafts. The people of Sumer are credited with inventing the wheel and a form of writing known as *cuneiform*. They built a pyramid-like temple known as a *ziggurat*.

It's a wheel!

Babylonia

In about 2000 B.C., the city of Babylon was built along the Euphrates River. A powerful Babylonian king, Hammurabi, was a talented administrator. He created a set of laws based on his concern for the welfare of his people. *Hammurabi's Code* set fair prices, fair taxes, rights for all citizens, and a system of punishment.

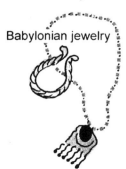

Babylonian jewelry

Assyria

Beginning in about 1800 B.C., the Assyrians lived in southern Mesopotamia. Their culture was based around the capital city of Nineveh on the Tigris River. The Assyrian empire grew wealthy from the lands captured by their fierce armies. A king of Assyria was known to begin the first library, containing writings on many subjects preserved on clay tablets. The first Assyrian Empire flourished from 1814 to 1754 B.C. The second empire lasted from 911 to 609 B.C.

153

Hebrews

The Hebrews are the ancestors of modern-day Jews. The earliest Hebrews were from the land of Canaan, between the Jordan River and the Mediterranean Sea. A shortage of food forced them to go to Egypt, where they were taken as slaves and lived in slavery for many years. The Hebrews, led by the prophet Moses, escaped from Egypt in about 1250 B.C. The Hebrew people wandered in the desert for over 200 years, enduring many wars and hardships. Finally they arrived in Canaan and settled in Palestine. In about 1000 B.C., the Hebrews made Jerusalem their capital. After that, Palestine was invaded many times by different groups.

Phoenicians

From about 1200-800 B.C., the Phoenicians lived in the Fertile Crescent area, in the region that is now Lebanon. They were some of the first and most successful sailors and traders. They sailed around the Mediterranean Sea, building cities and colonies at places such as Carthage, Byblos, Beirut, and Tyre. The successful trade brought them great wealth. They are also known for their artistic skills, and their alphabet, which formed the basis for Greek, Latin, and modern Roman writing.

Persian Warrior

Persians

Another culture of the ancient Middle East was Persia, which began in the area that is now Iran. A powerful king, Cyrus II, united Persia with the kingdom of Media and expanded his empire by conquering areas west to the Fertile Crescent. A later king named King Darius I, expanded the empire further. One of the accomplishments of King Darius was the building of a strong government that established a fair legal system and built roads throughout the entire empire. The Persian Empire flourished from about 700 to 330 B.C.

Minoans & Mycenaens

Minoan bull

The first known European civilization developed in Crete between 2500 and 1450 B.C. It was named after King Minos. The Minoans were traders in the Mediterranean Sea. They built well-planned towns and impressive palaces and developed a form of writing known as *Linear A.* Another culture, the Mycenaen civilization, developed in Greece from 1600 to 1200 B.C. Like the Minoans, these people were traders in the Mediterranean area. They developed a form of writing known as *Linear B.*

Hittites

The Hittites lived in the mountains north of the Mediterranean Sea. Their empire was a chief power and cultural influence in western Asia from about 1400 to 1200 B.C. They were one of the first cultures to successfully smelt iron, giving them the ability to make stronger tools and weapons. They were also one of the first civilizations to establish a treaty. They agreed with Egypt to respect each other's borders, not to attack one another, and to help each other if attacked by someone else.

Indus Valley Civilization

The Indus Valley civilization flourished in India from along the Indus River 2500 to 1800 B.C. The people built large cities such as Mohenjo-Daro and Harappa. Archaeologists have found remains of hundreds of cities. They are known for the organization of their cities, well-developed drainage and sewage systems, farms with complex irrigation systems, and advanced tools and crafts. About 1500 B. C., the civilization of the Indus River Valley mysteriously disappeared.

What happened to the people of the Indus Valley?

There are several theories . . .

- The land was over-farmed and no longer yielded enough food, so the people moved.
- The people scattered due to an invasion.
- A big flood destroyed the civilization.
- Drought caused widespread famine, and the civilization died out.

How Egyptian Mummies Were Made:

1. Remove the brain and throw it away.

2. Remove the internal organs and save them in canopic jars.

LUNGS   STOMACH   LIVER   INTESTINES

3. Fill the body cavity with an embalming chemical called natron.

4. Cover the body completely in natron and let it dry for 40 days.

5. Wrap the body in strips of linen moistened with resin glue. This process often requires as many as 20 wrappings before completed.

6. Place the dried, wrapped mummy into three gilded coffins.

Egypt

A remarkably complex and successful civilization grew up along the banks and delta of the Nile River, where the flooding of the river creates rich soil. The ancient Egyptian civilization began about 3300 B.C. and lasted almost 3000 years. The Nile River provided transportation, food, and work for the people. Warrior kings (*pharaohs*) in ancient Egypt conquered a vast empire. The Egyptians also produced amazing works of architecture and feats of engineering. They are known for their development of a calendar, for a system of weaving cloth, for building boats and temples, and for making paper and many objects of art. They used their paper and system of writing (*hieroglyphics*) to enable them to become the first civilization with a written history.

The ancient Egyptians are perhaps best remembered for their pyramids. The religion gave great honor to the dead; they wanted to make sure the dead had a good life in the next world. So they built huge and magnificent stone tombs (*pyramids*) for their kings and other important people. They filled the pyramids with valuable items and food for the dead to use in the next life. The bodies were preserved by *mummification*. Many of the great pyramids remain, displaying the skills of the Egyptian engineers and builders.

Get Sharp: Early Civilizations

Classical Greece

During the period of 500 to 330 B.C., Greece was divided into great *city-states*. Each city was like a separate nation. This is known as the *Classical Period* in Greek history. Developments in politics, art, science, and philosophy that originated from Greece during this period left a lasting influence on future civilizations in Europe and the rest of the world. Athens and Sparta were two particularly prosperous and influential city-states. Sparta was a military city-state that conquered many people and made slaves. The Spartans became rich from the trade and the work of the slaves. In Athens, great learning, writing, and art flourished. Thinkers such as Plato, Aristotle, and Socrates discussed ideas that became the basis for modern philosophy. The Athenian system of government was the beginning of *democracy*, a form of government in which citizens rule. The Greeks are also credited with great advances in medicine, drama, architecture, literature, and poetry. Eventually, rivalries between the city-states ended the classical period in Greece.

The Roman World – A.D. 138–235

Rome

The city of Rome began as a group of small villages in Italy built along the edge of the Tiber River. By about 750 B.C. the villages had grown into one great city, Rome. This city became the center of one of the greatest ancient civilizations and the largest empires in the ancient world. Kings ruled Rome until 510 B.C. when the people set up a republic. A *republic* is a form of government where citizens choose representatives to run the government. Under a series of generals and emperors, the Roman Empire conquered all the lands around the Mediterranean Sea and spread from North Africa and the Middle East to England. The achievements of the Romans include a system of representative law that is a foundation of many democratic societies today, great roads and aqueducts, spectacular architecture and sculpture, and advances in literature and poetry. The Roman Empire lasted until around A.D. 476, when Germanic tribes and Mongol people *(Huns)* invaded and conquered parts of the empire.

Alexander the Great

Alexander the Great was a brilliant military leader who ruled in northern Greece. His father, King Philip II of Macedonia, defeated the Greek city-states that had been weakened by fighting among themselves. Alexander became king at age 20 when his father was murdered. He built a great empire—the largest one in the ancient world. His empire stretched from Greece to India, establishing cities and spreading Greek ideas and language throughout a wide area.

Greek temple

The Development of Christianity

During the era of the Roman Empire, a Jewish boy named Jesus was born in the Roman province of Judea. He grew up to become a religious teacher who claimed to be the Son of God. His followers called him *Christ*, which means *the anointed one*. His teachings became very popular in the later years of the Roman Empire, and spread throughout the empire, even though the Romans tried to stop it. Christians, including Jesus, were persecuted and even killed, but the religion continued to spread. In A.D. 337, the Roman emperor Constantine became a Christian and made the religion legal. After that, Christianity became a prominent religion in the empire.

Japanese art

African mask

China

Civilizations grew up along two large rivers in China: the Huang He (Yellow River) and the Chang Jiang (Long River). The history of ancient China is the story of a succession of dynasties. China had over ten major dynasties before the revolution in 1911 which put an end to dynastic rule. Different conditions prevailed under different dynasties. Some of them are credited with cultural, artistic, and societal advances. Some were warlike; others ruled periods of peace. The first known dynasty, the Shang dynasty, ruled China from 1766-1027 B.C. During this time, writing was invented, art flourished, and silkworms were cultivated. The Great Wall of China was built under the Qin (or Ch'in) dynasty (221-206 B.C.) to protect China from invaders. Some important achievements of the ancient Chinese civilizations were the invention of gunpowder and paper, advances in astronomy and engineering, and the development of acupuncture.

Japan

The early history of Japan is mostly legend. Supposedly, Japan was founded in 660 B.C. under Emperor Jimmu, a descendent of the Sun goddess. Reliable records only date back to A.D. 400, however. In the early centuries, Japan was inhabited by many clans or tribes ruled by priests. The first control over some of Japan came in the 5th century with the power of the Yamato clan. The Yamato chief-priest took the position of emperor. The society developed rapidly over the next 300 years, with strong Chinese influence on the culture.

Kush

The Kush civilization was one of the first in Africa. From about 2000 B.C. to A.D. 350, the Kush people lived along the Nile River south of Egypt. They raised crops and cattle, and mined copper and gold. For many years, the Egyptians invaded Kush and took slaves, gold, and other resources. In 752 B.C., the Kush invaded and conquered Egypt, ruling Egypt for about 100 years, until the Assyrians pushed them back. The Kush moved their capital to Meroe and developed iron-making skills. The city of Meroe became one of the ancient world's foremost centers for the production of iron.

Ghana

One of the first empires of Africa was the Ghanaian Empire, located on the grasslands of western Africa. Ghana became a great, wealthy trading empire. Although Ghana had little of the valuable metal resources gold and iron, it acted as an agent in the exchange of these metals between other cultures. Ghanaians used the iron to make weapons, and built a powerful army. The empire of Ghana lasted from about A.D. 700 to 1200.

Get Sharp: Early Civilizations

Adenas and Hopewells

The Adena people made up one of the first known civilizations in North America. They lived in small groups, farming from about 100 to 300 B.C. in what is now the Ohio River Valley. They were skilled pottery makers. In addition, the Adena are known as the *Mound Builders* because they built large mounds of earth to cover the graves of the important members of their society. The Hopewell people lived in the Ohio and Mississippi River valleys from 2000 B.C. until A.D. 400. They were influenced by the Adena, and also built mounds. Their mounds took many different shapes and sizes.

Mayans

The Mayan culture was one of the most sophisticated civilizations of the ancient times in the Americas. The culture arose in about 300 B.C. and continued until about A.D. 900 in the Yucatan Peninsula of Central American. The Mayan people were farmers who built many cities deep in the jungles. Some of the most developed centers of their civilizations were the great cities of Copán El Tikal and Uaxactún and Uxmal in the regions that are now Honduras, Mexico, and Guatemala. They developed a calendar, a system of writing, and a system of numbers. The Mayans were skilled mathematicians and astronomers. Their architects built splendid buildings and monuments, and their artists produced elaborate murals, paintings, and carvings.

Chavins and Moches

The Chavin civilization was the first in South America, developed in the Andes Mountains of Peru and lasting from about 1200–300 B.C. The people were skilled stoneworkers who built large temples and spectacular sculptures. They were the first people in South America to make things from gold. The Moche civilization also developed in the Andes of Peru. From about A.D. 200 to 800, its people built pyramids from adobe bricks. The most famous of these is the *Temple of the Sun.*

Olmecs

The Olmec people developed one of the first civilizations in the Americas. This civilization grew up along the coast of the Gulf of Mexico between 1500 B.C. and A.D. 200. The Olmecs were farmers ruled by priests. They developed a system of hieroglyphic writing, began a counting system, and created calendars. They are known for their great temples, monuments, and pyramids built to honor their rulers. They carved huge heads from stone which are believed to be representations of their rulers.

158

Toltecs

The Toltec civilization flourished in the Valley of Mexico beginning in about 900 and lasting into the 1200s, with their capital at Tollan. Their culture had been influenced by the Olmec culture. The tools and arts of the Toltecs were advanced; they smelted metals and worked with highly developed stonework. (The name Toltec means *master builders*.) They also had a well-developed system for studying astronomy. The Toltecs worshipped many gods, and human sacrifice was a part of their religious practice.

Aztecs

The Aztec civilization replaced the Toltecs as the dominant culture in central Mexico. The capital of the Aztec Empire was the magnificent city of Tenochtitlan, near the site of present-day Mexico City. The Aztecs had well-developed engineering skills—building roads, irrigation channels, and a water system for the city. The Aztec arts of weaving, metalwork, sculpture, and music were also highly developed. The organization of the society was also highly organized, with one ruler, nobles that ruled cities, and priests to perform religious duties. Religion was a major part of the lives of the Aztecs. They built grand pyramids and ornate temples to honor their gods. They are known as Sun worshippers; their main god was a god of Sun and war. Human sacrifice was a part of the religious practice of the Aztecs. They believed that the shedding of blood was necessary for agricultural bounty and strength of the civilization. A strong army and years of conquests led to the conquering of their neighbors.
By about 1400, the Aztecs ruled a mighty empire throughout central and southern Mexico.

Incas

In the 1300s and 1400s, the Inca civilization gained control of the Peruvian area in South America. By the early 1500s, they controlled a huge empire, stretching along the coast of South America in the Andes Mountains. The Incas were skilled agricultural engineers, building terraces for farming and ditches and canals for drainage and irrigation. Their engineering also extended to construction of buildings, temples, and an elaborate network of roads and bridges. They domesticated animals such as llamas and alpacas. The Incas were also fine artists and metal workers. They mined copper, gold, silver, and tin, and made extensive use of metals in their artistic designs and temples. The Incas are also known for using many different kinds of fiber to produce beautiful multicolor tapestries.

Incan artifact

Get Sharp: Early Civilizations

Timeline of Key Events

40,000-35,000 B.C. – The Old Stone Age begins; humans emerge in southern Europe.

15,000 B.C. – The first people migrate to the North American continent, crossing from Asia on land and ice.

10,000 B.C. – Agriculture begins in the Fertile Crescent.

9000-5000 B.C. – Towns, such as Jericho and Catal Huyuk, grow up in the Fertile Crescent.

6000-5000 B.C. – Lepenski Vir, one of the first villages in Europe, is built by the Danube River.

5000 B.C. – Farming begins in Egypt.

5000-4000 B.C. – Groups of people settle in the Huang He and Yangtze River Valleys in China.

4500-1500 B.C. – Large stone monuments, called *megaliths*, are built in areas of Europe. These structures are temples, tombs, and stone circles (*henges*) used for ceremonies.

Stonehenge, a huge megalith, is built between 300 and 1500 B.C. in Britain.

4000-3000 B.C. – Sumerians build the first cities in Mesopotamia.

4000 B.C. – People settle in communities in the Indus River Valley in India.

3500-3300 B.C. – The Sumerians invent the wheel and a system of writing called *cuneiform*.

3300 B.C. – A strong Egyptian civilization grows along the banks of the Nile River.

3118 B.C. – King Menes unites Egypt and becomes first pharaoh.

3100 B.C. – Egyptian culture begins a form of writing called *hieroglyphics*.

2700 B.C. – Cultivation of silkworms for the production of silk begins in China.

2686-2181 B.C. – The pyramids are built in Egypt.

In the 2500s B.C., the Great Sphinx is built to line up with the Pyramid of Khafre.

2500-1800 B.C. – A strong civilization flourishes in the Indus River Valley in India.

2500-1200 B.C. – The Minoan and Mycenaean civilizations flourish in southern Europe.

2000-900 B.C. – Peruvians gain skills in farming, metalworking, and pottery making. Permanent settlements form by 300 B.C.

2000 B.C. – Horses are used in Europe.

2000 B.C. – The city of Babylon is built.

2000 B.C. – The kingdom of Kush arises in Africa, south of Egypt.

1800-1200 B.C. – The Assyrian Empire grows and flourishes in the Middle East.

1766 B.C. – The first known dynasty, the Shang dynasty, rules China.

1792 B.C. – Babylonians develop the first system of written laws: the *Code of Hammurabi*.

1500-600 B.C. – Religious poems known as *Vedas* are created and spread throughout India. These ideas form the basis for the Hindu religion.

1500 B.C. – AD 200 – The Olmec culture thrives in Mexico.

The Olmecs carved heads of stone, possibly replicas of their rulers. Cobata, the largest one discovered, stands 11 feet tall.

1400 B.C. – The Chinese begin a system of writing on bones, creating *oracle bones* (bones thought to predict the future).

1400-1200 B.C. – The Hittite civilization thrives in Turkey.

1250 B.C. – The Trojan Wars between the Greek Mycenaens and Trojans from Troy, Turkey, bring the destruction of Troy.

According to the story of the Trojan War, the Greeks deceive the Trojans to get their army into the enemy's city. They build a huge wooden horse, hide warriors inside it, and leave it as a gift outside the gates of Troy. While the Trojans are sleeping, the Greek soldiers come out and conquer the city.

1200-300 B.C. – The Chavin civilization is the first in South America.

1200 B.C. – The Hebrew people settle in Palestine after fleeing captivity in Egypt.

1500 B.C. – The Hindu religion begins to spread throughout India.

1200-1000 B.C. – The Phoenician civilization arises and thrives in Lebanon.

1010 B.C. – The Hebrews unite in one kingdom under King David.

1000 B.C. – The Hebrews make Jerusalem their capital.

800 B.C. – The Greek poet Homer writes the *Iliad* and the *Odyssey*. These writings are epic poems about the Trojan Wars.

776 B.C. – The first Olympic Games begin in Greece.

753 B.C. – Rome is founded.

700-300 B.C. – The Persian Empire flourishes and grows under King Cyrus II and King Darius I.

600-200 B.C. – The Adena civilization flourishes in North America. The people construct burial mounds and earthen buildings.

563 B.C. – Siddhartha Gautama is born in India. He establishes the Buddhist religion and becomes known as the *Buddha*.

510 B.C. – Rome becomes a republic. A Senate is established as the ruling group.

508 B.C. – In Greece, reforms in the political system lead to the establishment of a democracy in Athens.

500-338 B.C. – A classical period thrives in Greece; important ideas and advancements develop in politics, literature, architecture, arts, drama, science, and philosophy.

500 B.C. – The Nok civilization develops in Nigeria, West Africa.

The Noks make unique terra-cotta sculptures of heads, the earliest known African sculptures.

161

336 B.C. – Alexander becomes king in Macedonia. He begins a great empire, spreading Greek culture through a wide area.

300 B.C.-A.D.900 – The Mayan civilization rises to its peak on the Yucatan Peninsula of Mexico.

214 B.C. – The Qin leader of China, Shi Huangdi, begins building the Great Wall of China.

27 B.C. – Augustus becomes emperor of Rome. His rebuilding and organization leads to a long period of peace (200 years) called *Pax Romana*.

6 B.C. – Jesus Christ is born in Bethlehem.

1-100 – Buddhism spreads throughout Asia.

100 – Paper is invented in China.

100-552 – Buddhism spreads to China and from China to Japan.

29 – Jesus Christ is crucified in Jerusalem. Afterward, Christian followers spread the teachings of Jesus.

50 – Teotihuacan is built in Central America, in the area of present-day Mexico City. It becomes a center of civilization. By 500, it is a rich and powerful city.

Great pyramids are a part of the city. The largest is the Pyramid of the Sun. At 216 feet, it is the tallest pyramid in present-day Mexico.

300-1200s – Ghana has great power in western Africa, controlling the trade in gold.

320-550 – The Gupta Empire controls a large part of northern India. The period is marked by advances in art, mathematics, philosophy, and law.

300-349 – Constantine the Great rules and reunites the east and west Roman Empires, with a capital at Constantinople.

350-399 – The Huns (Mongols) invade Europe from central Asia.

400s-500s – The legendary King Arthur supposedly lived and fought with his Knights of the Round Table during this time period.

In medieval history, knights are private armed warriors that gave service to nobles. Knights wear protective plates of armor, shields, helmets, and suits of mail.

400 – The first towns appear in sub-Saharan Africa.

400-1500 – *The Middle Ages* begins in Europe. This is generally understood to be the time from after the fall of Rome until the Renaissance. This period is marked by a system of *feudalism* where powerful lords rule areas of land and give lands to nobles in exchange for their military service. Peasants work fields in large estates owned by lords.

410 – Barbarian tribes from northern Europe, including the Visigoths, invade and conquer lands throughout Europe that are part of the Roman Empire.

476 – The Roman Empire falls.

500 – Most of Japan is controlled by Yamato emperors.

527-565 - The Byzantine Empire, the eastern half of the Roman Empire, survives long after the fall of Rome with its capitol in Constantinople (now Turkey). Under the leadership of Justinian, the empire extends its power into Italy, North Africa, and Spain.

594 - The plague subsides after killing almost half the population in Europe.

611 - The prophet Muhammad of Mecca dictates the *Koran*. These teachings of Muhammad teachings begin and spread the religion of Islam.

618-907 - The Tang dynasty rules in China, bringing a period well known for poetry, art, music, and silk trade.

632 - Muhammad, founder of Islam, dies. By this time, Islam is spreading fast across North Africa and Arabia.

632-850 - Through conversion and conquering, a vast Islamic empire is established across Asia.

768 - Charlemagne becomes King of the Franks, ruling a large kingdom in northern Europe.

700s - The Mississippi Valley civilization develops in North America.

771 - Charlemagne becomes king of the Franks.

800 - Feudalism begins to rise as a system of control in Europe.

800-1000 - Viking warriors and traders from Scandinavia invade Britain, France, and other parts of Europe.

The Vikings are warriors, traders, or farmers. Some Vikings raid and loot because of food shortages at home. Others are skilled shipbuilders traveling in search of new homes.

800-1400 - The Khmer dynasty establishes a kingdom in Cambodia. Its center is Angkor.

900 - The Vikings discover Greenland.

900-1200 - The Toltec civilization controls much of Mexico.

982 - Eric the Red establishes a colony in Greenland.

1000 - The Anasazi people establish settlements called *pueblos*, or *cliff dwellings*, in the southwestern part of North America.

1000 - The Samurai people gain control in Japan.

1000 - The Chinese invent gunpowder.

1000 - Maori people settle in New Zealand.

1000-1600 - Inhabitants of Easter Island in the southern Pacific build huge stone monuments in the shape of heads.

Giant stone monoliths, known as "maoi," dot the coastline of the island.

1066 - William of Normandy (known as *William the Conqueror)*, invades England, takes power after winning the Battle of Hastings, and proclaims himself king.

1096 - A group of kings in Europe send armies to the Middle East to try to capture the city of Jerusalem. The purpose of these invasions, or *Crusades*, is to regain areas for Christianity and stop the spread of the Islam religion into Europe. A series of crusades continues until 1291. Jerusalem is recaptured in the First Crusade, but it is later lost. The eight Crusades have limited military success.

1150 - A magnificent temple, Angkor Wat, is completed by the powerful Khmer civilization in Cambodia.

Angkor Wat is the largest of many temples built by the Khmers over a period of 300 years. Ruins of 100 temples can still be seen in Burma and Cambodia.

1170 - Oxford University is established in England. Universities are established in Bologna in 1119 and in Paris in 1150.

1162 - Archbishop of Canterbury Thomas Becket is murdered under instructions from King Henry II.

1179 - The great Mayan city of Chichen Itza in Mexico is destroyed.

1200s - The Mongols, warlike nomadic tribes, form a large empire and seize control of large areas of Asia. In 1206, a Mongol warrior is named Genghis Khan (meaning *the Great One*). Khan leads the Mongols in many conquests.

1215 - Nobles of the court of King John of England force the king to sign the *Magna Carta*, an agreement limiting the king's powers and giving the nobles a right to be involved in decisions.

The Magna Carta is seen as the beginning of a parliamentary form of government.

1230 - The Mali Kingdom becomes powerful in North Africa, with its center of activity in Timbuktu.

1275 - Parliamentary government takes hold in England.

1290 - The Ottoman Empire, under the control of Muslim Turks, expands and controls large areas of the Middle East, North Africa, and parts of Europe.

1300 - The Incan people settle in Peru around Cuzco. Machu Picchu, the *Lost City of the Incas*, is built as a religious retreat sometime in the 1400s.

1325 - The Aztec Indians in Mexico build the city of Tenochtitlan, which becomes the center of a huge and powerful empire.

1333 - China suffers a terrible drought, losing millions of people to starvation and disease.

1337 - The Hundred Years' War begins between France and England, lasting until 1453.

1347-1353 - A terrible disease, known as the *Black Death* or the *plague*, strikes Europe and kills as much as one-third of the population.

1350 - The Renaissance (meaning *rebirth*) begins in Italy, starting a period of renewed interest in the arts, learning, and literature, and blossoms into new scholarship, invention, and discovery. The Renaissance spreads throughout all of Europe over the next 150-200 years.

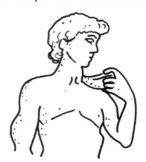

Michelangelo's 1504 sculpture, David, is one of the most famous creations of the Renaissance period.

1400s – Europeans begin explorations around the globe that continue for more 200 years. In this *Age of Exploration*, new territories for commerce develop rapidly. By 1700, European countries have explored and founded colonies in most of the Americas.

1436-1464 – The powerful Montezuma I rules the Aztec people in Central America.

1440 – Portuguese explorers take African slaves, beginning hundreds of years of slave trade.

1429 – Jeanne d'Arc, a young French peasant girl, leads the French against the English at Orleans, France. She is burned at the stake as a witch in 1431.

1450 – Under the support of the Medici family, Florence becomes the center of Renaissance art. Medici family members, as *patrons* of the arts, financially support many artists, allowing them to work in the city.

1452-1519 – Leonardo da Vinci, an artist in Florence, lives a life full of long-lasting artistic accomplishments. He is famous for many pieces of art, in particular, the painting of the *Mona Lisa*.

1455 – Johann Gutenberg develops printing presses and prints the first book in Europe, the *Gutenberg Bible*.

1478 – Russian Ivan II frees Moscow from Mongol rule and establishes himself as the first Czar of Russia.

1492 – Christopher Columbus, an Italian explorer, sails from Europe to the Caribbean Sea, founding the first European settlements in the Americas.

1498 – Spanish explorer Vasco da Gama sails around Africa.

1500s – The Turkish empire of the Ottoman Turks is at its peak in these years, controlling most of the Middle East and all of Egypt.

1503 – Leonardo da Vinci paints the Mona Lisa.

The Mona Lisa is believed to be the portrait of the wife of a Florentine merchant. In the 21ˢᵗ century, the painting hangs in the Louvre Museum in Paris, France.

1509 – Michelangelo paints the ceiling of the Sistine Chapel.

1593 – Spanish explorer Ponce de Leon discovers Florida.

1517 – The Reformation begins as an attempt to reform the Roman Catholic Church, but results in a church split—leading to the formation of Protestant sects. Martin Luther, a Catholic monk, posts 95 theses on a church door, objecting to some practices and beliefs of the Catholic Church.

1519 – Portuguese explorer Ferdinand Magellan sets out on a journey to sail around the world. Natives in the Philippines kill him, but one of his ships completes the circumnavigation of the globe in 1522.

1534 – Jacques Cartier of France discovers and explores Canada.

1534 – King Henry VIII leaves the Roman Catholic Church and establishes himself as the head of the English Church (the Anglican Church).

1543 – Nicolaus Copernicus publishes his theory that Earth revolves around the Sun.

1588 – Spain tries to invade England, but the English navy defeats the entire fleet of warships (the *Spanish Armada*).

Get Sharp: Early Civilizations

1607 - English colonists settle in Jamestown, Virginia, in North America.

1608 - Quebec is founded by the French.

1619 - African slaves arrive in North America for the first time.

1618 - The Thirty Years' War begins in Europe and causes great destruction to Europe over the thirty years of its duration.

1620 - The Pilgrims land at Plymouth Rock in North America after a 3-month voyage on the *Mayflower*.

1632 - Italian astronomer Galileo publishes ideas about his discoveries in science, math, and astronomy.

1639-1850 - Japan becomes isolationist, forbidding foreigners from entering Japan and forbidding citizens from traveling abroad.

1642-1647 - Civil War rages in England.

1650 - Dutch settlers, known as *Boers*, arrive in the southern part of Africa.

1665 - A great plague sweeps London.

The plague takes 75,000 lives.

1666 - A great fire sweeps through London for five days. The fire virtually destroys the city.

1679 - French explorer, Robert de la Salle, explores the Great Lakes of North America.

1682 - Peter the Great takes the throne in Russia at age 10. He is one of the most successful rulers in Russian history, leading Russia to become a major power in Europe.

1685 - Ports in China open to foreign trade.

1600s-1700s - China has a heavy trade business, exporting fine fabrics, porcelain, and tea to Europe.

1750 - The Industrial Revolution begins in England and, over the next century, spreads to Western Europe and the United States. The Industrial Revolution radically affects the lives of people all over the world, drastically changing the way goods are produced.

The invention of machines, such as the spinning Jenny and steam-powered engines helped industries speed up production of goods.

1755 - A powerful earthquake destroys Lisbon, Portugal.

1762 - Catherine the Great becomes the Empress of Russia. The Russian Empire thrives and expands under her leadership.

1775-1783 - The American colonists, dissatisfied with the British rule, plan and declare independence from England.

1783 - In the Treaty of Paris, Britain recognizes the 13 colonies in North America as an independent country: The United States of America.

1789-1799 - The French Revolution begins with the storming of the Bastille Prison and spreads quickly through France.

1793-1794 - During the *Reign of Terror* in France, anyone suspected of being against the revolution is executed by guillotine.

1799 - Napoleon Bonaparte becomes dictator of France. Under his brilliant military leadership, France conquers much of Europe by 1812.

Quotations from History

1800 – British traders import opium from India into China.

1800s – The century sees a mad rush on the part of European countries to increase their influence in other continents. In this *Age of Imperialism*, Britain, Belgium, Spain, France, Italy, Portugal, and Holland colonize most of Africa, as well as large portions of southeastern Asia and islands in the South Pacific Ocean. The imperialism provides more raw materials for the new manufacturing and opportunities for people to move to new lands.

1802-1803 – English explorer Matthew Flinders is one of the first Europeans to explore Australia. Over the next several years, Australia becomes a place where Britain "dumps" criminals and other undesirable people.

1804 – Napoleon introduces the *Code Napoleon*, a document that gives peasants rights to the property they gained in the French Revolution.

1804 – Haiti, the first black nation to gain freedom from European control, ends its colonial status by declaring independence from France.

1808-1825 – In Central and South America, Argentina, Venezuela, Paraguay, Colombia, Uruguay, and Chile fight wars to gain independence from Spanish and Portuguese rule.

1810 – Colombian Simon Bolivar leads a revolt against Spanish control. After many years, ten South American countries gain independence from Spain.

1814-1815 – Napoleon is forced from power to exile on the island of Elba. He escapes and retakes power, but is defeated in a battle at Waterloo.

1819 – The British settle the colony of Singapore, which remained in Britain's control until its independence in 1959.

1823 – In the *Monroe Doctrine*, the U.S. president warns European nations not to interfere in the Western Hemisphere.

1830-1832 – British navigator John Biscoe circumvents and explores Antarctica.

1835-1843 – To escape British domination, Boer farmers begin the *Great Trek* from Cape Province in South Africa to find lands north and east.

1839-1842 – The Opium Wars break out between China and Britain after China bans the British trade of opium.

1841 – David Livingston, from Scotland, explores Africa. In 1852-1856, he is the first European to cross Africa on foot.

1843 – Samuel Morse develops an effective code for sending telegraph signals.

1845-1848 – A long famine in Ireland causes thousands of Irish to emigrate to the U.S. from their homeland.

1848 – Karl Marx and Friedrich Engels release the *Communist Manifesto*.

1848-1849 – Discovery of gold in California starts a rush of settlers to the western U.S.

The Gold Rush miners were called Forty Niners because they came to California in 1849, after hearing of the 1948 gold discovery.

1848 – In this *Year of Revolutions*, many European countries experience uprisings from their people to protest food shortages, harsh rule, or economic problems. Though the rebellions are unsuccessful, in many cases the rulers are forced to make changes.

1853 – Turkey, Britain, and Britain declare war on Russia for demanding the right to send ships through the Dardanelles Strait. A very bloody war follows, leading to the defeat of Russia and a treaty signed in Paris in 1856, ending the war.

1853 – American Naval officer Matthew Perry sails into Tokyo harbor with gunboats, forcing Japan to open its ports to outside trade. Japan had been closed off to foreign visitors for years.

1857-1858 – In the Indian Mutiny, people in India rise up against the British. The British regain power and, afterwards, begin to control India more directly.

1860-1880 – Westward movement and settlement in the U.S. leads to wars with Native American populations. Large portions of the Native Americans populations die from war and disease.

1861 – Southern states in the U.S. break away from the union and form the Confederate States of America. A civil war breaks out in the country.

1865 – U.S. President Abraham Lincoln is fatally shot by John Wilkes Booth.

1865 – The American Civil War ends.

1867 – Russia sells Alaska to the U.S. for $7 million.

1869 – The transcontinental railroad is finished in the U.S., making it possible for faster travel across the North American continent.

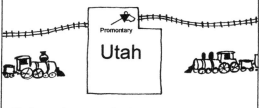

Promontary
Utah

The last spike was made of gold. It was driven into the railroad in Promontory Point, Utah.

1869 – Discovery of diamonds in South Africa leads to a rush of settlers and explorers hunting for diamonds.

1876 – The telephone is invented by Alexander Graham Bell.

1880 – Construction begins on the Panama Canal to connect the Atlantic and Pacific Oceans.

1880s – Jewish immigrants from Europe bean migrating to Palestine, with the purpose of returning to their historic homeland.

1885 – The first motorized car is built in Germany by Karl Benz.

The Benz auto has an internal-combustion engine, 3 wheels, electric ignition, differential gears, and a water-cooling system.

1886 – The Statue of Liberty, given to the U.S. by France, is set up in New York City harbor.

1889 – The Eiffel Tower is built in Paris.

1890 – The last uprising of Native Americans, the *Battle of Wounded Knee*, ends in their tragic defeat.

1893 – New Zealand becomes the world's first country to give women the right to vote.

1896 – The first modern Olympic Games are held in Athens, Greece.

1898 – Spain loses some of its colonies to the U.S. in the Spanish-American War.

1899 – The Boers in Transvaal and Orange Free State in Africa declare war against Britain to rid their countries of British interference.

1903 – The Wright Brothers succeed with the first powered flight at Kitty Hawk, North Carolina, U.S.

1908 – In the U.S., Henry Ford begins the first mass production of automobiles.

1912 – The *Titanic* sinks on its maiden voyage across the Atlantic.

1914 – World War I begins.

1915 – Mahatma Gandhi returns to India, beginning a long nonviolent campaign to win rights for the common people.

1917 – The Russian Revolution overthrows the czar, leaving the communists (called *Bolsheviks*) to take control.

1919 – World War I ends with a peace treaty signed in Versailles, France.

1919 – The League of Nations is formed.

1922 – The USSR is formed.

1927 – Charles Lindbergh successfully completes a solo flight across the Atlantic Ocean.

The flight took 33½ hours in Lindbergh's single engine, propeller plane named "The Spirit of St. Louis."

1929 – The Great Depression begins.

1930s – The Japanese military takes control of the government, and begins to invade neighboring countries.

1933 – Hitler becomes dictator of Germany.

1933 – Japan and Germany withdraw from the League of Nations.

1939 – World War II begins in Europe. Germany invades Poland and France.

1941 – Japan attacks the U.S. Naval Fleet at Pearl Harbor, bringing the U.S. into World War II.

1941 – Hitler sets up extermination camps to eliminate Jews.

1942 – In the *Manhattan Project*, U.S. scientists go to work to create an atom bomb.

1945 – The U.S. drops nuclear bombs on the Japanese cities of Nagasaki and Hiroshima.

1945 – World War II ends.

1945 – After World War II, a long period of tension develops between the U.S. and the Soviet Union, beginning a period called the *Cold War*.

1945 – The United Nations is established, replacing the League of Nations.

1947 – Pakistan and India gain independence from Great Britain.

1948 – Mahatma Gandhi is assassinated.

1948 – The state of Israel is created.

1948 – Several Arab states attack the new country of Israel, beginning the first Arab-Israeli war.

1948 – South Africa established the policy of *apartheid*, separating black and white citizens.

1948-1949 – The Soviet Union blockades West Berlin in an attempt to force it to be part of Eastern Europe; Britain and the U.S. airlift supplies into West Berlin; West Germany and East Germany become separate states.

1949 - Mao Zedong takes control of the Communist Party in China, forms the Communist Peoples' Republic of China.

1949 - The U.S. and 11 European nations form NATO (*the North Atlantic Treaty Organization*), signing agreements to protect each other against Soviet aggression.

1950s-1970s - The era of colonialism ends and most colonies in Africa gain independence.

1950-1953 - The U.S. and other nations join South Korea to fight against a North Korean invasion.

1953 - Scientists Francis Crick and James Watson discover the structure of DNA.

1954 - Vietnamese communists, led by Ho Chi Minh, defeat the French in Indochina.

1954-1973 - Civil war rages in Vietnam. Pro-communist forces fight against anti-communist forces in South Vietnam. The U.S. eventually becomes involved in supporting the South Vietnamese government.

1955 - In the U.S., Martin Luther King, Jr., leads a bus boycott in Alabama in a protest against segregation, expanding the American Civil Rights Movement.

A national holiday in the U.S. honors the work of Dr. King each January.

1956 - In the *Suez Crisis*, Egypt nationalizes the Suez Canal, triggering action by Israel, Britain, and France to retake control of the canal. International pressure ends the crisis. The canal is closed for six months.

1957 - The U.S.S.R. launches *Sputnik I*, the first satellite in space.

Sputnik I carries the first living creature in space, a small dog named Laika.

1958 - Fidel Castro takes power in Cuba and installs a communist government aligned with the Soviet Union.

1960 - OPEC (*the Organization of Petroleum Exporting Countries*) is formed to control oil production and prices.

1961 - Soviet Cosmonaut Yuri Gagarin becomes the first human to fly in space, orbiting Earth in his space ship, *Vostok I*.

1961 - The Berlin Wall is built around East Berlin to keep Germans on the east side from escaping to West Germany.

1961 - The U.S. begins sending troops to Vietnam.

1962 - In the *Cuban Missile Crisis*, the U.S. and Cuba have a standoff over Soviet nuclear weapons in Cuba.

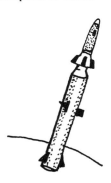

In response to Soviet military shipments to Cuba, Soviet bases in Cuba, and the presence of Soviet nuclear missiles there, the U.S. blockades Cuba and threatens war. For a few dangerous days, the world seems on the brink of nuclear war, before Russia backs down and gives into U.S. demands.

1963 - U.S. President John F. Kennedy is assassinated.

1965 - The U.S. begins bombing North Vietnam.

1966 – Mao Zedong, leader of China, begins the *Cultural Revolution*.

The Cultural Revolution is a period of time when any capitalist influences in China are brutally crushed and all citizens are encouraged to keep Communism pure. The young people in China are pressured to join the Red Guard, an organization that hunts for signs that anyone is not supportive of the revolution. The period ends in 1876 with the death of Mao.

1966 – The Seven-Day War between Israel, Egypt, and Syria ends with a victory for the Israelis.

1967 – Israel captures territory from Egypt, Syria, and Jordan in the Six Days War.

1969 – The U.S. successfully lands the first human on the Moon.

1969 – The peace movement grows in the U.S., with major demonstrations against the Vietnam War.

1970 – Egypt and Israel go to war over control of the Sinai Peninsula.

1971 – Pakistan gives up the control of East Pakistan, allowing it to become the independent state of Bangladesh.

1971 – The first space station, *Salyut I*, is launched by the U.S.S.R.

1972 – Israeli athletes are murdered at the Olympic Games in Munich by an Arab terrorist organization, *Black September*.

1972 – President Richard Nixon is the first U.S. president to visit Communist China.

1972 – The U.S.S.R. and the U.S. sign the SALT to reduce arms. (SALT is *the Strategic Arms Limitation Treaty.*)

1973 – The U.S. withdraws its troops from Vietnam.

1974 – U.S. President Richard Nixon resigns amidst the Watergate Scandal.

1975 – North Vietnam defeats and occupies South Vietnam.

1976 – The *Concorde*, a supersonic passenger plane designed by Britain and France, takes its first transatlantic flight.

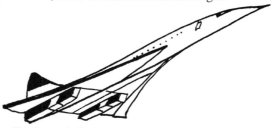

The Concorde flies at a speed of 1350 mph (twice the speed of sound) and holds 100 passengers. Twenty of the planes are built, at a cost of about $46 million each.

1978 – Israel and Egypt agree to terms of peace in the *Camp David Agreement*.

1978 – The U.S. begins diplomatic relations with China.

1978 – The Vietnamese invade Cambodia to help rebels overthrow their government.

1979 – Egypt signs a peace treaty with Israel agreeing to withdraw from the Sinai Peninsula.

1980s – The Cold War tensions between communist and noncommunist countries decrease.

1980 – The Iran-Iraq war begins.

1982-1985 – Israel invades Lebanon in an attempt to drive the Palestine Liberation Organization out of the country.

1986 – The U.S. and other nations begin economic sanctions against South Africa because of its *apartheid* policies.

1986 – The first major disaster at a nuclear power plant occurs in Chernobyl, U.S.S.R.

1986 – The Space Shuttle *Challenger* explodes immediately after liftoff.

1989 – Chinese students protest their government policies and march for democracy in Beijing's Tiananmen Square; the Chinese army crushes the protest.

1989 – The Berlin Wall is knocked down; Germany is reunified in 1990.

1990 – The Hubble Space Telescope is launched.

Hubble is the size of a school bus, and transmits enough data every day to fill 10,000 computer diskettes. It takes 97 minutes to circle the Earth at a speed of 17,500 mph.

1990s – Communist governments lose control of countries in Eastern Europe.

1990 – *Apartheid* ends in South Africa. Activist Nelson Mandela is released from prison after 27 years.

1991 – The Soviet Union collapses.

1991 – The U.S. and a coalition of Allies go to war with Iraq to push back Iraq's 1990 advances on its neighbor Kuwait.

1991 – A cyclone kills 125,000 people in Bangladesh and leaves many more homeless.

1993 – The European Union is established.

1993 – Yasir Arafat, leader of the PLO, and Yitzak Rabin, Israel's prime minister, sign a peace agreement in Washington, DC.

1994 – Nelson Mandela becomes the first black president in South Africa.

1994 – A civil war in Rwanda leads to the deaths of half a million citizens.

1997 – The British return control of Hong Kong to China.

1997 – The first sheep is cloned in Scotland. The sheep is named Dolly.

1998 – The European Union (except the U.K.) adopts a single currency, the *Euro*.

1998 – Terrorists bomb U.S. embassies in Kenya and Tanzania.

1999 – Northern Ireland wins the right to govern itself.

2000 – The first crew arrives at the International Space Station.

2001 – The UN and its secretary-general, Kofi Anaan, win the Nobel Peace Prize.

2001 – Terrorists crash planes into buildings in the U.S. on September 11, killing about 3000 people.

2002 – Suicide bombings and violence escalates in Palestinian-Israel conflict.

2002 – The U.S. and a coalition of allies go to war with Afghanistan to overthrow the ruling Taliban party and search for members of al Qaeda, the terrorist group responsible for the September 11 attacks.

2002 – Scientists and researchers complete a draft of the human genome sequence.

2002 – North Korea admits to developing nuclear arms in violation of a treaty with other world nations.

2002 – The UN Security Council passes a resolution requiring Iraq to disarm or face serious consequences.

2002 – UN inspectors return to Iraq.

Who Said It?

A banquet of historical quotes:

The future belongs to those who believe in the beauty of their dreams.

Eleanor Roosevelt (1884-1962)

Democracy is the worst form of government – except for all the rest.

Winston Churchill (1874-1965)

The human race has one really effective weapon – and that is laughter.

Mark Twain (1835-1910)

The only tyrant I accept in this world is the still voice within.

Gandhi (1869-1948)

The hunger for love is more difficult to remove than the hunger for bread.

Mother Teresa (1910-1997)

Men, their rights, and nothing more; women, their rights, and nothing less.

Susan B. Anthony (1820-1906)

We are not amused.

Queen Victoria (1819-1901)

The ballot is stronger than the bullet.

Abraham Lincoln (1809-1865)

Power tends to corrupt, and absolute power corrupts absolutely.

Lord Acton (1834-1902)

The great question, which I have never been able to answer – is, "What does a woman want?"

Sigmund Freud (1856-1939)

Let every nation know, whether it wishes us well or ill, that we shall pay any price, bear any burden, meet any hardship, support any friend, oppose any foe, to assure the survival and success of liberty.

John F. Kennedy (1917-1963)

Somewhere out in this audience may even be someone who will one day follow my footsteps and preside over the White House as the President's spouse. I wish him well.

Barbara Bush (1925-)

World History Personalities

Here are just a few of the people (other than myself) who made specific contributions to the amazing history of the world.

Cleopatra

Alexander the Great (356-323 B.C.) – King of Macedonia; conqueror of Greece and Persia

Alexander II (1818-1888) – Russian Czar from 1855-1881; abolished serfdom

Anaan, Kofi (1938-) – UN Secretary-General from 1987 to present; born in Ghana; recipient of the 2001 Nobel Peace Prize

Antoinette, Marie (1755-1793) – Queen of France from 1774-1792; killed by guillotine in the *Reign of Terror* during the French Revolution

Arafat, Yasir (1929-) – leader of the Palestine Liberation Organization (PLO) who signed 1993 peace accord with Israel; president of Palestine since 1994; recipient of 1994 Nobel Peace Prize

Aristotle (382-332 B.C.) – philosopher of Ancient Greece; made important contributions to mathematics

Balboa, Vasco de (1475-1517) – Spanish explorer who first reached the Pacific by crossing Panama (1513)

Barak, Ehud (1942-) – Peace-seeking Israeli military leader; prime minister from 1999 to 2001

Begin, Menachem (1913-1992) – Israeli prime minister who signed the Camp David Peace Accord (1978)

Benedict (480-543) – Italian monk who organized monasteries

Bolivar, Simon (1783-1830) – Venezuelan leader who drove Spanish out of northern South America

Bonaparte, Napoleon (1769-1821) – French emperor and military conqueror from 1804-1815

Brezhnev, Leonid (1906-1982) – head of the Communist Party of the U.S.S.R. from 1964 until his death

Caesar, Julius (100-44 B.C.) – Roman general, statesman, and historian

Calvin, John (1509-1564) – French-born Swiss Protestant reformer; one of the founders of Protestantism

Castro, Fidel (1927-) – Cuban revolutionary who took control of the country in 1959 and headed the country under a communist government

Catherine the Great (1729-1796) – Russian empress who poisoned her husband to gain control and greatly expanded Russia's territory; reigned from 1762-1796

Chaing Kai-shek (1886-1975) – Chinese national leader; led fight against the communists in 1930s and 1940s

Charlemagne (724-814) – Frankish king who spread Christianity through Europe emperor from 768-814

Churchill, Winston (1874-1965) – British prime minister from 1951-1955; led Britain during World War II

Cleopatra (69-30 B.C.) – powerful Egyptian queen during the rule of Caesar

Columbus, Christopher (1446-1605) – Italian explorer who arrived in the Americas in 1492

Confucius (551-479 B.C.) – Chinese philosopher whose teachings spread through China, beginning the philosophy-religion of Confucianism

Constantine (280-337) – Roman emperor from 312-337; legalized Christianity in the Roman Empire

Cook, James (1728-1779) – British explorer who first explored Australia

Copernicus, Nicolaus (1473-1543) – Polish astronomer who made many important discoveries in astronomy and argued that the Sun is the center of the solar system

Da Gama, Vasco (1469-1542) – Portuguese explorer; found a water route to the Indies

DaVinci, Leonardo (1452-1519) – successful Renaissance painter and inventor

DeKlerk, F. W. (1936-) – South African president from 1989 to 1994 who led the country during the end of apartheid; lifted the ban on the African National Council, and released Nelson Mandela from prison

Dias, Barthalomeau (1450-1500) – first European to sail around the southern tip of Africa (1487-1488)

Drake, Francis (1540-1596) – English military leader who led the defeat of the Spanish Armada in 1588

Einstein, Albert (1879-1975) – German scientist who published the *Theory of Relativity* in 1905

Eisenhower, Dwight D. (1879-1975) – supreme commander of Allied forces who organized the D-Day invasion in 1944; became U.S. president in 1953

Elizabeth I (1533-1603) – powerful Queen of England from 1558-1603 who reinstated the Anglican Church as the Church of England

Any intelligent fool can make things bigger, more complex, and more violent. It takes a touch of genius— and a lot of courage— to move in the opposite direction.

Albert Einstein

Ferdinand, Franz (1863-1914) – heir to the Austria-Hungary throne whose murder by a Serbian nationalist triggered World War I

Frank, Anne (1929-1945) – young Jewish girl who recorded a diary of her experiences hiding from the Nazis and, after being caught, died in a concentration camp

Galileo Galilei (1563-1642) – Italian astronomer and mathematician who made use of a telescope to observe the solar system and published new findings about astronomy

Gandhi, Mohandas (1869-1948) – Indian leader who taught civil disobedience and led India's independence movement (1920)

Gautama, Siddhartha (563-483 B.C.) – founder of Buddhism; known as *the Buddha*

Gorbachev, Mikhail (1933-   ) – leader of the Soviet Union from 1985-1991; began reforms that led to the fall of Communism in the U.S.S.R.

Gutenberg, Johann (1400-1468) – German printer credited with the invention of the printing press; published the first book made on printing presses, the *Gutenberg Bible*

Hammurabi (1800-1750 B.C.) – Babylonian ruler famous for first system of laws called *Hammurabi's Code* (1792 B.C.)

Hidalgo, Miguel (1752-1811) – Mexican priest who led a revolt that began the Mexican fight for independence

Hitler, Adolf (1889-1945) – German Nazi leader and dictator who led Germany into World War II

Ho Chi Minh (1890-1969) – North Vietnamese leader who led communist troops in the takeover of South Vietnam

Homer (950-900 B.C.) – Greek poet; writer of famous epic poems, *The Odyssey* and the *The Iliad*

Ivan the Great (1440-1505) – Russian ruler from 1462-1505; freed Russia from Mongolian control

Jesus Christ (6 B.C.-A.D.29) – 1st-century Jewish teacher who was crucified by the Romans; believed by Christians to be the Son of God

John (1167-1216) – King of England from 1199-1216; signed the *Magna Carta* in 1215

Khomeini, Ayatollah (1902-1989) – fundamentalist Islamic ruler of Iran who took control of the government from the Shah in 1979

Lenin, Vladimir (1870-1924) – Russian communist leader who founded the Soviet Union

Livingston, David (1813-1873) – Scottish missionary who ventured into the deepest parts of Africa where no white person had traveled

Louis XVI (1754-1793) – French king from 1774-1792; executed by guillotine during the *Rein of Terror* in the French Revolution

Luther, Martin (1483-1546) – German monk who demanded reforms in the Roman Catholic Church and whose efforts eventually led to the Protestant Reformation

Mandela, Nelson (1918-   ) – South African lawyer who led the struggle against the policies of *apartheid*; jailed from 1964-1990; became South Africa's first black president in 1994

Marcos, Ferdinand (1917-1989) – Philippine leader who became a dictator and was forced into exile in 1986 by the people of his country

Marx, Karl (1818-1883) – German writer whose ideas formed the basis for socialism and communism

Meir, Golda (1898-1978) – Zionist leader who helped to found Israel and served as Israel's prime minister from 1969-1974

Michelangelo (1475-1654) – Italian Renaissance painter and sculptor

Muhammed (570-632) – founder of the Islam religion

Nasser, Gamal Abdel (1819-1970) – Egypt's first president

Nehru, Jawaharlal (1889-1964) – India's first prime minister; follower of Gandhi's teachings

Newton, Isaac (1642-1727) – English scientist who discovered the *law of gravity* and formulated other laws about energy and motion

I took control of the French government in 1661 and ruled with absolute power. My friends and enemies called me the "Sun King."

Louis XIV of France

Peter the Great (1672-1725) – Russian czar from 1682-1725; built the capital at St. Petersburg

Plato (428-347 B.C.) – Greek philosopher who studied under Socrates

Roosevelt, Franklin (1882-1945) – U.S. president from 1933-1945; led the country during World War II

San Martin, Jose de (1778-1850) – South American leader of armies that won independence from Spain for Argentina and Chile

Shakespeare, William (1564-1616) – well known Renaissance English poet and playwright whose work has endured for centuries

Sharon, Ariel (1928-   ) – Israeli general who sparked controversy by visiting the Temple Mount in Palestinian East Jerusalem in 2000, triggering Arab demonstrations and derailing progress toward peace; prime minister of Israel since 2001

Socrates (470-399 B.C.) – famous philosopher and scholar of ancient Greece

Stalin, Joseph (1879-1953) – harsh Soviet dictator from 1924-1953; turned the U.S.S.R. into a totalitarian nation

Sun Yat-sen (1866-1925) – founder of the Chinese Republic and leader of the Chinese nationalist party

Walsea, Lech (1943-   ) – factory worker who led 1988 Polish protests against the communist government; won a Nobel Peace Prize in 1985 and became president of Poland in 1990

Zedong, Mao (1893-1976) – Chinese communist leader who founded the Cultural Revolution in China with the purpose of purging all noncommunist influences from China

Spectacular Inventions and Discoveries

Remarkable discoveries and amazing inventions have punctuated the story of human life on Earth. Over and over, new understandings, ideas, and technologies keep changing the way people live, think, work, and interact.

The propeller airplane was invented by American brothers, Orville and Wilbur Wright, in 1903.

Fortunately for early aviators, the parachute had already been invented by Jean Pierre Blanchard of France in 1785.

Transatlantic travel was revolutionized after the invention of the steam boat in 1807 by an American, Robert Fulton.

Englishman George Stephenson invented the steam locomotive in 1829, making trains the fastest, safest way to travel.

A prototype of the modern submarine was devised by Simon Lake of the U.S.A. in 1894.

In 1980, Scott Olson (U.S.), invented a truly innovative mode of transportation—rollerblades!

The gasoline powered automobile was first developed in the U.S.A. by Charles and Frank Duryea in 1892.

Driving *really* advanced, however, when Mary Anderson invented a practical little item called the windshield wiper.

Paper was invented by Ts' Lun in China in the year A.D. 105, and remained the most practical form of communication for centuries.

When Samuel F. B. Morse invented the telegraph in 1837, the world really started buzzing. In 1876, Alexander Graham Bell topped that invention with one of his own—the telephone.

The popular cellular phone was perfected by the Swedish company, Ericsson, in 1979.

One of the most important advancements in telecommunication was the development of the Internet in the 20th century.

The German astronomer Johannes Kepler (1571-1630) correctly theorized that the force of gravity governs the orbits of the planets around the Sun.

Albert Einstein (1879-1955) developed the Theory of Relativity which investigates the relationship between time, energy, matter, and space.

Lise Meitner (1878-1968) discovered nuclear fission, and theorized about the sort of chain reaction that would lead to the release of power in a nuclear bomb.

Food preservation and storage went through historic changes when the Englishman Jacob Perkins (1892-1961) invented refrigeration.

In 1924, American Clarence Birdseye invented prepackaged frozen foods, and during the same era, Frederick Jones invented refrigerated trucks to get those frozen foods to market.

And of course, Thomas Alva Edison (1847-1931), the genius of Menlo Park, was responsible for many inventions including the electric light bulb, a bright idea that helps people find frozen food inside their refrigerators.

Spectacles for reading date back to the 13th century (or even earlier) but Ben Franklin had the right idea when he invented bifocals in 1780.

The human desire to see other worlds far away, or tiny worlds under our noses, led to the development of the telescope and the microscope.

Many researchers believe that the Dutchman, Hans Lippershey, invented the telescope around 1600, but credit is usually given to the Italian genius, Galileo, who wrote a paper on its use in 1609.

The Hubbell telescope was launched in 1990 and continues to expand our view of the universe.

Conflicts & Connections

War is a major theme in the history of the world. Economic needs, desire for power and territory, human greed, self-defense, religious differences, and clashes in ideas are all factors that have motivated the wars and other conflicts that have affected history. Friendships, agreements, and alliances have also brought change to the world, often promoting peace and stability for cultures. These brief descriptions summarize some of the major conflicts and alliances in world history.

The Crusades (1095-1291) – For almost 200 years, European Christians launched a series of military campaigns to win the Holy Land (Palestine) back from Muslims. In the *First Crusade* (1096-1099), the crusaders took back Jerusalem, but the territories gained were later lost. Many other *Crusades* followed; but the Christians did not succeed in gaining and holding the Holy Land for the Christians. In 1212, a group of children tried to accomplish what the older crusaders could not. The crusade failed miserably, with many of the children dying from disease or hunger, and many others taken into slavery.

Hundred Years' War (1337-1453) – War began between England and France when William the Conqueror (of Normandy, France) conquered England, creating a state that included English and French land. The French wanted control of their own territory and the English believed they controlled France. Invasions and wars, with a back-and-forth struggle over power and land, continued for over a hundred years.

Oh, dear! There's more unrest in the world!

The American Revolution (1775-1783) – After years of dissatisfaction with British rule in the America colonies, representatives from the colonies met in Philadelphia in 1775 to form plans for independence. In 1776 they signed the *Declaration of Independence*, beginning a war with the British. The war ended in 1783 with the *Treaty of Paris*, in which Britain recognized the independence of the colonies and the United States of America was formed.

The French Revolution (1789) – In the late eighteenth century, the citizens of France rebelled against the poor living conditions, shortages of food, heavy taxes, and unfair government of the kings and his nobles. In 1789, the Commoners formed their own National Assembly which put forth the *Declaration of the Rights of Man*. Riots against the government began, and a mob stormed the Bastille Prison on July 14, 1789. The revolution continued and became more violent, even after France became a republic. During the Reign of Terror in 1793-1794, many leaders were put to death by guillotine.

180

Boer War (1899-1902) – The South Africa Republic (Transvaal) and the Orange Free State formed an alliance to protect their independence, in the face of their belief that Great Britain was threatening to take over their territories. Control of the diamond and gold mines was a part of the struggle in the area. A long guerrilla war waged, with many deaths on both sides. The Boers could not hold out against the more powerful British forces. The war ended in 1902 with the *Treaty of Vereeniging*.

I used to think the Boer War was a great big animal fight!

The Russian Revolution (1917) – The people of Russia, oppressed for years by czars who held absolute power, followed the leadership of Lenin (the head of the communist Bolshevik party) and overthrew the czar. The new government killed the czar and his family and centralized control of land and services.

World War I (1914-1918) –The war began when Archduke Francis Ferdinand, the prince of Austria-Hungary, was killed in Sarajevo in 1914. Because he was murdered by a Serbian, Austria declared war on Serbia. Russia joined in to defend Serbia. Greater causes of the war were the intense economic and territorial rivalries between the powers of Europe. In just a few weeks, the Central Powers (Germany, Austria-Hungary, Turkey, and Bulgaria) were at war with the Allies (Russia, France, and Britain). Fierce fighting took place for four years, with Italy, Japan, the United States, Turkey, and Bulgaria joining in. About 17 million people were killed in the war, which ended with the signing of several treaties.

World War II (1939-1945) - The war began when Germany, under Adolph Hitler, invaded Poland. Britain and France, who were part of an alliance with Poland (the Allied Powers), declared war on Germany. Over the next five years, the war moved across Europe and into northern Africa. Japan joined with the German alliance (the Axis Powers), and began taking control of areas in southeastern Asia and the Pacific. In 1942, the U.S. joined the Allies after Japan attacked the U.S. Naval fleet at Pearl Harbor, Hawaii. The Allies landed in Europe (at Normandy) in 1944 and turned the tide of the war against Germany. The U.S. dropped two atomic bombs in Japan in 1945, and the Axis powers were defeated both on the European and Pacific fronts in the same year.

The Arab-Israeli Wars (1948-Present) – Soon after the establishment of the state of Israel in 1948, conflicts arose between the Jews and the Arabs. Frequent wars, border raids, and other clashes have continued ever since. In 1948, several Arab nations invaded the new country until the UN established a truce. Fighting erupted again in 1956 (*the 1956 War*), when Israeli forces moved into Egypt's Sinai Peninsula. Israel withdrew from these positions in 1957. In the *Six Day War* in 1967, Egypt closed Israel off from the Gulf of Aqaba in response to Israeli raids across the borders of neighboring countries. In 1973-1974, Egypt attacked Israel on a Jewish holy day (*the Yom Kippur War*). This brutal siege ended through diplomatic efforts from the U.S. In 1979, Israel and Egypt signed the *Camp David Peace Accords*. In 1982, Israel launched an attack to destroy Palestinian bases in Lebanon. Under international pressure, Israel retreated and cease-fire agreements were reached. In 1988, Yasir Arafat, leader of the PLO (*Palestine Liberation Organization*) signed an accord with Israel leading to limited Palestinian self-rule in Jericho and the Gaza Strip. Further agreements to finalize borders and solve the dispute over Jerusalem were signed, but new violence, attacks, and suicide bombings that began in September of 2000 have stalled progress on these issues.

Korean War (1950-1953) – At the end of World War II, Korea was divided into two zones at the 38th parallel. In 1950, communist North Korean forces invaded noncommunist South Korea. Forces from the U.S. and UN joined under the command of U.S. General MacArthur to aid South Korea. After much brutal fighting with heavy casualties, a cease-fire agreement was signed in 1953. There was no official treaty ending the war, and U.S. troops still occupy the area near the North Korea-South Korea border. Tensions between the two countries continue.

Vietnam War (1950-1975) – After Vietnam won its independence from French colonial control in 1954, the U.S. began to support anti-communist efforts in South Vietnam. In this *Cold War* period, the U.S. had a belief in the *Domino Theory*, a fear that the North Vietnam's fall to Communism could result in the spread of Communism throughout the area. The anti-communist efforts grew into full-blown American military involvement in Vietnam, with thousands of U.S. troops taking part in a war against the communist forces. Even with heavy bombing and its military might, the U.S. was unable to stop the communists. Forces on both sides suffered heavy casualties, while inside the U.S., opposition to the war grew strong. American troops withdrew from Vietnam in 1973. South Vietnam surrendered to North Vietnam in 1975, and the country was reunited.

Iran-Iraq War (1980-1988) – This conflict began with an Iraqi invasion of Iran in 1980 following a dispute over a waterway that forms the Iran-Iraq border. Clashes continued for years, bringing huge death tolls and devastation to the countries, economies, and peoples of both countries. After Iran attacked Kuwaiti oil tankers in 1988, the UN forced a cease-fire. In 1990, Iraq withdrew its troops from Iran, but a formal peace treaty has never been signed.

Persian Gulf War (1991) – The war was sparked by Iraq's August, 1990 invasion of long-disputed territory in Kuwait. The U.S. and a coalition of allies launched *Operation Desert Storm* on January 18, 1991, and liberated Kuwait in February. Iraq withdrew from Kuwait, but Iraq's leader, Sadaam Hussein, remained in power.

Alliances are generally pretty good things.

Agreements & Alliances

Allies *(World War I)* – group of nations that supported one another in the war *(Britain, Russia, France, U.S., Belgium, Serbia, Greece, Romania, Montenegro, Portugal, Italy, Japan)*

Central Powers *(World War I)* – group of nations that supported one another the war *(Austria-Hungary, Germany, Bulgaria, and Turkey)*

Allies *(World War II)* – group of nations that supported one another in the war *(Britain, France, U.S.S.R., U.S., Australia, Belgium, Brazil, Canada, China, Denmark, Greece, Netherlands, New Zealand, Norway, Poland, South Africa, Yugoslavia)*

Axis Powers *(World War II)* – group of nations that supported one another in the war *(Germany, Italy, Japan, Hungary, Romania, Bulgaria)*

NATO *(North Atlantic Treaty Organization)* – an alliance formed in 1949 by several western European countries and the U.S. to stand against expansion by the Soviet Union and protect each other in the event of an attack by any other nation

Warsaw Pact – an alliance formed in 1955 by several eastern European countries in response to NATO

CIS *(Commonwealth of Independent States)* An organization formed in 1991 by independent European states, most of which were former republics of the U.S.S.R., to cooperate in matters of economics, defense, and foreign policy

Commonwealth of Nations – an association of Great Britain and its current and former dependencies formed to cooperate and consult on economic and foreign matters

European Union – a confederation of European countries with a purpose of cooperating in matters of security, foreign affairs, economics, and justice

ASEAN *(Association of Southeast Asian Nations)* – an organization formed to promote financial stability and socioeconomic progress, and to ban development of nuclear weapons among several nations

Arab League – an organization formed to give a unified political voice to Arab nations and to cooperate in matters of education, finance, law, trade, economic, defense, and foreign policy matters

GET SHARP →

on United States History, Government, & Citizenship

VOTE FOR SCHOOL OFFICERS HERE

Early Americans

Today, the North American continent is separated from Asia by the Bering Strait. Thousands of years ago during the Ice Age, glaciers froze so much of the water that the level of the oceans dropped. This exposed dry land (a land bridge) between the two continents, and allowed humans to migrate into America.

Early Cultures

By the 13th century, about a million people lived in the area that is now the United States and Canada. Cultures differed because of the land, climate, and resources in the areas where they lived. Some cultures were based on agriculture. Others were hunting cultures. Each group had to adapt to their particular environment, finding ways to get food, provide shelter, and meet the other basic needs of life. Most of the societies had little contact with other groups unless their trading and food-gathering needs brought them into contact or conflict with other groups.

The First Americans

The Eastern Woodlands

The native people of the Northeast lived between the Atlantic Ocean and the Mississippi River. The area extended to the Great Lakes and above the lakes into Canada. Cultures grew up in densely wooded areas. Their way of life included deer hunting, fishing, and farming. A group of tribes joined together in a tribal association known as the *Five Nations* or the *League of the Iroquois* in the area that is now New York. (These tribes were the Seneca, Mohawk, Onondaga, Cayuga, and Oneida.) Other tribes of the Eastern Woodlands were the Ojibwa (Chippewa), Potawatomi, Miami, Illinois, Shawnee, Ottawa, Algonquin, Shawnee, Powhattan, Huron, Penobscot, Susquehanna, Delaware, Narraganset, Massachuset, and Mohegan.

The Southeast

South of the Eastern Woodlands was a region stretching from the Ohio River to the Gulf of Mexico. This area, some of it in the Ohio River Valley, was rich with fertile soil and deep forests. Tribes that inhabited this area lived by hunting, fishing, farming, and gathering food. Some of them made pottery. After the year 500, some of the cultures in this area became *Mound Builders*, building earthen mounds in the shape of humans, birds, or other animals for burying their dead. This region was the home of several tribes: the Choctaw, Creek, Cherokee, Natchez, Timucua, and Chickasaw. The Calusa and Seminole tribes lived in the southernmost parts of the region.

The Great Plains

The Plains area extended from the Canadian border south to what is now Texas and spread from the Mississippi River to the foothills of the Rocky Mountains. The main tribes that lived in this area were the Crow, Cheyenne, Mandan, Dakota (Sioux), Arapaho, Pawnee, Osage, Kiowa, and Comanche. The people of some tribes were farmers who lived in permanent dwellings. Others tribes were nomadic, traveling to hunt buffalo. The horse, introduced to the region in the 18th century, changed life for the Indians. Horses made it easier for them to travel and hunt. It also brought them into more frequent contact with other tribes.

The Southwest

The people of the Southwest lived in an area that extended over present day Arizona, New Mexico, and parts of Utah and Colorado. The earliest Southwest people lived in pit dwellings or stone slab houses. Later, the Pueblo Indians created large community houses built in terraces on ledges of canyons (*cliff dwellings*). These tribes lived by farming and hunting. They were skilled potters and basket-weavers. Water was scarce in the region, so people had to find ways to keep a water supply. Some tribes brought water to their fields through irrigation ditches. The tribes that inhabited these areas were the Pueblo, Zuni, Hopi, Navajo, and Apache.

The Plateau

The Plateau area extended from above the Canadian border through the plateau area of the southwest, part of California, and the mountainous area of the Rockies. Tribes that lived in the area were the Cayuse, Nez Perce, Flathead, Chumash, Spokan, Paiute, and Pomo. They lived by hunting and gathering.

The Great Basin

In the Great Basin region (the area that is now Nevada, Utah, and parts of southern Oregon and Idaho), the land was harsh and dry. The Shoshone and Ute tribes were wanderers, hunting small animals and gathering seeds and plants. Other tribes were the Klamath, Modoc, and Paiute.

The Northwest

The inhabitants of the Northwest lived along the Pacific coast from northern California to Alaska. The area was thickly wooded with heavy rainfall. The natives fished for salmon and hunted land animals and sea mammals. In addition, they gathered fruit and berries. They used wood from the forests to build houses and canoes. The plentiful trees also supplied wood for totem poles. The tribes that lived in this area were the Maidu, Hupa, Yurok, Chinook, Satish, Kwakiutl, Haida, Tsimshian, and Nootka. In northern Canada and Alaska, ancestors of today's Eskimos lived from the bountiful animal life in the sea: walruses, seals, whales, and salmon. In the summer, they also hunted caribou.

Better Grades & Higher Test Scores / SOCIAL STUDIES
Copyright ©2003 by Incentive Publications, Inc., Nashville, TN.

Get Sharp: U.S History

Timeline of Key Events

Early history - 1635 ➡️

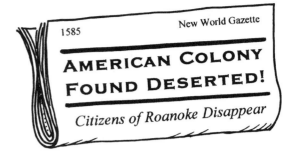

1585 New World Gazette

AMERICAN COLONY FOUND DESERTED!

Citizens of Roanoke Disappear

30,000-10,000 B.C. - The first people arrive on the North American continent, crossing from Asia on land and ice.

1000 B.C.-A.D. 1492 - Many different Native American cultures develop throughout North America.

1492 - Italian explorer Christopher Columbus reaches the West Indies and the Bahamas.

1497 - Explorer John Cabot, employed by the King of England, reaches Newfoundland.

1499-1502 - Italian Amerigo Vespucci explores the South American coast.

1507 - Martin Waldseemuller, a German mapmaker, names the New World *America*, after Amerigo Vespucci.

1513 - Spanish explorer Juan Ponce de Leon explores Florida.

1524 - Italian explorer Giovanni da Verrazano explores the North American east coast and enters New York Harbor.

1540-1541 - Spanish explorer Francisco de Coronado discovers the Grand Canyon and the Mississippi River.

1565 - The Spaniards establish the first European settlement at St. Augustine, Florida

1585 - Sir Walter Raleigh establishes the first English colony in America on Roanoke Island off the coast of North Carolina. By 1591, the colony is mysteriously deserted.

1607 - Captain John Smith founds the first permanent English settlement in North America at Jamestown, Virginia.

1609 - English-Dutch explorer Henry Hudson sails into New York Harbor and explores the Hudson River.

1619 - Virginia establishes the House of Burgesses, the first representative legislature in America.

1619 - Virginia imports slaves from West Africa, the first slaves brought to America.

1620 - Arriving on the *Mayflower* from England, Pilgrims found the colony of Plymouth, Massachusetts. They draw up the *Mayflower Compact* as the legal basis for governing themselves.

1622 - Colonists leaving Massachusetts found the colony of New Hampshire.

1624 - The colony of New Netherland (which later becomes New York) is established on the Hudson River.

1626 - Peter Minuit, a representative of the Dutch, buys Manhattan Island from the Manahata Indians for trinkets worth $24. The island is named New Amsterdam.

1630 - Colonists from Massachusetts, led by John Winthrop, found the city of Boston.

1630-1640 - Twenty thousand settlers join the Massachusetts Bay Colony.

1632 - Maryland is founded as a Catholic colony with religious tolerance for all.

1626 COLONIAL TIMES

GREAT BARGAIN!

MANHATTAN ISLAND PURCHASED FROM NATIVES

Get Sharp: U.S. History

Better Grades & Higher Test Scores / SOCIAL STUDIES
Copyright ©2003 by Incentive Publications, Inc., Nashville, TN.

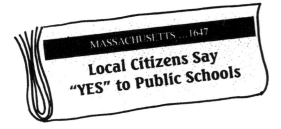

MASSACHUSETTS...1647
Local Citizens Say
"YES" to Public Schools

1636 – Harvard, the first college in the colonies, is founded.

1636 – After leaving Massachusetts, Roger Williams founds the colony of Rhode Island as a haven for religious freedom.

1636 – Thomas Hooker and followers, driven from Massachusetts, found the colony of Connecticut.

1638 – The colony of New Sweden (which later becomes Delaware) is founded on the Delaware River.

1647 – Massachusetts establishes the first colonial public school system.

1649 – Rhode Island becomes the first colony to outlaw slavery.

1660 – The British Parliament passes the first *Navigation Act* to regulate colonial commerce.

1663 – The colony of the Carolinas is founded.

1664 – The English take control of New Amsterdam from the Dutch and give the city a new name: New York.

1664 – The colony of New Jersey is founded on the land between the Hudson and Delaware Rivers.

1673 – French explorers Marquette and Jolliet reach the headwaters of the Mississippi River.

1682 – The colony of Pennsylvania is founded by William Penn, an English Quaker.

1699 – French settlements are established in Mississippi and Louisiana.

1703 – Delaware becomes a colony.

1704 – The first successful colonial newspaper, *The Boston Newsletter*, begins publication.

1729 – North Carolina and South Carolina become separate colonies.

1732 – Benjamin Franklin publishes the first issue of *Poor Richard's Almanack*.

1732 – The colony of Georgia is founded.

1740 – The Great Awakening, a great religious revival and force for religious tolerance, spreads through the colonies.

1750 – The Enlightenment spreads the belief that human reason will prevail—that by increasing their knowledge, people can improve themselves and the world.

1752 – Benjamin Franklin flies a homemade kite during a storm, proving that lightning is a form of electricity.

1754-1763 – The French fight against the English in the French and Indian War. They lose land in Canada and America to the English.

1763 – The *Proclamation of 1763* bans settlement beyond the Appalachian Mountains. Colonists dislike the limits on their westward expansion.

1764 – The British Parliament passes the *Sugar Act of 1764*, placing duties on lumber, foodstuffs, molasses, and rum in the colonies.

1765 – The spinning jenny, a mechanical spinning wheel, is invented; this leads to greatly increased cloth production.

1765 – The British Parliament passes the *Stamp Act*, taxing newspapers, legal documents, and other printed matter in the colonies. The act leads to protests in the colonies and a boycott of British imports.

DAILY BULLETIN   1649

Rhode Island Colonists Say
"NO" to Slavery

1766 - The British parliament repeals the *Stamp Act* and passes the *Declaratory Act*, declaring that the colonies are subordinate to the control of Parliament and Parliament can pass any law it desires.

1767 - The British government's *Townsend Acts* levy taxes on glass, painter's lead, paper, and tea in the colonies.

1770 - In the Boston Massacre, British troops fire on a group of colonists protesting English taxes.

1773 - The British Parliament passes the *Tea Act*. Colonists stage the Boston Tea Party to protest a tax on tea, dumping British tea into Boston Harbor.

1774 - The *Coercive Acts* (or *Intolerable Acts*) increase the power of the British government in the colonies, close Boston Harbor, and take other steps to punish the colonists.

1774 - The First Continental Congress meets in Philadelphia to condemn the *Intolerable Acts*.

1775 - *The Revolutionary War* begins between the colonists and the British with fighting at Lexington and Concord, Massachusetts.

1775 - The Second Continental Congress meets in Philadelphia to create an American army and make decisions about the war.

1776 - The colonists adopt the *Declaration of Independence* and form the United States of America.

1777 - The Second Continental Congress forms a government and drafts the *Articles of Confederation*, the first document of the U.S. central government.

1780 - Pennsylvania is the first state to abolish slavery.

1783 - The *Treaty of Paris* officially ends the Revolutionary War and recognizes the United States of America as an independent nation.

1787 - The Constitutional Convention begins writing the *U.S. Constitution*.

1789 - The *U.S. Constitution* is approved by all the states.

1789 - George Washington is chosen as the first U.S. President.

The Revolutionary Times
1773
Boston Protesters Dump Tea in the Sea

Confederation Chronicles
1789
Citizens Cheer Choice
Washington Becomes First American President

1790s-1900 - The Industrial Revolution leads to mass production of goods, a move toward an urban society, and a great change in the way of life for Americans.

1790s - The first U.S. political parties develop; a two-party system develops in 1796.

1791 - President Hamilton establishes the Bank of the United States, which issues paper money.

1791 - The *Bill of Rights* becomes law.

1792 - White House construction begins.

1793 - Eli Whitney invents the cotton gin, which leads to great increase in the production of cotton.

1793 - Congress passes a law requiring the return of runaway slaves.

1798 - Congress passes the *Alien and Sedition Acts* to protect the country against influence and dangers from foreigners.

1800s - Many Americans migrate west.

1800 - Washington, D.C. becomes the national capital.

1803 - The Louisiana Purchase, which includes most of the land between the Mississippi River and the Rocky Mountains, almost doubles the size of the U.S.

1804-1806 - The Lewis and Clark Expedition explores the northwestern U.S.

1807 - In response to the British practice of drafting American sailors, Congress passes the *Embargo Act*, prohibiting all U.S. exports to Britain.

1825 - The Erie Canal opens, providing a water route from the Atlantic Ocean to the Great Lakes.

1830s-1850s - The Age of Reform sees the developments of reform movements to end slavery, improve education and opportunities for women, offer free public education, give assistance to help needy children and the disadvantaged, increase power and improve conditions for workers, and reform the economic system.

1830-1930 - Almost 40 million immigrants come to the U.S., mostly from northern, central, and southern Europe.

The Early American Times....1804
Explorers Go West
Jefferson sends Louis and Clark on a Great Expedition

The Evening Gazette 1825
Erie Canal Opens!

1807 - Robert Fulton makes a trip up the Hudson River in the first practical steamboat.

1811 - Work begins on the National Road to link the eastern and the midwestern states.

1812-1814 - The U.S. and Britain fight the War of 1812 over a number of issues, including British meddling with the former colonies, interference with American trade, and clashes over land ownership. The war ends with the *Treaty of Ghent*.

1814 - Francis Scott Key writes *The Star Spangled Banner* during the Battle of New Orleans in the War of 1812.

1819 - The U.S. takes control of Florida from Spain.

1820 - The *Missouri Compromise* settles a slavery dispute by banning slavery west of the Mississippi River and north of the 36°30' parallel, except in Mississippi.

1823 - The *Monroe Doctrine* warns Europeans against interference in Western Hemisphere affairs.

1830 - The first steam-driven locomotive, the *Tom Thumb*, is built by Peter Cooper.

1830 - The *Removal Act* provides money to carry out President Jackson's policy of moving Indians from their lands.

1830s - Abolitionists speak out against slavery. William Lloyd Garrison and other abolitionists form the National Antislavery Society.

1834 - The National Trades Union is established as the first national union.

1834 - Cyrus McCormick patents the reaper.

1835 - Samuel Morse invents the telegraph.

1835-1836 - Texas fights and wins a war of independence from Mexico.

1838 - As a part of the government's Indian Removal Policy, the Cherokee Indians move from Georgia to Oklahoma. Thousands die of cold and disease on the long journey, called the *Trail of Tears*.

1840s – The attitude of *manifest destiny* takes hold in the country. This is the belief that the people of the U.S. should spread across (and control) the whole continent.

1841 – The first wagon train bound for California departs from Independence, Missouri, on May 1.

1842 – The Oregon Trail opens the way for more settlement of the west. In 1843, a large group makes the 5-month trip along the trail to the Wilamette Valley in Oregon.

1846-1848 – The annexation of Texas as a state (in 1845) leads to war with Mexico. As a result of the U.S. victory in the Mexican War, new U.S. territory is gained in the west.

1848 – Elizabeth Cady Stanton organizes a Women's Rights Convention in Seneca Falls New York. The convention produces *The Seneca Falls Declaration*, listing grievances of women.

1848-1869 – Gold is discovered in California. Over 80,000 people rush to California to find gold; the people are called the *Forty-Niners*.

1850s-1900 – The Industrial Revolution is at its height with the growth of invention, manufacturing, railroads, corporations, steel production, mass production, technology, communication, department stores, entrepreneurship, specialization in factories, and unionization of workers.

1850-1900 – The U.S. begins a period of expansionism, extending its influence and control into areas such as the Midway Islands in the Pacific, Japan, Hawaii, Alaska, and Latin America.

1850 – *The Compromise of 1850* temporarily ends a national crisis over the issue of slavery by banning slavery in some areas and allowing it in others.

1852 – *Uncle Tom's Cabin*, a novel about the injustices of slavery, is published by Harriet Beecher Stowe.

1854 – The *Kansas-Nebraska Act*, which allows for slavery to spread into new western territories, leads to fierce debate and turmoil over the issue of slavery.

1857 – In the case of *Dred Scott v. Sandford*, the Supreme Court rules that a slave cannot sue for his freedom because he has no rights.

1860-1890 – Settlers and the U.S. government battle Native American populations for control of western land, particularly in the Great Plains. The series of clashes ends with large numbers of Native Americans dead and most of the rest relocated to reservations.

1860 – Abraham Lincoln is elected President.

1860 – South Carolina is the first state to secede from the Union.

1860-1861 – South Carolina, Florida, Mississippi, Alabama, Georgia, Texas, Louisiana, Arkansas, North Carolina, Virginia, and Tennessee secede from the Union, forming the Confederacy.

1861-1865 – The Civil War begins when the Confederates fire on Fort Sumter, South Carolina. The war is fought between the Confederacy and the Union, resulting in over 600,000 people dead or wounded.

1850 Pamphleteer
Frederick Douglas To Speak Tonight
Abolitionist Addresses Slavery Issues

The Monitor 1852
H. Beecher Stowe's Novel Exposes Slavery Injustices!

1857
Highest Court Rules Against Dred Scott

1862 - The *Homestead Act* gives land to any settler who farms it for five years. This leads to an increase in movement to the Great Plains and western U.S.

1863 - President Lincoln issues the *Emancipation Proclamation*, declaring freedom for all slaves in Confederate-held territory.

1863 - In the bloody Battle of Gettysburg, the Confederate and Union forces fight on northern soil. Thousands of soldiers are killed and wounded before the Confederates retreat. After the battle, President Lincoln delivers the *Gettysburg Address*.

1865 - Confederate General Robert E. Lee surrenders to Union General Ulysses S. Grant at Appomattox Court House in Virginia, ending the Civil War.

1865 - President Abraham Lincoln is assassinated by John Wilkes Booth at Ford's Theater in Washington, D.C.

1865 - The *13th Amendment* outlaws slavery throughout the U.S..

1865-1867 - A period of Reconstruction follows the Civil War. Congress passes legislation and amendments giving black Americans rights and protections of law.

1866 - The *Civil Rights Act*, passed over the veto of President Andrew Johnson, makes black people citizens of the U.S..

1866 - The Ku Klux Klan is formed secretly. By 1867, there are units of the Klan in every southern state.

1867 - The U.S. buys Alaska from Russia.

1868 - The House of Representatives impeaches President Andrew Johnson for removing the Secretary of War without Senate approval. There are not enough votes in the Senate to remove him from office.

1868 - The *14th Amendment* guarantees equal protection of laws to all Americans.

1869 - The Transcontinental Railroad is completed.

1869 - The Knights of Labor union is founded in Philadelphia, becoming one of the first powerful labor unions in the U.S.

1870 - The *15th Amendment* gives black males the right to vote.

1872 - Congress establishes Yellowstone as the first national park.

1875 - Congress passes the *Civil Rights Act of 1875*, guaranteeing citizens of every race access to public places.

1876 - At the Battle of Little Bighorn, Sioux Indian Chief Sitting Bull is victorious over U.S. military officer, General Custer.

1876 - Alexander Graham Bell invents the telephone.

1881-1889 - States pass Jim Crow laws (laws that promote segregation in states).

1884 - Construction of the world's first skyscraper begins in Chicago.

1886 - The American Federation of Labor is founded. This becomes one of the most powerful labor unions in U.S. history.

1887 - Congress passes the *Interstate Commerce Act*, one of the first laws to regulate business.

Pioneer Gazette------------------1862

Homesteaders Stampede Across the Prairie

1865
The Daily Telegraph
Civil Wars Ends!
General Robert E. Lee Surrenders
Slavery Outlawed

Get Sharp: U.S History

1890 - The Battle of Wounded Knee, the last major battle between U.S. troops and Indians, is fought in South Dakota.

1890 - Congress passes the *Sherman Antitrust Act*, banning monopolies.

1893-1896 - A depression leads to severe unemployment.

1896 - The Supreme Court hears the case of *Plessy v. Ferguson* and gives a decision that makes segregation legal, even in public schools.

1898 - The U. S. defeats Spain in the Spanish-American War, gaining control of Guam, Puerto Rico, and the Philippines.

1900-1915 - During this period known as the Progressive Era, many Americans work to improve society (protect workers, protect children, regulate businesses, check the growth of monopolies, encourage prosperous people to share their wealth, expose evils of factories and city slum conditions, and reform corrupt city governments).

1903 - The Wright Brothers make the first successful motor-powered airplane flight at Kitty Hawk, North Carolina.

1908 - Henry Ford begins mass production of the Model T car.

1909 - William Du Bois and several white liberals form the National Association for the Advancement of Colored People (NAACP) to stop lynching and speak out for the rights of black Americans.

1912 - The *Titanic* sinks on its maiden voyage across the Atlantic.

1913 - The *16th Amendment* allows the federal government to collect income taxes.

1914 - The Panama Canal is completed.

1914 - World War I begins in Europe.

1917 - The U.S. enters World War I, declaring war on Germany after the sinking of ships carrying Americans, in particular the 1915 sinking of the *Lusitania*.

1918 - World War I ends with the German surrender and signing of an armistice.

1919 - The *18th Amendment* prohibits the manufacture, sale, or transportation of intoxicating liquors. The amendment is repealed in 1933 by the *21st Amendment*.

1920s - The decade is known as the *Roaring Twenties* because of a surge in entertainment and recreation such as music and dancing, a boom in spectator sports, advances in motion pictures and radio, and the mass production of automobiles.

1920 - The *19th Amendment* gives all citizens, including women, the right to vote.

1920 - Proposed by U.S. President Woodrow Wilson, the League of Nations is formed as an organization for keeping peace among the world's nations.

1921 - In an isolationist mood, Congress passes the *Emergency Quota Act* to limit the number of immigrants by nationality.

1921 - The heightened fear of foreigners is demonstrated in the Sacco-Venzetti murder trial of two Italian immigrants. They are convicted and executed with little evidence against them and apparent prejudice on the part of the judge.

1924 - Congress passes another immigration quota law, the *National Origins Act*, to limit the number of immigrants that can enter the U.S..

1925 - The Scopes Trial in Dayton, Tennessee, upholds the right of a state to ban the teaching of Evolution in public schools.

1912 — Evening Post

Titanic Sinks!

The ship they called 'unsinkable' hits iceberg.

May 7, 1915
Transatlantic Telegraph

Lusitania Hit by Torpedo!

German Aggression Kills 1200

Who Said It?

Quotations from U.S. History

Get Sharp: U.S History

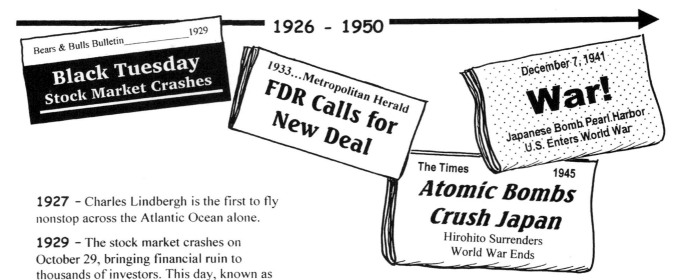

1926 - 1950

Bears & Bulls Bulletin _____ 1929

Black Tuesday
Stock Market Crashes

1933...Metropolitan Herald
FDR Calls for New Deal

December 7, 1941
War!
Japanese Bomb Pearl Harbor
U.S. Enters World War

The Times   1945
Atomic Bombs Crush Japan
Hirohito Surrenders
World War Ends

1927 – Charles Lindbergh is the first to fly nonstop across the Atlantic Ocean alone.

1929 – The stock market crashes on October 29, bringing financial ruin to thousands of investors. This day, known as *Black Tuesday*, sparks the Great Depression.

1930s – The U.S. suffers through the Great Depression.

1931 – The Empire State Building opens in New York City.

1933 – President Franklin D. Roosevelt begins the New Deal. President Roosevelt states the three aims of the New Deal: relief, recovery, and reform. He proposes legislation to end the depression, help people hurt by the depression, and stabilize the economy.

1935 – Congress passes the *National labor Relations Act*, guaranteeing the right of workers to organize and bargain collectively.

1937 – Aviator Amelia Earhart and her co-pilot Fred Noonan are lost somewhere in the Pacific on a flight around the world.

1939 – World War II begins in Europe with Hitler's invasion of Poland.

1941 – The U.S. enters World War II after Japan attacks the U.S. Naval Fleet at Pearl Harbor, Hawaii, on December 7.

1944 – The U.S. and Allied forces invade Europe at Normandy on D-Day, June 6.

1945 – The U.S. drops the first atomic bombs used in warfare on Hiroshima and Nagasaki, Japan.

1945 – Japan and Germany surrender, ending World War II.

1945 – The United Nations is formed as an organization to foster world peace.

1945 – At the Yalta Conference, the Big Three (President Roosevelt of the U.S., Winston Churchill of Britain, and Soviet dictator Joseph Stalin) meet to decide the fate of Europe after the war.

1945 – Tensions rise between communist and anticommunist ideologies after the war, (particularly between the U.S. and the Soviet Union). This period is called the *Cold War*.

1947 – President Truman announces the *Truman Doctrine*, pledging American aid to nations threatened by Communism.

1947 – The *Marshall Plan* offers to provide American money for European nations affected by the war.

1947 – Congress passes the *Labor Management Relations Act* (*Taft-Hartley Act of 1947*) restricting strikes that endanger the health, safety, or welfare of the nation.

1948 – The Soviets blockade roads leading to Berlin in an effort to force the Allies to give up their zones in the city. The U.S. and Allies respond with the *Berlin Airlift*, bringing supplies into West Berlin by plane.

1949 – The U.S. and several western European nations form the North Atlantic Treaty Organization (NATO). The purpose of the alliance is to protect each other in the event of Soviet attack.

1949-1950 – A number of Cold War events produce a widespread fear of Communism (called the *Red Scare*) within the U.S..

COURT REVIEW..................1954

SEGREGATION ENDS
Highest Court Rules that Segregated
Schools are Unconstitutional

1950 - Senator Joseph McCarthy of Wisconsin charges that the state department is full of traitors, setting off a "hunt for communists" known as *McCarthyism*.

1950s-1960s - The country sees a major population shift from cities to suburbs.

1950-53 - The U.S. supports South Korea against North Korean communist forces in the Korean War.

1954 - In the case known as *Brown v. Board of Education of Topeka*, the Supreme Court rules that school segregation is unconstitutional.

1955 - Rosa Parks, a black woman, is arrested for refusing to give up her seat on a city bus to a white man in Montgomery, Alabama. This sparks the year-long Montgomery Bus Boycott.

1955 - Martin Luther King, Jr. begins organizing a movement to protest discrimination against blacks.

1957 - The space race begins with the Soviet launch of the first satellite, *Sputnik I*.

1957 - The Governor of Arkansas calls out the National Guard to prevent the Little Rock schools from admitting black students to a white high school. President Eisenhower sends 10,000 soldiers to enforce the desegregation ruling of the Supreme Court.

1958 - *Explorer I*, the first U.S. satellite to go into orbit, is launched in Florida.

1960 - In the *U-2 Affair*, a U.S. plane spying over the Soviet Union is shot down.

1960 - John F. Kennedy becomes president.

1961 - The Berlin Wall is built to keep people from crossing out of Eastern Europe.

1961 - The *Bay of Pigs* invasion, a U.S.-backed plan by Cuban refugees to overthrow Fidel Castro fails miserably.

1961 - Astronaut Alan B. Shepard, Jr. becomes the first American in space.

1962 - In the *Cuban Missile Crisis*, President Kennedy demands that the Soviet Union remove missiles from Cuba. The standoff puts the world on the brink of nuclear war until the Soviets back down.

1962 - Cesar Chavez organizes the National Farm Workers Association to fight for improvement in working and living conditions for migrant workers.

1963 - President John F. Kennedy is assassinated on November 22; Lyndon Johnson becomes president.

1963 - Martin Luther King, Jr. leads a campaign against segregation in Alabama. The rough treatment of demonstrators by police sets off nationwide protest. Soon afterwards, 200,000 people demonstrate peacefully for civil rights in the March on Washington.

1963 - The publication of *The Feminine Mystique* by Betty Friedan, attracts wide-spread attention to the Women's Liberation Movement.

1964 - Congress passes the *Civil Rights Act of 1964* prohibiting racial discrimination in restaurants, hospitals, hotels, theaters, and all kinds of public facilities, and making it safer for southern blacks to register and vote. The act bans discrimination on the basis of gender as well as race.

1965 - American combat troops enter the Vietnam War.

Daily Tidings-----November 22, 1963

JFK SLAIN!
The nation is stunned when the 35th President is shot in Texas.

1966 - 1984

Chronicle 1969

Touchdown – Moon!
American Astronauts Walk on the Moon

Midwest Monitor 1970
Thousands Protest Vietnam War

1981 UPS
Hostages Freed After 444 Days
The Iranian hostages are finally freed just before the presidential inauguration.

1966 – Betty Friedan helps found the National Organization for Women (NOW).

1968 – Martin Luther King, Jr. is assassinated on April 4; Senator Robert F. Kennedy is assassinated on June 5.

1969 – Astronauts Neil Armstrong and Buzz Aldrin walk on the Moon.

1970 – National Guard Troops kill 4 students during a war protest at Kent State University in Ohio. State police at Jackson State kill 2 students during student protests.

1971 – The *26th Amendment* lowers the voting age to 18.

1972 – In the Watergate Affair, members of the Republican Party are involved in a break-in to the campaign headquarters of the Democratic candidate for president.

1972 – Richard Nixon becomes the first U.S. president to visit Communist China.

1972 – Congress passes the *Equal Rights Amendment*, stating that equal rights cannot be denied to anyone because of gender. Opposition blocks its ratification.

1973 – Several suspects in the Watergate Affair are put on trial; most plead guilty.

1973 – American Indian Movement (AIM) members hold the town of Wounded Knee, South Dakota, in a protest that lasts several weeks.

1973 – The U.S. removes the last of its troops from Vietnam.

1973 – During the Yom Kippur War, Arab-controlled oil exporting countries (OPEC) ban oil shipments to the U.S., causing a shortage of petroleum products.

1973 – The Supreme Court hears a controversial case, *Roe v. Wade*, and decides that a woman has the right to have an abortion in the first 3 months of pregnancy.

1974 – Nixon becomes the first American president to resign from office after members of Congress take steps to impeach him over the Watergate Affair.

1975 – The Vietnam War ends with North Vietnam defeating and occupying South Vietnam. The country of Vietnam is united.

1976 – The U.S. celebrates its bicentennial.

1978 – President Jimmy Carter brings rival nations Israel and Egypt together and helps to form a peace agreement between the two countries (the *Camp David Accords*).

1979 – In Iran, a mob holds 53 Americans hostage for 444 days.

1981 – The Iran hostages are released.

1981 – Congress agrees to provide weapons to a counter-revolutionary group in Nicaragua (the Contras) who are seeking to overthrow the procommunist controlling party (the Sandinistas).

1981 – Sandra Day O'Connor is the first woman appointed to the Supreme Court.

1984 – Congress passes the *Boland Amendment*, banning aid to the Contras and other such counter-revolutionary groups. President Reagan plans a secret sale of American arms to Iran in hopes that hostages will be freed. The man who arranges the deal, Colonel Oliver North, uses the profits from the arms sale to supply aid to the Contras in Nicaragua, in violation of the *Boland Amendment*.

1986 - The U.S. space shuttle *Challenger* explodes, killing all 7 members of the crew.

1988 - The U.S. and the U.S.S.R. sign a treaty eliminating some nuclear missiles.

1989 - The Berlin Wall falls, signaling the end of the Cold War.

1990 - The *Americans with Disabilities Act* outlaws discrimination against the handicapped.

1991 - The U.S. allies attack Iraq, beginning the Persian Gulf War in response to Iraq's 1990 invasion of Kuwait.

1992 - Riots break out in Los Angeles following the acquittal of 4 white policemen whose beating of African American Rodney King was caught on videotape.

1993 - President Bill Clinton signs the *North American Free Trade Agreement* (NAFTA) to reduce trade barriers among the U.S., Canada, and Mexico.

1993 - Federal agents raid cult Branch Davidian headquarters in Waco, Texas; 70 cult members and 6 federal agents are killed in the raid.

1993 - The World Trade Center in New York City is bombed.

1993 - U.S. troops join a UN peacekeeping force in Bosnia.

1995 - A truck bomb kills 168 people in the Federal Building in Oklahoma City.

1995 - The U.S. reestablishes diplomatic relations with Vietnam.

1998 - The House of Representatives votes to impeach President Bill Clinton. Clinton is acquitted in 1999.

1998 - Terrorists bomb the U.S. Embassies in Tanzania and Kenya.

1999 - In Littleton, Colorado, 2 students kill 12 other students, 1 teacher, and themselves at Columbine High School.

World Events ——————————— 1989

The End of the Wall

The Berlin Wall comes down. Fifty years of Communist rule ends in East Germany

2000 - Elian Gonzales, a 6-year old Cuban boy whose mother died trying to get him into the U.S. illegally, returns to Cuba with his father after a federal raid removes him from the home of his Miami relatives.

2000 - George W. Bush is declared the winner of the contested presidential race after the Supreme Court stops the recounting.

2000 - 2 Russians and 1 American arrive at the new International Space Station.

2000 - Officials of the U.S. government and representatives of a private company announce that they have completed mapping the DNA sequence of the human genome.

2001 - On September 11, over 3000 people are killed in terrorist attacks on the Pentagon in Washington, D.C., and the World Trade Center in New York City.

2001 - Letters containing anthrax are sent to different government and media offices. Several people, including postal workers, die after handling the letters.

2002 - U.S. and Afghan troops launch Operation Anaconda—a war in Afghanistan aimed at ending the Taliban control and finding al Qaeda terrorists.

2002 - Under pressure from the U.S., the UN Security Council passes a resolution demanding that Iraq disarm or "face serious consequences."

September 11, 2001

Twin Towers Collapse

The World Watches in Horror as 3000 Lives Are Lost

Get Sharp: U.S History

The Last Word
In Famous Quotes

Wit has truth in it; wisecracking is simply calisthenics with words.

Dorothy Parker, humorist (1893-1967)

Our flag is red, white and blue, but our nation is a rainbow—red, yellow, brown, black and white—and we're all precious in God's sight.

Rev. Jesse Jackson, politician (1941-)

There is nothing to fear but fear itself.

Franklin D. Roosevelt, U.S. President (1882-1945)

Once I knew only darkness and stillness...my life was without past or future...but a little word from the fingers of another fell into my hand that clutched at emptiness and my heart leaped to the rapture of living.

Helen Keller, writer and educator (1880-1968)

Progress might have been all right once, but it has gone on too long.

Ogden Nash, humorist (1902-1971)

That's one small step for man, one giant leap for mankind.

Neil Armstrong, astronaut (1930-)

To die for an idea; it is unquestionably noble. But how much nobler it would be if men died for ideas that were true!

H. L. Mencken, writer (1880-1956)

The buck stops here.

Harry S. Truman, U.S. President (1884-1972)

If a free society cannot help the many who are poor, it cannot save the few who are rich.

John F. Kennedy, U.S. President (1917-1963)

Anyone who hates children and dogs can't be all bad.

W. C. Fields actor/comedian (1890-1946)

Those who dwell among the beauties and mysteries of the earth are never alone or weary of life.

Rachel Carson, environmentalist (1907-1964)

The income tax has made more liars out Americans than golf.

Will Rodgers, humorist (1879-1935)

A nickel ain't worth a dime anymore.

Yogi Berra, baseball player (1925-)

I'm not worried about the deficit. It's big enough to take care of itself.

Ronald Reagan, U.S. President (1911-)

Good thing we've still got politics in Texas—finest form of entertainment ever invented.

Molly Ivins, journalist (1944-)

Money doesn't talk, it swears.

Bob Dylan, song-writer/musician (1941-)

Sometimes I think we're alone in the universe; and sometimes I think we're not. In either case the idea is quite staggering.

Arthur C. Clark, science fiction writer (1917-)

All the good music has already been written by people with wigs and stuff.

Frank Zappa, musician (1940-1993)

United States Presidents

The song, **"Hail to the Chief,"** is used to announce the arrival of the U. S. President.

Number	President	Vice President	Party	Term
1st	George Washington	John Adams	None	1789–1797
2nd	John Adams	Thomas Jefferson	Federalist	1797–1801
3rd	Thomas Jefferson	Aaron Burr, George Clinton	Republican	1801–1809
4th	James Madison	George Clinton, Elbridge Gerry	Republican	1809–1817
5th	James Monroe	Daniel D. Tompkins	Republican	1817–1825
6th	John Quincy Adams	John C. Calhoun	Republican	1825–1829
7th	Andrew Jackson	John C. Calhoun, Martin Van Buren	Democratic	1829–1837
8th	Martin Van Buren	Richard M. Johnson	Democratic	1837–1841
9th	William Henry Harrison	John Tyler	Whig	
10th	John Tyler		Whig	1841–1845
11th	James K. Polk	George M. Dallas	Democratic	1845–1849
12th	Zachary Taylor	Millard Fillmore	Whig	1849–1850
13th	Millard Fillmore		Whig	1850–1853
14th	Franklin Pierce	William R. King	Democratic	1853–1857
15th	James Buchanan	John C. Breckenridge	Democratic	1857–1861
16th	Abraham Lincoln	Hannibal Hamlin, Andrew Johnson	Republican	1861–1865
17th	Andrew Johnson		Republican	1865–1869
18th	Ulysses S. Grant	Schuyler Colfax, Henry Wilson	Republican	1869–1877
19th	Rutherford B. Hayes	William A. Wheeler	Republican	1877–1881
20th	James A. Garfield	Chester A. Arthur	Republican	1881
21st	Chester A. Arthur		Republican	1881–1885
22nd	Grover Cleveland	Thomas A. Hendricks	Democratic	1885–1889
23rd	Benjamin Harrison	Levi P. Morton	Republican	1889–1893
24th	Grover Cleveland	Adlai E. Stevenson	Democratic	1893–1897
25th	William McKinley	Garret A. Hobart	Republican	1897–1901
26th	Theodore Roosevelt	Charles W. Fairbanks	Republican	1901–1909
27th	William H. Taft	James S. Sherman	Republican	1909–1913
28th	Woodrow Wilson	Thomas R. Marshall	Democratic	1913–1921
29th	Warren G. Harding	Calvin Coolidge	Republican	1921–1923
30th	Calvin Coolidge	Charles G. Dawes	Republican	1923–1929
31st	Herbert C. Hoover	Charles Curtis	Republican	1929–1933
32nd	Franklin D. Roosevelt	John Nance Garner, Henry A. Wallace, Harry S. Truman	Democratic	1933–1945
33rd	Harry S. Truman	Alben W. Barkley	Democratic	1945–1953
34th	Dwight D. Eisenhower	Richard M. Nixon	Republican	1953–1961
35th	John F. Kennedy	Lyndon B. Johnson	Democratic	1961–1963
36th	Lyndon B. Johnson	Hubert Humphrey	Democratic	1963–1969
37th	Richard M. Nixon	Spiro T. Agnew	Republican	1969–1974
38th	Gerald R. Ford	Nelson A. Rockefeller	Republican	1974–1977
39th	Jimmy Carter	Walter Mondale	Democratic	1977–1981
40th	Ronald Reagan	George Bush	Republican	1981–1989
41st	George Bush	J. Danforth Quayle	Republican	1989–1992
42nd	Bill Clinton	Albert Gore, Jr.	Democratic	1992–2001
43rd	George W. Bush	Richard B. Cheney	Republican	2001–

Better Grades & Higher Test Scores / SOCIAL STUDIES
Copyright ©2003 by Incentive Publications, Inc., Nashville, TN.

Get Sharp: U.S. History

Important Places & Spaces

Events in history can be labeled with dates to show **when** they happened. In addition to being set in time, events are set in places and spaces; they all happened **somewhere**. Refresh your knowledge about the locations of some of America's historical events.

Alabama – where the first shots of the Civil War were fired

Alaska – state bought from Russia for $7 million

Arizona – home state to the Navajo National Monument and preserved cliff dwellings of the Anasazi culture

Arkansas – home state to Maya Angelou, Bill Clinton, and Johnny Cash

California – site of a major gold discovery in 1848

Connecticut – home of the nation's oldest newspaper still being published, *The Hartford Courant*

Delaware – first state to join the union

Florida – site of St. Augustine, the oldest city in the U.S.

Georgia – home state to Martin Luther King, Jr.

Hawaii – site of the Japanese attack on Pearl Harbor (December 7, 1941)

Idaho – part of the Louisiana Purchase, explored by Lewis and Clark in 1805-1806

Illinois – state to see Lincoln's boyhood home and the country's tallest building (Sears Tower)

Indiana – site of many Indian uprisings, including battles at Fallen Timbers in 1794 and Tippecanoe in 1811

Iowa – home to Effigy Mounds National Monument, a prehistoric Indian Burial Site at Marquette

Kansas – state that earned the name *Bleeding Kansas* because of the pre-Civil War disputes over slavery

Kentucky – state caught in the middle in the Civil War, supplying soldiers to both sides

Visit Martha's Vineyard, Massachusetts, to ride on the oldest operating merry-go-round in the U.S. (built in 1876).

Louisiana –site of the Battle of New Orleans and magnificent Mardi Gras celebrations

Maine – site of the first naval action of the Revolutionary War

Maryland – site of a colony formed by Catholics for religious freedom

Massachusetts – home to Plymouth Rock and the Salem Witch Trials

Michigan – home to the Mackinaw Bridge and the Sault Ste. Marie locks and canals

Minnesota – state settled by fur traders and French explorers

Mississippi – one of the country's largest producers of cotton throughout its history

Missouri – starting point of the Oregon Trail and home to the Gateway Arch

Montana – state famous for The Little Bighorn Battlefield and Glacier National Park

Nebraska – home to William James Bryan, Willa Cather, Buffalo Bill Cody, and Dick Chen

Nevada – site of discovery of the Comstock Lode in 1869, the richest-known deposit of silver

New Hampshire – state whose delegates were the first to vote for the *Declaration of Independence*

New Jersey – site of Princeton, one of the oldest universities in the nation

> Visit Altoona, Pennsylvania, to ride **Leap the Dips**, the world's oldest operating roller coaster. Built in 1902, it's a national historic landmark.

New Mexico – state acquired by the U.S. in the Mexican War (1848) and by the Gadsen Purchase (1853)

New York – home to the Empire State Building and the Statue of Liberty

North Carolina – the site of pirate raids in its early days as a colony

North Dakota – home to the Garrison Dam, Theodore Roosevelt National Park, and the Badlands

Ohio – site of severe fighting with the Indians in the 1790s

Oklahoma – site of the 1995 bombing of the Federal Building in Oklahoma City

Oregon – the end of the Oregon Trail

Pennsylvania – where both the *Constitution* and the *Declaration of Independence* were written

Rhode Island – site of Dorr's Rebellion in 1842, protesting property requirements for voting

South Carolina – home to the first Confederate capital

South Dakota – place to visit Mt. Rushmore, the Crazy Horse Monument, and the site of the Battle at Wounded Knee

Tennessee – site of extensive federal reservoirs on the Tennessee River, built to bring affordable electricity to citizens

Texas – place to remember the Alamo

Utah – where the last spike was hammered into the Transcontinental Railroad

Vermont – state where Ethan Allen and the Green Mountain Boys captured Ft. Ticonderoga from the British in 1775

Virginia – George Washington's home state

Washington – site of the most recent major volcanic eruption (Mt. St. Helen's)

West Virginia – state that split off from Virginia when 40 delegates disputed the secession from the union

Wisconsin – the first state to enact an unemployment compensation act (1932)

Wyoming – home to the nation's first national park, Yellowstone

Important Documents

The Declaration of Independence

By 1776, the colonists in America had given up hope of persuading England to treat them more fairly, and many Americans had been killed fighting the British on American soil. The Continental Congress met to draft a document explaining why independence was necessary. The document, mostly written by Thomas Jefferson, was called the *Declaration of Independence*. Congress officially approved it on July 4, 1776.

Get Sharp Tip # 14

Not all Americans supported the *Declaration of Independence*. Loyalists to England (*Tories*) believed that those in favor of it were traitors.

When, in the Course of human events, it becomes necessary for one people to dissolve the political bands which have connected them with another, and to assume, among the powers of the earth, the separate and equal station to which the laws of nature and of nature's God entitle them, a decent respect to the opinions of mankind requires that they should declare the causes which impel them to the separation.

We hold these truths to be self-evident, that all men are created equal, that they are endowed by their Creator with certain unalienable Rights, that among these are Life, Liberty, and the pursuit of Happiness.

That, to secure these rights, Governments are instituted among Men, deriving their just powers from the consent of the governed.

That, whenever any Form of Government becomes destructive of these ends, it is the Right of the People to alter or to abolish it, and to institute new Government, laying its foundation on such principles, and organizing its powers in such form, as to them shall seem most likely to effect their Safety and Happiness.

The Main Points of the Declaration of Independence . . .

- All people are born with certain rights, including life, liberty, and the pursuit of happiness.
- Governments are formed to protect these rights.
- When a government does not protect these rights, it is the right of the people to end or change the government.
- The colonists have been patient a long time with the unfair treatment, taxes, and insults of the British king and government.
- The British government has not been willing to listen or adjust to the complaints of the colonists.
- The people of the colonies claim their independence from Britain and their right to set up a separate state.

The Articles of Confederation

The first government of the United States was called a ***confederation***. It consisted of the first thirteen states. After the Revolutionary War, the new government had the tasks of turning the colonies into states and joining the states under one central government. The first constitutional document, written in 1777, was called *The Articles of Confederation*. This document put into writing the processes and powers the Continental Congress was already using. It gave each state one vote, required laws to be approved by at least nine of the thirteen states, and gave the national government several powers (to declare war and make peace, to make and borrow money, to operate post offices, and to make foreign policy). It did not give the national government power to levy taxes, to form armies, to enforce laws, or to establish a court system.

The Constitution

Problems that developed in the early years of the new nation brought many leaders to believe that the United States needed a stronger central government in order to maintain better order, gain more unity, and increase prosperity. In May of 1787, delegates from every state except Rhode Island met in Philadelphia to write a new constitution. The meeting became known as the Constitutional Convention. The *Constitution* was ratified in 1788 and went into effect in 1789. With this change, the thirteen states truly became one nation.

The Preamble is a short statement beginning the *Constitution*, stating clearly the intention to be a unified nation.

The beginning words, "We the people . . ." rather than, "We the states . . .", showed a change from power in individual states to a stronger power for the nation.

We the people of the United States, in Order to form a more perfect Union, establish Justice, insure domestic Tranquility, provide for the common defense, promote the general Welfare, and secure the Blessings of Liberty to ourselves and our Posterity, do ordain and establish this Constitution for the United States of America.

The Articles describe the structure and procedure of the government. The articles establish a government with *three branches*. They also establish a system of *checks and balances*. The powers of each branch can be controlled by the other two branches. The Articles also describe the processes for ratifying and amending the *Constitution*. There are seven articles.

Article I   The Legislative Branch *(creates the two houses of Congress and describes their powers and functions)*
Article II   The Executive Branch *(creates the office of the President and the Electoral process)*
Article III   The Judicial Branch *(creates the Supreme Court and process for lower courts, and defines the courts' power)*
Article IV   Relations Among States *(describes the states' powers and the relationship between states)*
Article V   Amending the Constitution *(describes how the Constitution can be changed)*
Article VI   Role of the National Government *(makes the Constitution the supreme law over state laws)*
Article VII   Ratification *(describes the process for approving the Constitution)*

The amendments are changes or additions to the Constitution, added after the *Constitution* was ratified. The first ten amendments are known as the *Bill of Rights*. Twenty-seven amendments have been added between 1791 and the present.

The Bill of Rights

The first ten amendments were added to the *Constitution* because the people demanded them. Many people in the new country feared that the central government would have too much power. The people wanted safeguards to assure their rights and liberties. These amendments, which guarantee basic liberties, are known as the *Bill of Rights*. It was ratified in 1971, three years after the *Constitution*.

Some Other Amendments

Get Sharp Tip # 15

In order to pass, an amendment must be approved by a two-thirds majority in the House of Representatives and in the Senate. After that, the amendment must be approved by three-fourths (38) of the states.

The **13th** Amendment prohibits slavery in the United States.

The **14th** Amendment guarantees equal protection of the law for all citizens, and guarantees that the *Bill of Rights* protects citizens' rights against actions taken by a state.

The **15th** Amendment guarantees that no person (including me) can be denied the right to vote because of race or color.

The **16th** Amendment gives the federal government the power to collect tax on my income.

The **17th** Amendment says that any state I live in will be represented in the Senate by two Senators.

The **19th** Amendment assures me and all other female citizens the right to vote.

The **25th** Amendment gives the president the power to appoint a new vice president if a vice president dies or leaves office in the middle of a term. The appointment must be approved by Congress.

The **26th** Amendment gives me— an 18-year old—the right to vote. (It lowers the voting age from 21 to 18.)

The **27th** Amendment says that any pay increases Congress members give themselves will not take effect until after the next election.

The **22nd** Amendment says that, if I am elected president, I can serve no more than two 4-year terms of office.

The **24th** Amendment makes it illegal for anyone to charge me a poll tax in a federal election.

Get Sharp: Historical Documents

The Legislative Branch

The chief responsibility of the legislative branch of the government is *to make laws for the country*. The legislative branch is also responsible to decide how money will be collected and spent. The legislative branch is made up of two groups, or houses: the House of Representatives and the Senate. The members of the two houses meet in different chambers on opposite sides of the Capitol Building. In order to pass, a law must receive a majority of votes in each of the two houses of Congress.

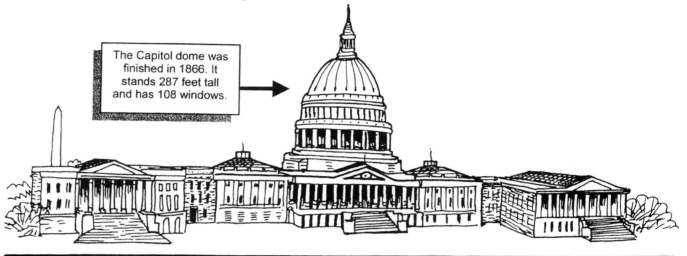

The Capitol dome was finished in 1866. It stands 287 feet tall and has 108 windows.

General powers of Congress:

- decide on all federal laws
- provide for the common defense and general welfare of the United States
- make all laws which shall be "necessary and proper" for carrying out other duties given to Congress
- impose and collect taxes and duties
- borrow money
- regulate trade among states and with foreign nations
- coin and print money
- establish post offices
- declare war
- raise armed forces
- control funds for use by armed forces

The Capitol building was built in 1793. Since then it has been burned, rebuilt, expanded, and restored.

Limits on the power of the legislative branch:

- The President can veto a bill passed by the Congress.
- The court system can decide that a law passed by Congress is unconstitutional.
- Supreme Court Justices are appointed for life. Congress cannot remove any of them.

What if

someone thinks the president has committed a crime or is violating the oath of office? *Impeachment* means charging an official with serious crimes in order to remove him or her from office. The House of Representatives is the only government body that can vote to impeach an official. Once someone is impeached, the Senate acts as a jury for trying the case. The chief justice of the Supreme Court acts as the judge. A vote of two-thirds of the members of the Senate is needed for impeachment.

The House of Representatives

The House of Representatives is the largest house of Congress. The number of representatives each state sends to the House of Representatives depends on the population of the state; each state has at least one. There are currently 435 members in the House of Representatives.

Requirements for a Representative:
- must be 25 years or older
- must be a U.S. citizen
- must be a resident of the state he or she is representing

> The first Chinese congressman was David Wu, elected to the House of Representatives in 1998.

Representative's term:
- 2-year term; no limit on number of terms

> Joseph Rainey, elected to the House of Representatives in 1879, was the first African-American congressman.

Presiding officer in House of Representatives:
- the Speaker of the House, selected by the members of the House, usually a member of the majority party

Duties and powers of the House of Representatives:
- vote on laws
- begin impeachment proceedings on government officials

The Senate

The Senate has two members from each state, with a total of 100 members.

> The first Hispanic U.S. Senator, Octavio Larrazolo, was elected in 1928.

Requirements for a Senator:
- must be 30 years or older
- must be a U.S. citizen
- must reside in the state he or she is representing

> In 1931, Hattie W. Caraway was the first woman appointed to the U.S. Senate.

Senator's term:
- 6-year term; no limit on number of terms

Presiding officer in the Senate:
- the Vice president of the United States
(The Vice President can vote only if there is a tie between the senators.)

Duties and powers of the Senate:
- vote on laws
- approve people the president appoints for jobs such as federal judges, Supreme Court justices, cabinet members, and ambassadors
- approve all treaties *(by a two-thirds vote)*
- act as jury in the impeachment process

207

How a Bill Becomes a Law

Step 1: A member of Congress proposes a law. This proposal is called a *bill*. The person who proposes it is the *sponsor*.

Step 2: The bill is introduced into both houses of Congress.

Step 3: The bill is sent to committees for discussion. Both houses of Congress have several committees, each specializing in a particular area of government.

Step 4: Committees in each house of Congress discuss the bill and change it if they wish.

Step 5: The committees vote on the bill.

Step 6: If the committee has approved a bill, it goes to the full House of Representatives or Senate for debate and vote.

Step 7: The bill is debated in both houses of Congress. A majority in both houses of Congress passes the bill.

Step 8: If the House and Senate pass different versions of the same bill, members of the two houses meet in a conference committee to try to agree on one version.

Step 9: The bill, with final changes, goes back to the houses for a vote.

Step 10: If both houses pass the bill, it is sent to the president.

Step 11: If the president signs the bill, it becomes law.

Step 12: The president can *veto* the bill. The vetoed bill does not pass.

Step 13: Members of both houses of Congress may vote on the bill again. If two-thirds of the votes in both houses are in favor of the bill, it can *override* the president's veto.

Step 14: The bill then becomes law without the president's signature.

I want my congressman to sponsor a bill naming pizza as the national food.

Powers & Limits on Power

The *Constitution* grants many important powers to the Congress (such as the power to coin money, declare war, and fund armed forces). The *Constitution* also says that there are some things Congress cannot do.

- Congress may not take away a person's right of *Habeas Corpus*. This is the right of a person charged with a crime to be seen and heard in a courtroom by a judge (except in cases of rebellion or invasion).
- Congress may not pass *bills of attainder*. This is a law that convicts a person of a crime and punishes them without a trial.
- Congress may not pass *ex post facto laws*. These are laws that punish someone for a crime that was not a crime when the person did it.
- Congress cannot tax products from a state.
- Congress cannot spend money without passing a law.
- Congress cannot issue titles of nobility.

Officer, you can't arrest me. *Ex post facto!* When I tied my alligator to the fire hydrant last week, it wasn't against the law. That law just passed yesterday.

I wonder why my congressman won't return my calls. I only asked him to make me a knight.

Enumerated powers are powers that are specifically given to Congress by the *Constitution*.

Implied powers are general powers that are stated in the *Constitution* but are not clearly outlined.

Inherent powers are unlisted powers that Congress must have simply because it is a government and needs to run its affairs smoothly.

Delegated powers are powers specifically given to the federal government (such as the power to declare war).

Concurrent powers are powers that are shared by the federal and state governments (such as the power to levy taxes).

Reserved powers are powers that are only held by the states (such as the power to create school systems).

It's illegal to push a moose out of a moving airplane in Alaska.

Was this law passed in the interest of public safety— or was it for the safety of the moose?

Some powers reserved for the states:

- establish public schools
- conduct of elections
- maintain public schools
- make marriage laws
- establish local governments
- creation of corporation laws
- regulate business within the state
- provide for public safety
- assume other powers not delegated to the federal government or prohibited to the states

---

209

The Executive Branch

The chief responsibility of the executive branch is *to enforce laws*. The president heads the executive branch of the federal government. This branch also includes the vice president, the staffs of the president and vice president, and several departments and agencies. The cabinet is made up of the heads of major departments. The president and vice president and many of their staff members work in the White House. The president and family also live in the White House.

> The White House was completed in 1880. The first president to move in was John Adams.

> There are 6 floors, 132 rooms, 412 doors, 147 windows, 35 bathrooms, 8 staircases, and 3 elevators in the White House.

What if

a president dies in office, or is not able to complete a term? The vice president becomes president. This might be temporary if the president is able to take over the job again. After the vice president, the next person in line for the presidency is the Speaker of the House of Representatives.

Requirements for President:

- must be 35 years or older
- must be a natural-born U.S. citizen
- must be a U.S. resident for at least 14 years

President's term:

- A limit of two 4-year terms

President's duties:

- **Commander-in-Chief of the armed forces**
  acts as top military person
  makes decisions regarding the use of armed forces
  can call the National Guard from individual states

- **Chief Executive**
  chooses people to head up departments that run the government
  oversees the operations of the government
  appoints judges and ambassadors

- **Chief of State**
  takes charge of foreign relations
  represents the U.S. to foreign nations
  hosts foreign dignitaries visiting the U.S.
  makes treaties with foreign governments

- **Chief Legislator**
  can suggest laws to Congress
  can veto laws passed by Congress

- **Chief of the Party**
  leads his/her own political party

Limits on the powers of the Executive branch:

- Congress can override a presidential veto.
- Congress must approve funds for armed services.
- Congress is the only body that can declare war.
- The Senate must confirm presidential appointments.
- The Senate must approve treaties with foreign governments.
- The House of Representatives can impeach the president or vice president.

The Cabinet

The *cabinet* is a group of people that advise the president. It is made up of the vice president, heads of departments, and other top officials. The heads of most cabinet departments have the title of *secretary* of their department.

State (foreign affairs)	**Labor** (workers, working conditions)	**Homeland Security** (protection against terrorism)
Treasury (money, taxes)	**Transportation** (roads, transportation systems)	
Education (public schools)	**Energy** (research on energy, energy use)	
Defense (armed forces)	**Veterans Affairs** (services for war veterans)	
Commerce (business, trade)	**Justice** (court system, legal issues)	
Agriculture (farming)	**Health and Human Services** (health, welfare)	
Interior (U.S. lands)	**Housing and Urban Development** (housing, cities)	

The Department of Homeland Security is the most recent addition to the president's cabinet. It was approved by Congress in 2003.

Cabinet Departments

Agencies and Organizations

Over two hundred different agencies or organizations make up the executive branch. Here are a few of the many agencies that administer programs which touch many areas of American life.

NASA *(National Aeronautic Space Administration)* – oversees space research

IRS *(Internal Revenue Service)* – collects taxes

FBI *(Federal Bureau of Investigation)* – investigates crimes against U.S. government

CIA *(Central Intelligence Agency)* – gathers clues about international crimes

FTC *(Federal Trade Commission)* – regulates trade and commerce

FHA *(Federal Highway Administration)* – plans and builds interstate highways

BIA *(Bureau of Indian Affairs)* – oversees matters to do with Native Americans

BLM *(Bureau of Land Management)* – manages national lands

FDA *(Food and Drug Administration)* – regulates quality and safety of food and drugs

FAA *(Federal Aviation Administration)* – ensures safety in air travel and at airports

DEQ *(Department of Environmental Quality)* – oversees environmental clean-up

INS *(Immigration and Naturalization Service)* – oversees immigrants and those who become citizens

The Judicial Branch

The chief responsibility of the judicial branch is to *interpret the laws*. The Supreme Court is the highest and most important court in the country. A decision of the Supreme Court is final. (This means that the decision cannot be appealed to any other court.) The nine justices of the Supreme Court are appointed by the president and confirmed by the Senate. The Supreme Court meets in the Supreme Court Building. In addition to the Supreme Court, there are 91 District Courts, 12 Courts of Appeal, the Court of Military Appeals, the United States Claims Court, and the United States Tax Court that are all parts of the federal judicial system.

Supreme Court Justice's term:
- appointed for life

Presiding officer in the Supreme Court:
- the Chief Justice (one of the nine justices)

Duties of the Chief Justice:
- preside over all meetings of the Supreme Court
- act as judge in impeachment proceedings

Duties and powers of the Supreme Court:
- review and decide cases involving federal law
- review and decide cases involving treaties of the U.S.
- review and decide cases that involve actions of presidents
- review and decide the constitutionality of state laws

Limits on the power of the Supreme Court:
- Congress can make new laws after a law is found unconstitutional.
- Justices must be appointed by the executive branch.
- Justices must be confirmed by the Senate.
- The House of Representatives can impeach a Supreme Court Justice.

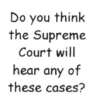

JUDGE KNOT

Do you think the Supreme Court will hear any of these cases?

- • I was arrested in Baltimore for taking a lion to a movie. I didn't know that was illegal.
- • How was I supposed to know it's against the law in Tennessee to sell hollow logs?
- • How surprising to get a ticket in Hartford, Connecticut, for walking across the street on my hands!
- • I took my French poodle to the opera in Chicago, and now I have to pay a fine.
- • In Vermont, it's against the law to whistle under water. I didn't see the sign.
- • In Florida, an unmarried woman can be arrested for parachuting on Sunday. Will I go to jail?
- • Was I supposed to know that it's against the law to tease a skunk in Minnesota?

Historic Supreme Court Decisions

Some court decisions stand out in history because of their impact on the society. These are a few of the better-known cases that have come before the Supreme Court.

Marbury v. Madison (1803) – This ruling stated that the Supreme Court can overrule a law of Congress. It was the first time the court struck down an act of Congress.

Dred Scott v. Sandford (1857) – The Supreme Court ruled that, whether slave or free, an African-American person had no right to bring a lawsuit.

Plessy v. Ferguson (1896) – The Supreme Court declared that requiring African Americans to ride in separate railroad cars did not deprive black people of their rights under the 14th amendment, so long as the facilities were equal. This was called the "separate but equal" ruling.

Brown v. the Board of Education of Topeka (1954) – The Supreme Court ruled that school segregation is unconstitutional. This overturned the previous Supreme Court decision of *Plessy v. Ferguson*.

Engel v. Vitale (1962) – This case ended with a Supreme Court decision to forbid prayer in public schools.

Miranda v. Arizona (1966) – The Supreme Court ruled that anyone arrested must be read a statement of their rights before being questioned, or their statements can't be used as evidence against them. These rights have come to be known as *Miranda rights*.

In the 1969 case of *Tinker v. Des Moines School District*, high school students who wore black armbands to school to protest American participation in the Vietnam War had been suspended from school. The court overturned the suspension, declaring that students cannot be asked to leave their constitutional rights to freedom of speech or expression at the door of the school.

Roe v. Wade (1973) – This ruling by the Supreme Court protects a woman's right to end a pregnancy with an abortion.

U.S. v. Nixon (1974) – The Supreme Court ruled that executive privilege for the president has limits. President Nixon was ordered to turn over tapes of personal conversations as evidence in the Watergate investigation.

Board of Education v. Pico (1982) – The Supreme Court ruled that a public school board couldn't ban a book from a school library because someone doesn't agree with the ideas in the book.

Texas v. Johnson (1989) – The Supreme Court ruled that a state government couldn't stop a person from a dissenting view or action because it finds it offensive. In this case, the offensive action was desecration (burning) of an American flag in Texas.

Bush v. Palm Beach County Canvassing Board – (2000) The Supreme Court refused to rule on issues related to the Florida recount of votes in the 2000 presidential election. This decision led to the victory of George W. Bush in the election.

Citizenship and Voting

The people, or citizens, are a powerful force in a representative democracy like the United States. In order for democracy to work, the citizens must participate. Voting is the one of the most important ways for a citizen to take part in the democratic process.

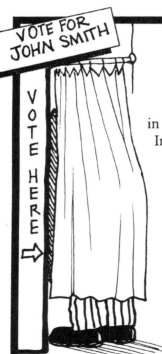

Get Sharp Tip # 17

A president can win the election without getting the majority of the popular vote. *This happened in 1876 (Hayes), 1888 (Harrison), and 2000 (Bush).*

Some things for good citizens to do:

Be informed! Learn about political issues, both in Washington, D.C., and in your own backyard. Pay attention to the news, ask questions, and read about things that affect your life. Find out what's going on in the world, the nation, your state, and your community. Think about your own views on the issues. Discuss them with friends and family members. Get to know about the elected officials who represent you in your city, county, state, and country.

Vote! It is the primary right of a citizen. A person cannot have a voice in the choices or operations of the city, state, or nation if he or she does not vote. Even if you are too young to vote, you can think about how you would vote on an issue or which candidates you would support.

Get involved! Volunteer for a community service or other organization that you think deserves help and attention. A good citizen gives something of herself or himself to make the country or local area a better place. When you become an adult, think about running for a public office. You can run for president, mayor, or a position in the U.S. Congress, state government, city council, school board, or many other government offices.

VOTE FOR JOHN SMITH

VOTE HERE ⇨

How a President is Elected

VOTE FOR JILL JONES

Every four years, American voters elect a president and vice president. This election is somewhat different from elections for other officials, in that the president and vice president are not chosen directly by the people. In the presidential election, the votes people cast actually choose electors. The president is then chosen by these electors (the Electoral College).

The **Electoral College** is a group of 538 members (called **electors**) that have been chosen by the states. Each state has a number of electors equal to its total number of U.S. senators and representatives. In December, after the election, the Electoral College members meet to cast their votes for the president. Usually, the party that got the most votes in the November election wins all the electoral votes for the state. In January, the votes are presented during a session of Congress. To win the presidential election, a candidate must get a majority (270) of the electoral votes. If no candidate wins a majority, the House of Representatives chooses the president. This happened in 1800 (with the election of Thomas Jefferson) and 1824 (with the election of John Quincy Adams).

VOTE FOR TIM GARCIA

VOTE FOR:

president
vice president
U.S. senators
U.S. representatives
state senators
state representatives
county commissioners
state district attorney
state school superintendent
mayor
city council members
school board members
parks commissioners
judges
sheriff

VOTE FOR:

class president
Homecoming Queen
best cafeteria food
best music album
favorite movie star
class mascot

Some things for good citizens to know:

- **A democracy** is a government that is governed by its people, all of whom have the same basic rights and freedoms.

- **A representative democracy** is a democracy in which the people vote for officials to represent them in certain government positions.

- **The *Constitution*** is the document that describes the structure of the government. It also assures and protects citizens' rights, including the right to vote.

- **Political parties** are organizations that put candidates forward for political offices.

- **The platform** of a political party is a statement of the party's policies and principles for voters to consider.

- **An election** is the process of voting to choose public officials.

- **A primary election** is an election held to choose candidates for the main election.

- **Candidates** are people who are running for political offices.

- **To register** is to officially sign up to vote. (Citizens must register before they can vote.)

- **A residency requirement** is a length of time that someone must live in a state before being able to vote there.

- **A ballot** is a list of candidates used by the voter to place his or her vote.

- **A voting district** is the place where a citizen lives and is registered to vote.

- **A polling place** is the location people go to vote in their district.

- **Absentee ballots** are votes mailed in by people who cannot be present at the polls on the election date.

- **The popular vote** is the number of votes cast by individual voters in a presidential election.

- **Electoral College votes** are votes cast in a presidential election by electors chosen by each state (See page 214).

- **The turnout** is the number or percentage of eligible voters who actually vote in an election.

- **An initiative** is an issue placed on the ballot for citizens to decide by vote.

- **A recall election** can be held to decide whether to remove an elected public official from office before the end of his or her term.

- **A recount** is a second counting of the ballots when the outcome of an election is very close.

- **A referendum** is a vote on a specific issue, such as a city's budget or a building project.

Symbols & Traditions

Red stands for hardiness and courage.

White stands for purity and innocence.

Blue stands for vigilance, perseverance, and justice.

The American Flag

The *Stars and Stripes* is the popular name for the red, white, and blue national flag of the United States. Francis Scott Key first called this flag the *Star-Spangled Banner* in 1814 when he wrote the poem that later became the national anthem. A Massachusetts sea captain, William Driver, gave the name *Old Glory* to the United States flag in 1824.

The flag represents the land, the people, the government, and the ideals of the United States. The seven red and six white stripes represent the thirteen original colonies. The stars represent the states. In 1777, Congress stated that the flag have thirteen stars. In 1795, Congress directed that the flag should have stars on a blue field and fifteen stripes. In 1818, Congress resolved that the flag have thirteen stripes and that a new star be added for each new state. Today, the flag has 50 stars.

I pledge allegiance to the flag of the United States of America and to the Republic for which it stands, one Nation under God, indivisible, with Liberty and Justice for all.

The pledge (to the flag) is a promise of allegiance to the United States. Francis Bellamy of Boston wrote the original pledge. Public school students fist recited it in 1892. In 1942, Congress made the pledge part of its code for use of the flag.

Flag Terms to Know:

badge – an emblem or design, usually on the fly

battle flag – carried by armed forces on land

bunting – cloth decorated with stripes of the national colors

canton – the upper corner of a flag where a special design appears

color – a special flag carried by a military unit or officer

field – the background color of a flag

fly – the free end of a flag, farthest from the staff

halyard – a rope used to hoist and lower a flag

national flag – the flag of a country

pennant – a triangular or tapering flag

staff – the pole on which the flag hangs

standard – a flag around which people rally

The Great Seal

The Continental Congress adopted the Great Seal in 1782 as a symbol of the nation. The eagle is a symbol of sovereignty. The eagle holds a ribbon in its mouth with the Latin words *e pluribus unum,* meaning *out of many, one.* The olive branch held by the eagle stands for peace, and the arrows stand for war. The constellation symbolizes the nation as a sovereign republic. The pyramid on the back of the seal represents strength. The eye on the pyramid represents the eye of Providence. The Great Seal is kept in the United States Department of State and its image is printed on many government documents.

The National Anthem

The national anthem of the United States comes from a poem called, "The Star Spangled Banner." The poet, Francis Scott Key, was inspired by the U.S. flag flying during a battle in the War of 1812. Mr. Key's poem was later set to music composed by John Stafford Smith. Congress officially approved the song as the national anthem in 1931. The song has four verses, but ordinarily, only the first verse is used.

> *O say, can you see, by the dawn's early light,*
> *What so proudly we hailed at the twilight's last gleaming?*
> *Whose broad stripes and bright stars, through the perilous fight,*
> *O'er the ramparts we watched, were so gallantly streaming!*
> *And the rockets' red glare, the bombs bursting in air,*
> *Gave proof through the night that our flag was still there:*
> *O say, does that star-spangled banner yet wave*
> *O'er the land of the free and the home of the brave?*

The Eagle

The United States chose the bald eagle as its national bird in 1782. The bald eagle has powerful wings, and its white head feathers give it the appearance of baldness. Its tail is also white.

The Liberty Bell

The Liberty Bell is a symbol of American independence. The bell was made in England in 1752 and sent to the State House in Philadelphia. It broke after its arrival and was recast. The bell was rung along with other church bells on July 8, 1776, to announce the adoption of the *Declaration of Independence.* The Liberty Bell was rung each year until 1835, when it cracked as it was ringing during the funeral of Chief Justice John Marshall. The bell is no longer rung. It is housed in Liberty Bell Pavilion, just north of Independence Hall in Philadelphia.

The Statue of Liberty

The Statue of Liberty is a 151-foot tall copper statue located in New York Harbor. It is a symbol of American liberty under a free form of government. France presented the monument to the United States in 1884 as a symbol of friendship, and in commemoration of the two countries' alliance during the American Revolution. The statue's title is "Liberty Enlightening the World." It has become a symbol of freedom for oppressed people everywhere.

217

Holidays

The United States Congress has established several federal holidays. They are holidays for Washington, D.C. and for federal offices and buildings, banks, and some schools. Each state decides on its own holidays. Many states honor several or all of the federal holidays.

Calendar of Federal Holidays	New Year's Day	Martin Luther King, Jr. Day
	(January 1st) In the U.S., the first day of the new year is commemorated. Most places of work are closed on this day.	(the third Monday in January) This holiday honors the January 15th, 1929, birthday of Martin Luther King, African-American Civil Rights Leader.
Presidents' Day (the third Monday in February) This day celebrates the birthdays of Presidents George Washington (February 22, 1732) and Abraham Lincoln (February 12, 1809).	**Memorial Day** (the last Monday of May) Also known as *Decoration Day*, this holiday honors men and women who died while serving their country in the military.	**Independence Day** (July 4th) This day is regularly celebrated as a day to honor and remember American independence and the events that made it possible. July 4th is the anniversary of the 1776 adoption of the *Declaration of Independence*.
Labor Day (the first Monday in September) This day honors America's workers with a day off work for many.	**Columbus Day** (the second Monday in October) This day is the anniversary of the day Christopher Columbus supposedly arrived in the Americas (October 12, 1492).	**Election Day** (the first Tuesday after the first Monday in November) Election day is a day for voting in federal elections.
Veterans Day (November 11) Also called *Armistice Day*, this holiday honors veterans who fought in wars. It celebrates the armistice that ended World War I (signed on November 11th, 1918).	**Thanksgiving** (the fourth Thursday in November) The Pilgrims celebrated the first Thanksgiving in 1621. It was, and still is, a day to give thanks for the harvest and for other blessings.	**Christmas** (December 25) This is a religious holiday of the Christian religion. It has also become a secular holiday.

Better Grades & Higher Test Scores / SOCIAL STUDIES
Copyright ©2003 by Incentive Publications, Inc., Nashville, TN.

GET SHARP →

on Economics

Money

Get Sharp Tip # 18

A medium of exchange can be anything that the group agrees has a certain value.

Bazaar

BIG DVD SALE Today Only!

I'm out of money, but I'll buy your DVD player for two camels.

Money is bills and coins, right? Not necessarily! Throughout history, many other things have been used as money around the world. People have exchanged things like shells, beans, stones, feathers, and even cows or camels for the goods and services they need or want. ***Money*** is a ***medium of exchange*** (anything that a society or group of people accepts in exchange for goods or services). ***Goods*** are things you want or need, such as clothing, food, toys, and vehicles. A ***service*** is work that someone does for you—such as fixing plumbing, serving food, giving haircuts, or providing medical care. Any kind of money used as a medium of exchange in a country is called the country's ***currency***.

Today, coins and paper bills serve as the medium of exchange for most countries. In 1792, the U.S. Congress established a money system using the ***dollar*** as the main unit of currency. In 1793, the government began minting coins. To ***mint*** a coin means to stamp it out of metal. A ***mint*** is also a place where coins are made.

Coins

Over thirteen billion coins are minted in the U.S. each year. All the coins are produced at two government mints: The U.S. Mint in Philadelphia and the U.S. Mint in Denver. At one time, there were also mints in San Francisco and New Orleans. The first coins minted in the U.S. were made of gold and silver, but coins are no longer made from these precious metals. Today's coins are made from nickel and copper alloys. Metal is melted and poured into bars called ***ingots***. After the ingots are flattened, the coin shapes are cut from the flat sheets. Machines then add edges and stamp designs on the coins.

Dimes and quarters are ***milled coins*** (coins with ridges around the edges). When coins were made of silver and gold, people would shave the edges off the coins and sell the scraps. The ridges were added to stop this practice.

Look for a tiny letter on any coin. This will tell you where the coin was minted.

P stands for Philadelphia.

D stands for Denver.

S stands for San Francisco.

O stands for New Orleans.

Every coin minted in the U.S. has two sayings on it. One saying is in Latin: *E Pluribus Unum*, which means, *Out of many, one.* The English saying is: *In God We Trust.*

Paper Money

The official unit of paper currency in the U.S. is the **dollar**. All the paper currency in the country is produced in Washington, D.C., at the Bureau of Engraving and Printing. Each bill is called a **Federal Reserve Note**, and is issued by one of the branches of the **Federal Reserve**, the government's bank. Dollars are made in several **denominations** (or specific values): one, five, ten, twenty, fifty, and hundred dollar bills are currently printed in the U.S.

Did you ever examine a real dollar closely? Look at all the information!

1. This mark tells which Federal Reserve Bank first issued the bill.

2. This number is the serial number, unique to this bill.

3. This is the date that the particular bill design was first used.

4. This is the signature of the U.S. Treasurer at the time the bill was printed.

5. The phrase *Annuit Coeptis* means, "He has favored our undertakings."

6. The phrase *Novus Ordo Seclorum* means, "new order of the ages."

7. This number shows the bill's denomination.

8. These show the two sides of the Great Seal of the United States.

Whose face is that?

$1	George Washington
$5	Abraham Lincoln
$10	Alexander Hamilton
$20	Andrew Jackson
$50	Ulysses S. Grant
$100	Benjamin Franklin

To discourage people from making counterfeit (fake) money, the government uses special tricks such as individual serial numbers, secret formula inks, color-shifting inks, watermarks, microprinting, and invisible fibers.

Paper money is not really paper. U.S. dollars are made from a blend of 25% cotton and 75% linen. These fabrics are stronger and last longer than paper.

Get Sharp: Money

Getting Money

People can get money in several ways. Money can be gained by earning interest on savings or investments. Some people inherit money; it is passed to them from a family. Some people get money from the government. Most people, however, get most of their money by doing some kind of work. Here are a few things to know about getting money.

- **Income** is money earned or received from someone else. It can be gained from working or from investments.

- **An employer** is a person who runs a business of some kind.

- **An employee** is a person who works for someone else.

- **A wage** is the amount of money someone is paid for doing a job. Wages are often paid at a certain rate per hour of work.

- **A minimum wage** is the lowest amount of money per hour that the laws of a state allow a worker to be paid.

- **A salary** is a fixed sum of money that an employer pays to an employee.

- **Benefits** are additional awards, other than pay, given to workers by an employer.

- **An investment** is the risk of money or time taken for the hope of getting something in return (such as a profit).

- **Interest** is money earned when a bank or other borrower pays someone for use of their money.

- **A dividend** is a share of a company's profits that is paid to stockholders.

- **A profit** is money made on an investment or money a business makes after all the expenses are paid.

- **Welfare** is income given by the government to some people who are not able to earn enough money to live.

Some ideas for making money by selling cheesecakes:

Chelsea's Cheesecakes

Sell to big stores.

Sell door-to-door.

Will I earn more in a year if I bake 500 cheesecakes in a month and sell them for $6 profit each, or if I work as a chef on a yearly salary of $31,000?

Depending, of course, on how many of the cheesecakes I eat myself.

Advertise in newspapers, radio and TV.

Donate free samples to charities.

Using Money

There are so many things to do with money once you have it! You have to decide whether to spend it or whether to save it. If you spend it, you must choose how, when, and where to spend. Here are a few things to know about using money.

- **A need** is something necessary for survival or a healthy life, such as food, clothing, or housing.

- **A want** is something that you would like to have but don't really need.

- **A consumer** is someone who uses or consumes goods and services. If you buy anything or pay for any services, you are a consumer. Consuming costs money.

- **A producer** is someone who makes goods or provides services. If you are a producer, you are hopefully earning money or making a profit. Usually a producer must spend some money in order to create a product or offer a service.

- **Advertising** is any method used to convince consumers to part with their money to buy something, invest, lend, or donate.

- **A donation** is a contribution of money, time, services, or goods that is given to a charity or other worthy cause.

- **Interest** is an amount of money paid to borrow money.

- **Disposable income** is money earned that is left over after the you've paid for necessities.

- **Saving** is holding on to money (not spending it), usually by putting it somewhere that it earns interest.

- **Investing** is risking some money for the possibility of making a profit.

- **A budget** is a plan for keeping track of all the money coming in going out.

- **A balanced budget** is a budget in which the money going out is equal to or less than the money taken in.

Where Does the Money Go?

housing
telephone
cellular phone
electricity and water
heating gas or oil
homeowner's insurance
food and clothing
car payments and insurance
education and school supplies
business expenses
medical care
health insurance
savings or investments
entertainment
travel and vacations
gifts and donations
child care
pet care

$200 a month for sugar!

$300 a month for eggs!

$1000 a month for cream!

HELP!

$250 a month for electricity!

Am I wrong, or does the money go out faster than it comes in?

223

Banking

A bank is a place that keeps money for people and businesses. It's a safe place to keep money that you are planning to use soon or money that you want to save for later. Your money doesn't just sit in the bank. Like any business, banks try to make a profit. They use their customers' money in many ways to bring in profit for the business.

Banking Know-How

To do business with a bank, I need to open some kind of an **account**. **A checking account** is a good place to keep money that I will need soon. I can take money out of it by writing a check. **A savings account** or **CD** (certificate of deposit) is a good place to put money that I don't need right away. The bank will pay me **interest** on the money in a savings account. My bank requires a **minimum balance** for some accounts. This is the least amount of money that must be kept in the account at all times.

Any business I do at a bank is called a **transaction**. Basically, there are two kinds of transactions: **Deposits** (putting money in the bank) and **withdrawals** (taking money out of the bank). **Debit** is another word used to describe the removal of money from my account. If I do these transactions at a bank, I go to a **teller** (the person who handles money at a bank window). I can also do transactions at an **ATM** (an Automatic Teller Machine). In order to use an ATM, I need a special card and a **PIN** (a Personal Identification Number. My bank also has a system for customers to do transactions over the telephone or the Internet.

When I **deposit** money, I fill out a **deposit slip** that tells the bank where I want to put my money. If I deposit a check that someone has written to me, I need to **endorse** it (sign my name) on the back of the check first. Sometimes it is possible to make a **direct deposit**. To do this, I arrange for my employer to send the money by **electronic transfer** directly to my account at the bank.

I can **withdraw** money in several ways. I can write a **check**. This is a written order that tells my bank to pay a specific amount of money to a person, a business, or myself. This money is removed from my account. I can also use a **debit card**. This is a bankcard that allows me to tell the bank to transfer funds electronically from my account and pay it to a business. I can also withdraw money with my ATM card, or I can go into the bank and take money out of my account after filling out a **withdrawal slip**. This slip tells the bank how much money I want to take out. Sometimes I do withdrawals over the telephone or Internet. In these cases I give permission for money to be taken directly from my checking account by electronic transfer.

Every month, my bank sends me a **bank statement** for each account. The statement is a monthly summary of all the transactions on the account. But I always keep my own records of the **balance** in my accounts. (The balance is the amount of money in the account.) I have a **register** for each account. This is a place to keep a record of my deposits, checks, or debits.

The bank keeps a considerable amount of cash on hand. Most of this is stored in a **vault** or safe for safekeeping. These are rooms with thick steel walls and doors and heavy locks.

I can purchase special checks from the bank. One kind of check is a **cashier's check**, where the money comes from the bank's account after I've given them the money. **Traveler's checks** are other special checks I can purchase. A traveler's check works just like money, but it can only be used with my signature. Use of traveler's checks is a safe way to carry money on a trip.

There are different kinds of **loans** available at my bank. A loan is sum of money that someone borrows for a certain amount of time. The bank offers **credit cards** to its customers, too. With a credit card, I can buy things now and pay for them later. The bank charges interest and other fees for this privilege of using a credit card.

I rent a **safe-deposit box** for a small fee at my bank. This is a box that is kept locked in the bank's vault. I keep valuable possessions such as important papers and jewelry in mine. Two keys are needed to open a safe-deposit box. I have one key and the banker keeps the other. The bank provides me with a room where I can have plenty of privacy to put things in or take things out of my safe-deposit box.

Checks and Balances

Charlie took his friends out to eat pizza and wrote a check for $30.

That restaurant sent his check back. They wanted the original $30 and another $25!

What's going on? Charlie's bank bounced his check because he didn't have enough money in his account to cover it. The restaurant got NO money from Charlie. They want the $30 and a penalty for their trouble.

I guess I've learned my lesson! If I'm going to write a check, I'd better make sure I have enough money in the bank to cover it, or I'll just go Dutch treat!

225

Credit

Credit is a way to get money when you don't have it. It's also a way to buy things without money at all. It's not exactly free, though. Having credit means someone is willing to lend you money and let you pay it back later, usually charging a fee or interest for the use of the money.

What's Happening Here?

Charlie has been given a **mortgage** (a loan given for a house or building). He put his house up for **collateral** against the loan. This means that if Charlie doesn't pay the loan, the bank will keep his house.

Charlie's bank has signed an agreement with Charlie that he can borrow up to $5000 from the bank whenever he needs money.

A bank has agreed to loan Charlie the money to buy a ski chalet, but they are holding the title to his house until the loan has been paid off.

Charlie has just arranged for a **line of credit**.

Charlie went to his bank and borrowed $6000 by giving only a credit history and his signature.

Charlie has been given an **unsecured loan**. This means he does not have to give the bank something valuable in return for the loan.

When Charlie gets his credit card bill, he sees that the bank is requiring him to pay at least $50 on the account.

The bank has set $50 as the **minimum payment** due on his credit card balance for this month.

Charlie paid $2000 to the car dealer for his new car. The car company will loan him the remaining $13,000 for 5 years at 6% interest. He'll pay about $250 a month.

Charlie made a **down payment** of $2000. He now has a **debt** of $13,000 to the car company. The $250 is a **monthly payment**. The 6% interest is the **finance charge** on his loan.

Wow! This is a lot of debt. I'll be paying a load of money in interest.

226

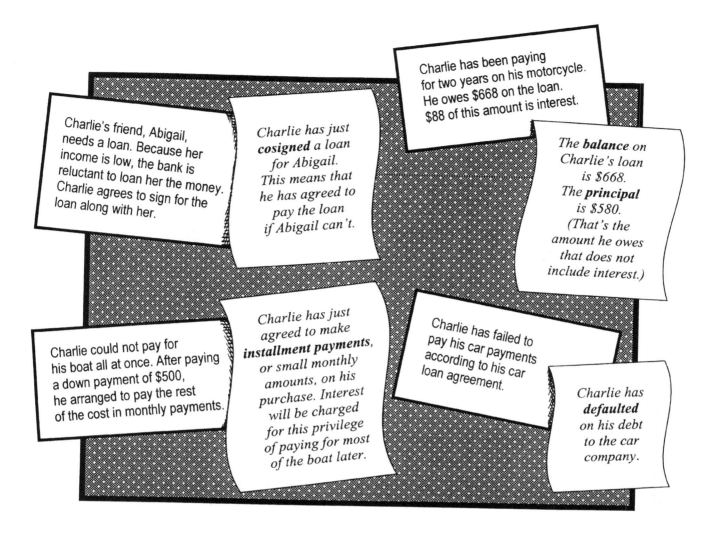

Charlie's friend, Abigail, needs a loan. Because her income is low, the bank is reluctant to loan her the money. Charlie agrees to sign for the loan along with her.

Charlie has just **cosigned** a loan for Abigail. This means that he has agreed to pay the loan if Abigail can't.

Charlie has been paying for two years on his motorcycle. He owes $668 on the loan. $88 of this amount is interest.

The **balance** on Charlie's loan is $668. The **principal** is $580. (That's the amount he owes that does not include interest.)

Charlie could not pay for his boat all at once. After paying a down payment of $500, he arranged to pay the rest of the cost in monthly payments.

Charlie has just agreed to make **installment payments**, or small monthly amounts, on his purchase. Interest will be charged for this privilege of paying for most of the boat later.

Charlie has failed to pay his car payments according to his car loan agreement.

Charlie has **defaulted** on his debt to the car company.

Hey, Sally. Can you believe it? My credit card was refused. The credit card company won't let me charge my ski trips any more. Why not?

Well, Charlie, I do believe that you have reached your **credit limit**. That's the total amount of money the bank thinks you will be able to pay back.

In that case, Sally, may I borrow $125?

Get Sharp Tip # 19
There is always a cost when you buy on credit. Watch out for interest— it adds up fast.

Making Choices

You can't have anything to do with money without making choices. Since most people do not have unlimited money, they have to choose when to say, "yes," or "no" to different purchases. They also have to choose between saving and spending. Even people with plenty of money must make choices about how to use it.

For every decision you make about earning, spending, saving, investing, or donating money, there is a **cost** or **consequence** (something you give up) and a **benefit** or **gain** (something you get). The costs and benefits might not always be financial.

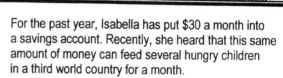

Isabella has been searching for a job so she can buy a car. She's been offered one job at a fast food restaurant for $8.00 an hour. The schedule is a hard; the job hours will take up every afternoon after school and all day Saturday. In this job, she is guaranteed steady work 20 hours a week for the next year. Her other offer is a house-sitting job. The pay is better ($10 an hour), and the schedule is more flexible. She would work about 50 hours a month over two weekends. The work is not very hard, and she could do her homework while she takes care of the house. There is no guarantee about how long the job will last.

The choice: Isabella chooses the house-sitting job.

The benefits of this choice:
• She can set her own schedule and choose which weekends to work.
• The job won't be as tiring.
• The job won't interfere with her schoolwork.

The consequences of this choice:
• She will earn less money.
• She will have to give up two whole weekends a month.
• She will work alone.
• The job has no guarantee of lasting.

For the past year, Isabella has put $30 a month into a savings account. Recently, she heard that this same amount of money can feed several hungry children in a third world country for a month.

The choice: Isabella decides to donate $30 a month to the agency that helps feed the children instead of saving that amount.

The benefits of this choice:
• She feels good about helping someone.
• This choice can help her to be more careful with the money she has left.

The consequences of this choice:
• She is not building her savings.
• She feels less secure with a smaller savings.

With ski season coming up, Isabella is excited about getting the latest style in a new ski outfit. She finds a great outfit for $180. It's the right color for the season, made of highly water-proof fabric, and the same style that her friends are buying. Then she sees another outfit on sale for half the price. It's last year's style and last year's color, and it's not rated quite as high for being waterproof, but it fits her perfectly and will keep her just as warm on the ski hill.

The choice: Isabella chooses the more expensive outfit.

The benefits of this choice:
• She will look as stylish as her friends on the ski hill.
• She gets an outfit that will probably keep her drier than the cheaper outfit.

The consequences of this choice:
• She misses the chance to save $90.
• She trades good money for something that will go out of style in a year anyway.

Everywhere you turn, there are powerful influences trying to convince you to spend, save, invest, or give away money. Although some influences are not very obvious, but there are plenty of people and things that affect your choices. These influences that encourage or pressure you to make one kind of choice are called **incentives**. Some incentives come from outside. Others come from inside yourself. There are **positive incentives** (incentives that cause you TO DO something with your money) and **negative incentives** (incentives that cause you NOT TO DO something with your money.

Grandpa Jake's car is in bad shape. It looks so bad that he's embarrassed to drive it. It gets him where he needs to go most of the time; but it is unreliable. He frequently needs to call a service to get it started. About once a month, he spends money to get it fixed. His neighbors all have newer, fancier cars. He keeps seeing advertisements showing senior citizens in luxury cars or SUVs. His wife does not want to spend the money, but he would like a new car. To get one, he'd have to get a bank loan, pay interest, and have high monthly payments. All these things worry him.

The positive incentives to keep his old car:
- His wife doesn't want him to borrow money.
- He won't have to borrow money.
- He won't have any car payments.

The negative incentives to keep his old car:
- Advertising leads him to think a new car will make him happier.
- The appearance of his old car leaves him feeling inferior to his friends.
- He thinks a new car might be safer.
- Worries about constant breakdowns and costly repairs leave him feeling insecure when he's driving.

Jake's grandson, Louie, has a great idea for a new business. He has perfected a new technology that makes strong, fast snowboards. He has done all the research and has a good business plan for manufacturing and selling the boards. He's found a great location for the shop, right in the area where a new ski and snowboarding hill is about to open. There is a large snowboarding club in the town, and the members are excited about the possibility of this new business. Louie wants Grandpa Jake to invest $20,000 to help in his business, in return for 30% of the profits. Louie's mother, Jake's daughter, is asking Grandpa to take a chance on this. Jake's wife thinks it's important for him to support his grandson. Jake's banker friend thinks it's a very big risk. Grandpa Jake does have that much money available, but he will have to take it out of his retirement fund.

The positive incentives for Grandpa to invest:
- The new ski hill, support from the local snowboarding club, and solid business plan are signs the business might succeed.
- Family members are pressuring him. It would make them happy if he agreed.
- The investment would encourage his grandson.
- There's a chance he could make a good profit on his money.

The negative incentives for Grandpa to invest:
- There are no guarantees that the new business will succeed.
- The friend who is knowledgeable about investments is encouraging him not to take the risk.
- Removing the money from his retirement fund will make his retirement income less secure.

Economically Speaking

What's the answer?

What is the economy?
It's the way the people in a society use resources and work together to produce the goods and services that they need and want.

What is profit?
It's the goal of most businesses—an amount of money earned that exceeds the expenses of running the business. Some businesses exist to provide a service, but do not intend to make a profit. A business that makes no profit is called a *non-profit business*.

What kinds of resources are used in an economy?
There are natural resources (such as land, water, minerals, and wood), human resources (such as people's time, energy, and ideas), and financial resources (such as money).

What is an entrepreneur?
An entrepreneur is the person who has an idea for a business, creates the business, and operates it.

What is the concept of scarcity?
This is a key idea in economics; it is the idea that there is a limit to all resources. If a resource is heavily used for one purpose or group, there will be less of that resource available for other uses or for other groups.

What is capital?
Capital usually refers to the money an investor puts into starting a business. Sometimes capital is not financial. The investment of time and energy that people put into starting a business venture is called *human capital*.

What is a business?
A business is any enterprise that brings in money from selling goods or services.

What is a market economy?
This is the term used to describe an economy in which making a profit is the main incentive for producing goods or offering services.

Why do governments collect taxes?
Taxes are money that a government collects from people and businesses. People or companies pay taxes on earnings, profits, inheritances, and certain goods. Taxes are used to run the government. They are also used for schools, parks, roads, libraries, armed forces, medical care, and many other government services.

. . . between producers and consumers?

Producers are people or businesses that create or provide goods and services. **Consumers** are people who buy and use goods and services. Just about everybody in an economy is a consumer.

. . . between the private sector and the public sector?

The **public sector** is the part of the economy that is produced or controlled by the government. The **private sector** is the part of the economy produced by businesses or individuals.

. . . between supply and demand?

Supply is the amount of goods and services that are available in the economy at any one time. **Demand** is the amount of desires consumers have for goods and services. In general, prices fall when supply is high, and prices increase when demand is high. If the price of a product or a service gets too high, it is likely that the demand will decline.

. . . between recession, depression, and inflation?

Recession is a condition in the economy when the flow of money slows down. Generally, unemployment rises and demand for goods and services declines. **Depression** is a severe form of recession, when business declines to an extreme low and unemployment is very high. In periods of **inflation**, prices show a continued increase.

. . . between monopoly and competition?

A company has a **monopoly** on a product or service when it is the only source of that product or service. **Competition** occurs when more than one business supplies the same product or service. In general, competition leads to lower prices and more varied products.

. . . between a free enterprise system and a socialistic system?

In a **free enterprise** economic system, the federal government generally has somewhat of a "hands-off" approach. This means there is a moderate or minimal amount of government regulation of business. Private individuals are likely to control most of the businesses and industries in the society. In a **socialistic** system, government is likely to control most of the businesses and industries and have strong regulation of private businesses.

. . . between stocks and bonds?

A **stock** is a part of the ownership of a company that is available for sale to the public. Owners of stock are called *stockholders*. A **bond** is a certificate showing that someone has loaned money to a business or to the government. People buy bonds because of the promise of a profit, or dividend, on the money they loan.

Money & the Government

The Fed

The United States government collects, controls, and spends a huge amount of money. All this money is managed by the Federal Reserve System, known as **The Fed**, which is the bank of the U.S. government. The headquarters of the Fed is in Washington, D.C.. The Fed has 12 regional banks across the country. The biggest of the branches is the Federal Reserve Bank of New York. All the checks written in the country pass through the Federal Reserve System.

The Fed's main job is to control the amount of money in circulation. It controls the flow of money by requiring banks to hold more money in reserve, or by making more money available for loans. The Federal Reserve can raise or lower interest rates. This affects the amount of money people borrow, so it is a tool to control the flow of money.

In periods of rapid economic expansion, the Fed would probably raise interest rates to slow down the flow of money and keep inflation from rising. In periods of recession, the Fed is likely to lower interest rates. This loosens up the flow of money and encourages people to buy and businesses to grow. The Fed works to keep just the right balance between having too much money in circulation and too little money in circulation.

I never knew!

Wow!

The U.S. has by far the highest GDP in the world. In the year 2000, the worth of goods and services produced in the country was almost 10 trillion dollars.

The Federal Deposit Insurance Corporation is a U.S. government agency that acts as a huge insurance company for banks. This corporation assures bank customers that their money will be safe in any bank in America. All banks must insure each customer account for an amount up to $100,000. If the bank goes out of business, runs out of money, or gets robbed, the bank customers will not lose their money.

The GDP (Gross Domestic Product) of a country is a measure of the amount of goods and services produced within a country in a given period, even those produced by companies that are not owned by citizens of country.

The GNP (Gross National Product) of a country is a measure of all the production of goods and services by businesses owned by the nation's citizens during a given period, even if the businesses are not located within the country.

The balance of trade is the relationship between the value of a country's imports and its exports. A country has a *favorable balance of trade* if the value of the exports is greater than the cost of the imports.

Index

A

abolition, 189, 190
above water mountain range, longest, 101
absentee ballot, 215
absolute location, 94
account, 224
acculturation, 61
Acton, Lord, 174
Adams, Abigail, 193
Adenas, 158, 161
advertising, 223
Adi Granth, 73
advice,
    to parents, 11-12, 17
    to students, 11-12, 14
    to teachers, 11-12
Afghanistan War, 173, 197
Africa, ancient, 118, 160-162, 164
Age of Exploration, 165
Age of Imperialism, 168
Age of Reform, 189
airport, busiest in U.S., 149
Aldrin, Edwin, 196
Alexander the Great, 156, 162, 175
Alexander II, 175
Alien and Sedition Acts, 188
Allies, World War I, 181, 182
Allies, World War II, 181, 182, 194
almanac, 37
Al Qaeda, 173, 197
amendments to the U.S. Constitution, 188, 191, 192, 196, 203-205
American,
    Civil Rights Movement, 171
    colonies, 166, 168, 186-188
    flag, 216
    independence, 166
    Indian Movement (AIM), 196
    Revolution, 180, 188
Americans, early, 184-185
Americans with Disabilities Act, 197
Anaan, Kofi, 173, 175
analyze, 35
Anasazi cliff dwellings, 146, 163
Anderson, Mary, 178
Angkor, 163, 164
Angkor Wat, 164
Anthony, Susan B., 174
anthropology, 62
anthrax, 197
Antoinette, Marie, 175
apartheid, 170, 173
aquarium,
Audubon Aquarium
    of the Americas, 147
    biggest in world, 128
Arab-Israeli Wars, 170, 172, 181, 196
Arab League (AL), 182
Arafat, Yasir, 173, 175, 181
archaeology, 62
Archimedes, 167
archipelago, 98

arguments, 36
Aristotle, 167, 175
area, world nations, 104-113
Armstrong, Neil, 196, 198
Articles of Confederation, 202
articles of the U.S.Constitution, 203
artifacts, 152
Asia, 117
assimilation, 61, 64
assignments, 22
Association of Southeast Asian Nations (ASEAN), 182
Assyria, 153, 160
atlas, 37, 78
atoll, 98
atomic bomb, 170, 194
Augustus, 162
Australia, 119, 168
authority, 31, 70
automatic teller machine (ATM), 224
Axis Powers, 181, 182
Aztecs, 158, 164, 165

B

Babylon, 153, 169
balance, 225, 227
balance of trade, 232
Balboa, Vasco de, 175
ballot, 215
bank, 224-225
Barak, Ehud, 175
Barbarians, 162
Barnum, P. T., 193
Battle of Little Big Horn, 191
Battle of New Orleans, 189
Battle of Wounded Knee, 169, 192
bay, 98
Bay of Pigs invasion, 195
beach, 98
Becket, Thomas, 164
Begin, Menachem, 175
Bell, Alexander Graham, 169, 191
Benedict, 175
benefit, 228
benefits, 222
Benz, Karl, 169
Berlin Airlift, 170, 194
Berlin Wall, 171, 173, 195, 197
Bible, 72
Big Apple, 149
bill, 208
Bill of Rights, 188, 204
biographical references, 37
Birdseye, Clarence, 179
Black Death, 164
Black September, 172
Black Tuesday, 194
Blanchard, Jean Pierre, 178
Boers, 166, 168, 169, 181
Boer War, 181
Boland Amendment, 196
Bolivar, Simon, 168, 175

Bolsheviks, 181
Bonaparte, Napoleon, 166, 168, 175
bonds, 231
Bosnia, 197
Boston Newsletter, 187
Boston Massacre, 188
Boston Tea Party, 188
Brahman, 73
Branch Davidians, 197
Brezhnev, Leonid, 175
bridge, longest suspension, 128
Brown v. Topeka Board of Education, 195, 213
Buddha, 72, 161, 176
Buddhism, 72, 162, 176
budget, 223
buildings,
    tallest in U.S., 148
    tallest in world, 128
Bush, Barbara, 174
Bush, George, 197
business, 230
butte, 98
Byzantine Empire, 163

C

cabinet, 211
Cabot, John, 186
Caesar, Julius, 167, 175
Calvin, John, 175
Camp David Accords, 172, 181, 196
canal, 98
    longest in world, 128
candidates, 215
canyon, 98
    biggest in U.S., 149
    deepest in world, 100
    longest in world, 101
cape, 98-99
capital cities,
    U.S., 134-135, 136-140
    world, 104-113
capital, 230
Capitol, U.S., 206
card catalog, 40
careful reading, 45
Carlsbad Caverns, 146
Carnegie, Andrew, 193
Carson, Rachel, 198
Carter, Jimmy, 196
Cartier, Jacques, 165
Carnival, 75
castle, 128
Castro, Fidel, 171, 175
Catherine the Great, 166, 175
cause and effect, 33
cave, 100, 101
celebrations, 74-75
Central Powers, 181, 182
Chaing Kai-shek, 175
channel, 98
Charlemagne, 163, 175

elaborate, 33
election, 214, 215
Electoral College, 215
electors, 215
electronic transfer, 224
elevation map, 87
Emancipation Proclamation, 191
Embargo Act, 189
Emergency Quota Act, 192
Empire State Building, 146, 194
employee, 222
employer, 222
enculturation, 61
encyclopedias, 38
Engels, Friedrich, 168
Enlightenment, 187
entrepreneur, 230
environment, 95, 122
Equal Rights Amendment, 196
equator, 81-83
Eric the Red, 163
Erie Canal, 189
Esala Perahera, 74
ethnocentrism, 61
euro, 173
Europe, 116
European Union (EU), 123, 182
evaluate, 35
Evolution, 192
excuses, 27
executive branch, U.S. government, 210-211
expansionism, 190
explorers, 163, 165, 166, 168, 186
expressions of culture, 62
extend, 33
extremes,
        U.S., 148-149
        world, 100-101

F

fact and opinion, 34
Famous First Facts, 39
faulty,
        arguments, 36
        generalizations, 32
Feast of St. Lucia, 74
Federal Deposit Insurance Corporation (FDIC), 232
Federal Reserve (Fed), 221, 232
Federal Reserve Note, 221
federation, 71
Ferdinand, Franz, 176, 181
Fertile Crescent, 153, 160
feudalism, 162, 163
Fields, W. C., 198
finance charge, 226
fjord, 98
        longest in world, 101
flag, U.S., 216
Flinders, Matthew, 168
floor plans, 90
foothills, 98-99
Ford, Henry, 170, 192, 193
Frank, Anne, 176
Franklin, Benjamin, 178, 187

free enterprise system, 231
French and Indian War, 187
French Revolution, 166, 180
Freud, Sigmund, 174
Friedan, Betty, 195
Fulton, Robert, 178, 189

G

gain, 228
Gagarin, Yuri, 171
Galileo, 166, 176
Gandhi, Mahatma, 170, 174, 176
Garrison, William Lloyd, 189
Gateway Arch, 125, 126
Gautama, Siddhartha, 72, 161, 176
gazetteer, 39
generalize, 32
generalizations,
        broad, 32
        faulty, 32
        safe, 32
geography, 93-150
        cultural, 94
        human, 94
        physical, 94
        themes, 94-95
        U.S., 129-150
        world, 93-128
get,
        healthy, 24
        motivated, 14-16
        organized, 18-23
Gettysburg Address, 191
geysers, 148
Ghana, ancient, 157, 162
glacier, 98, 100, 101
global connections, 31, 122-124, 182
globes, 78, 80
glossaries, 38
goals, setting, 15-16
Golden Gate Bridge, 147
Gold Rush, 168, 190
Gonzales, Elian, 197
goods, 220
Gorbachev, Mikhail, 176
government, 31, 71, 202-215
GPS, 95
Grand Canyon, 146
Grant, Ulysses S., 191
Great Awakening, 187
Great Depression, 170, 194
Great Lakes States, 144
Great Seal, U.S., 217
Great Sphinx, 125, 127, 160
Great Trek, 168
Great Wall of China, 125, 127
Greece, classical, 156, 161
Greeley, Horace, 193
grid,
        Earth's, 83
        maps, 79, 88
gross domestic product (GDP), 232
gross national product (GNP), 232
groups, social, 66-67, 70
Guinness Book of Records, 39
gulf, 98-99

Gutenberg, Johann, 165, 176

H

habits, study, 25-28
Hammurabi, 153, 160, 176
Hammurabi's Code, 153, 160
Hanukkah, 75
Harvard, 187
health, 24
Hebrews, 154, 161
hemispheres, 80
Hidalgo, Miguel, 176
hieroglyphics, 155, 158, 160
hill, 98
Hinduism, 73, 161
historical events,
        U.S. timeline, 186-198
        world timeline, 160-174
history,
        U.S., 183-218
        world, 151-182
Hiroshima, Japan, 170, 194
Hitler, Adolf, 170, 176, 181
Hittites, 154, 161
Ho Chi Minh, 171, 176
holidays, U.S., 218
Homer, 161, 176
Homestead Act, 191
Hopewalls, 158
House of Representatives, U.S., 206-209
Hubble Space Telescope, 173, 179
Hudson, Henry, 186
human,
        genome, 173
        geography, 94
        interaction with environment, 95
        migration, 95
        movement, 95
Hundred Years' War, 164, 180
Huns, 156, 162
hurricane, 148
Hussein, Sadaam, 182

I

iceberg, 100
        biggest, 101
identify,
        biases, 36
        faulty arguments, 36
        propaganda, 36
        stereotypes, 36
immigrants, 189
impeachment, 191, 196, 197, 206
Incas, 158, 164
incentives, 229
income, 222
independence,
        African, 171
        America, 167
        Latin American, 168
index, 39
Indian Mutiny, 169
Industrial Revolution, 166, 188
Indus Valley Civilization, 155, 160
infer, 33

Better Grades & Higher Test Scores / SOCIAL STUDIES

Index

Better Grades & Higher Test Scores / SOCIAL STUDIES
Copyright ©2003 by Incentive Publications, Inc., Nashville, TN.

Better Grades & Higher Test Scores / SOCIAL STUDIES
Index